12/09

D0934335

HURRICANE KATRINA

JUSTICE AND SOCIAL INQUIRY

SERIES EDITORS

Jeremy I. Levitt

Matthew C. Whitaker

Hurricane Katrina

AMERICA'S UNNATURAL DISASTER

EDITED AND WITH AN INTRODUCTION BY
JEREMY I. LEVITT
AND
MATTHEW C. WHITAKER

UNIVERSITY OF NEBRASKA PRESS LINCOLN & LONDON

Library of Congress Cataloging-
in-Publication Data

Hurricane Katrina : America's unnatural
disaster / edited and with an introduction by
Jeremy I. Levitt and Matthew C. Whitaker.
p. cm. — (Justice and social inquiry)
Includes bibliographical references and index.
ISBN 978-0-8032-1760-7 (cloth : alk. paper)
1. Hurricane Katrina, 2005. 2. Disaster
relief—Louisiana—New Orleans. 3. African
Americans—Louisiana—New Orleans—Social
conditions. 4. Social justice—Louisiana—
New Orleans. I. Levitt, Jeremy I., 1970–
II. Whitaker, Matthew C.
HV636 2005 .N4 L48 2009
976'.044—dc22
2008045278

For the victims of Katrina's unnatural disaster, and for the hope of a better tomorrow

In loving memory of the benevolent Donda West, her son Kayne West, and ten others whom Jeremy Levitt led on a three-day humanitarian mission to visit, support, and lift the spirits of thousands of Katrina victims housed in the Houston Astrodome, Reliant Center, George R. Brown Center, and several churches shortly after the storm in September 2005

CONTENTS

FIGURES

TABLES

ACKNOWLEDGMENTS

First and foremost we thank the many contributors to this book. Their intelligence, insight, and commitment to justice are whole and complete, and we truly appreciate their willingness to lend their names and expertise to this volume. Essential to the preparation of this book were various forms of support, financial and strategic, provided by our institutions, Florida International University College of Law and Arizona State University Department of History. We are particularly appreciative of R. R. Donnelly, the world's premier full-service provider of print and related services, including document-based business process outsourcing, which provided FIU College of Law with a general and unrestricted grant to support Hurricane Katrina relief activities, which were, in part, used to underwrite this book. In this regard we especially thank former R. R. Donnelly CEO Mark Angelson for organizing the grant. Nevertheless, we do not, in any way, shape, or form, attribute the book project or the views expressed herein to R. R. Donnelly.

Several people at the University of Nebraska Press, especially Heather Lundine, took a keen interest in this project from its initial stages and have maintained their support throughout the editorial process. The idea for the book was inspired by our desire to help scholars, activists, and everyday people understand the social, economic, and political forces that made so many people, particularly African Americans, so vulnerable to destruction and death before, during, and after Hurricane Katrina. If knowledge truly is power, perhaps our efforts will offer a modest bulwark against the kind of repudiation and neglect that undermine the well-being of black people and all victims of racism and poverty.

We would not have been able to complete this book without the love and support of our families and close friends. In recognition of their sacrifices and confidence, we extend a sincere and heartfelt thank-you to Latrice Levitt and Gidget Whitaker. We also thank Darlene Clark Hine and Brooks Simpson for their encouragement, inspiration, critical eyes, and passion for service-based scholarship. Megan Falater edited the manuscript with eagerness, precision, and a deep concern for those who were affected by the storm. Her assistance was invaluable. Finally, we are truly grateful for all of the inspirational and desperately needed work rendered by Sly Stone's everyday people and institutions in areas damaged by Katrina and the human failures associated with it. In appreciation of their work, we have elected to donate a portion of the royalties from the sale of this book to Common Ground Relief, a group that symbolizes the aforementioned dedication.

Common Ground Relief's charge is to provide temporary aid for victims of hurricane disasters in the Gulf Coast region and long-term support for reconstructing communities affected by Katrina in the Greater New Orleans area. Common Ground Relief is a grassroots organization that offers various kinds of assistance and mutual aid. It does not administer to communities; rather, it gives hope to communities by working with them in sustainable ways to meet their most basic and pressing needs. We thank you, Common Ground Relief, for standing at the forefront of the rebuilding process and for showing us the way forward.

"Truth Crushed to Earth Will Rise Again"

Katrina and Its Aftermath

JEREMY I. LEVITT AND MATTHEW C. WHITAKER

What we saw unfold in the days after the hurricane was the most na-
ked manifestation of social policy towards the poor, where the message for decades has been: "You are on your own." Well, they really
were on their own for five days in that Superdome, and it was Dar-
winism in action—the survival of the fittest. People said: "It looks like
something out of the Third World." Well, New Orleans was Third
World long before the hurricane.—CORNEL WEST, "Exiles from a
City and from a Nation," *Observer*, September 11, 2005

Hurricane Katrina was one of the deadliest and most costly hurricanes in U.S. history. It was the sixth strongest Atlantic hurricane
ever recorded and the third strongest on record that reached the
continental United States. Katrina formed on August 23, 2005, during the Atlantic hurricane season. It devastated much of the north-
central Gulf Coast of the United States. The most severe loss of life
and property damage occurred in New Orleans, Louisiana, which
was largely devoured by floodwaters after the levee system suffered a calamitous failure. Katrina's floodwater exposed as much

as it covered, however. The storm caused destruction not only in New Orleans, but across the entire Mississippi coast and into Alabama (as far as a hundred miles from the storm's center), uncovering weaknesses, prejudices, and inequalities throughout the Gulf Coast and within the whole of American society.[1]

Katrina was the eleventh tropical storm, fifth hurricane, third major hurricane, and second Category 5 hurricane of the 2005 Atlantic hurricane season. It formed over the Bahamas on August 23, 2005, and made its way past southern Florida as a moderate Category 1 hurricane, where it caused some deaths and flooding, before growing rapidly in size and strength in the Gulf of Mexico, where it became one of the more powerful hurricanes recorded at sea. The storm weakened somewhat before hitting land for a second and third time, on the morning of August 29, in southern Louisiana and at the Louisiana/Mississippi state line, respectively, as a Category 3 storm. The storm surge caused catastrophic destruction along the Gulf Coast. In Louisiana, the flood protection system in New Orleans failed in fifty-three different places. Nearly every levee in metro New Orleans breached as Hurricane Katrina's 140-mile-an-hour gale force winds, torrential rain, and thunderous floodwaters rolled eastward through the city, flooding 80 percent of the city and many areas of neighboring parishes for weeks. Along the Mississippi coast, Katrina overwhelmed the cities of Bay St. Louis, Biloxi, Gulfport, Long Beach, Ocean Springs, Pascagoula, Pass Christian, and Waveland.[2]

More than a million Gulf Coast residents were displaced by Katrina, relocating in cities in all fifty states. Many of Katrina's so-called refugees were living well below the poverty line before the storm struck, which made them extremely vulnerable to the storm's wrath and the many human failures that followed. At least 1,836 people were killed by Hurricane Katrina and in the subsequent human floods that ravaged the Gulf Coast, making it the deadliest in the United States since the Okeechobee Hurricane in 1928 and the hurricane that hit the island city of Galveston, Texas, in 1900. Katrina caused an estimated $81.2 billion in damage, making it the costliest natural disaster in U.S. history.

Criticism of the federal, state, and local governments' reaction to the storm was widespread and resulted in an investigation by the U.S. Congress and the resignation of the Federal Emergency Management Agency (FEMA) director Michael Brown. The storm also prompted Congressional review of the U.S. Army Corps of Engineers and the failure of the levee protection system. Hurricane Katrina revealed as much about American society and the inextricable link between race, class, gender, and age in our nation as it did about nature's fury. Indeed, Katrina uncovered not only the devastating penalty for structural racism and classism but also their loathsome underbelly. As the world watched the coverage of Hurricane Katrina and its desolation in horror, America's racial inequality and shocking levels of poverty, vulnerability, and dislocation, particularly among African Americans, were laid bare before the world.[3]

The purpose of this book is to offer a critical assessment of the local, national, and international impact of Hurricane Katrina on the lives of African Americans in the social, cultural, political, economic, environmental, religious, and legal spheres. The chapters in this collection are multidisciplinary and comparative, and draw principally from the following disciplines: law, political science, history, economics, sociology, and religion. The chapters introduce polemic and critical ideas and question the efficacy of the national and global responses to Katrina's central victims, African Americans. The essays, which reveal the multifarious impacts of Hurricane Katrina on black people, combine research and advocacy by some of the most experienced scholars and activists working on cutting-edge Katrina-related issues of race, ethnicity, and class of real-world significance. This book underscores the extent to which black people and others were and are being impacted by the natural and human-engineered forces that have engendered and maintained intense suffering associated with Katrina and its aftermath.

Although this introduction places Katrina in its proper historical context, the current socioeconomic condition of Katrina's victims will be the primary focus of this book. Since Katrina, in fact, its survivors continue to be confronted by the racial, economic, and political injustices that marginalized their existence before the storm; discrimination placed them squarely in harm's way during the hurricane and continues to undermine their ability to rebuild their often shattered and scattered lives after the storm. This reality requires political leaders, scholars, and activists to address these problems assertively and in intelligent and practical ways. Failure to engage these issues has created and enabled political obfuscation, cutthroat capitalism, unchecked market forces, avarice, racism, classism, sexism, and basic apathy to undermine relief and rebuilding efforts in housing, education, employment, contracting, and infrastructure.[4]

Such neglect has also adversely affected many people, particularly immigrants who have come to the United States seeking work in the Gulf Coast redevelopment industry. They are also facing manipulation, xenophobia, and racism and are arguably allowing themselves to be used in perpetuation. Following Hurricane Katrina, the Gulf Coast region played host to the arrival of larger numbers of immigrant and non-immigrant workers who were lured to the area by contractors with promises of well-paying jobs and housing. Yet, in New Orleans and throughout the Gulf Coast region, many found themselves mired in poverty without shelter, advocates, or representation. The Advancement Project, the National Immigration Law Center, and the New Orleans Worker Justice Coalition demonstrated how complicated and divisive these issues were when they revealed that African American survivors were often denied employment opportunities, even as migrant and especially immigrant workers secured jobs (positions that were often quite exploitive and unsafe).[5]

The most enduring and jarring stories associated with Hurricane Katrina, however, are the abject poverty and racism that has marked the region for generations. Television cameras from around the world captured indelible images of people walking, floating, and sometimes drowning in contaminated water. Once the water receded, the same cameras captured frightening images of dead bodies on deserted streets, crowds of people dying slowly of hunger and dehydration, and people fainting and thrashing about in pain for want of desperately needed medication for chronic illness. As Michael Eric Dyson recently observed:

> Photo snaps and film shots captured legions of men and women huddling in groups or hugging corners, crying in wild-eyed desperation for help, for any help, from somebody, anybody, who would listen to their unanswered pleas. The filth and squalor of their confinement—defecating where they stood or sat, or, more likely, dropped, bathed in a brutal wash of dredge and sickening pollutants that choked the air with ungodly stench—grieved the camera lenses that recorded their plight.

Scores of people took to the streets dotted by deserted shops and restaurants, scavenging for food, water, and clothing. The hordes were multiracial in orientation, but the overwhelming majority of the displaced and disinherited were black. At first glance, many people would have assumed that the sight they were seeing was taking place in some other corner of the so-called Third World, such as Liberia, Rwanda, or Sierra Leone. Many people asked, could this be happening in the United States of America? Could the wealthiest and most powerful country in the world abandon some of its poorest citizens at a time when they needed their government the most?[6]

It is precisely these questions, and others, that this anthology answers. What formed the pre- and post-Katrina Gulf Coast? What were the public and private sectors' responses to the disaster? How should a post-Katrina America be constructed? How do we get there? Since Hurricane Katrina has become synonymous with socioeconomic circumstances that mark many communities throughout the country, what lessons can be learned from pre- and post-Katrina failures that will help ameliorate many of the problems associated with pre- and post-Katrina America? The pre-Katrina Gulf Coast, especially New Orleans, like many other American regions and cities, was characterized by racism, racial segregation, and acute poverty levels well before the storm. The antebellum and post–Civil War South, particularly New Orleans, was populated by indigenous peoples, enslaved people of African descent, free blacks, Creoles of various hues and status, and whites, including Cajuns and European ethnics, who embodied the area's native, African, Spanish, French, and English roots.[7]

Despite the multiracial nature of the New Orleans heritage, the metropolis has been characterized by acute racial segregation. People of African descent were marketed, sold, purchased, exchanged, and treated as chattel. Black people were raped, mutilated, ridiculed as aberrant and inferior, and denied the freedoms set forth in the Declaration of Independence that America claimed to embrace. Even after legal slavery ended in the United States in 1865, black people, by virtue of their race and class, were relegated to sharecropping and other wage-earning forms of work and forced to live in the poorest areas of New Orleans. At the time of Katrina, according to the Brookings Institution, New Orleans was one of the most racially segregated among the largest U.S. metropolitan cities. Moreover, post–World War II suburbanization and white flight from the city's core led to the African Americanization of New Orleans. As the city became blacker, it also became poorer as blacks were systematically denied work and a living wage. In 1960 New Orleans was 37 percent black; in 1970 it was 43 percent black; in 1980 it was 55 percent black; in 1990 it was 62 percent black, and in 2000 it was over 67 percent black.[8]

The poverty rate was 28 percent in New Orleans in 2000, compared to 12 percent for the nation. By the time Katrina hit New Orleans, the city claimed the second highest percentage of its residents (38 percent) living in high-poverty census tracts, in which more than 40 percent of its residents were living at or below the poverty line. In addition, the city's black poverty rate was 35 percent, three times the rate of 11 percent for whites. White people who remained in New Orleans fled to areas such as Jefferson Parish, which is 70 percent white; St. Bernard Parish, which is 88 percent white; and St. Tammany Parish, which is 87 percent white. "By 2000," the Brookings Institution argues, "the city of New Orleans had become highly segregated by race and developed high concentrations of poverty. . . . [B]lacks and whites were living in quite literally different worlds before the storm hit."[9]

Such racial disparities and poverty are the result of individual choices and actions. They are also the result of a long history of institutional structures and arrangements that have helped create our contemporary sociopolitical and economic order. Slavery and its racialized effects on wealth accumulation, family life, and white attitudes toward and treatment of people of African descent are the historical root causes of black poverty in New Orleans. Another century of legalized segregation, informal barriers to racial equality, and so-called progressive policies such as the New Deal actually sustained and exacerbated racial inequality. Social Security excluded agricultural workers and domestics, occupations that were dominated by African Americans. Federal housing programs severely restricted their aid to people of color, which reinforced racial segregation. The celebrated G.I. Bill that was passed following World War II offered extremely restricted housing and education assistance to black people, even as it subsidized upward mobility for millions of whites. It must be noted that when African Americans did receive these benefits, schools, housing authorities, and employers, more often than not, did not allow blacks to freely exercise them.[10]

History does not repeat itself, but it certainly rhymes, and the socioeconomic pulse of race and class discrimination continues to reverberate. For example, poor people, regardless of color, are often ignored, marginalized, and exploited. People of color, especially women of color, however, often find themselves disproportionately represented among the poor and dispossessed. Even as racial discrimination was eliminated officially between 1954 and 1970, the government and the private sector circumvented anti-discrimination laws. "Redlining" by loan-granting institutions, for example, is still widespread, and de facto school segregation since *Brown v. Topeka Board of Education* has lead to gross inequities in educational opportunities. Employment and housing discrimination remains, prejudicial zoning regulations endure, racialized bank lending and real estate practices flourish, while federally financed highways that privilege predominantly white suburbs and tax breaks for wealthier home owners facilitate this inequitable system. Disparities in lending and health care along race lines thrive, and the criminal justice system practices ardent favoritism in terms of sentencing patterns and incarceration rates. These matters are of utmost importance because extreme poverty and racial segregation undercuts opportunity, and as sociologist Douglas Massey maintains, "any process that concentrates poverty with racially isolated neighborhoods will simultaneously increase the odds of socio-economic failure."[11]

Regrettably , there are "haves" and "have-nots," and race, which is inextricably linked to class, still plays a significant role in determining the social status (and corresponding opportunities) into which all of us are born. The haves in New Orleans and the Greater Gulf Coast, therefore, had the resources to escape or withstand Katrina's wrath, while the have-nots were fully exposed to destruction, dislocation, injury, and death. As Hartman and Squires argue:

> [The wealthy have] access to personal transportation or plane and train fare, money for temporary housing, and in some cases second homes. Guests trapped in one luxury New Orleans hotel were saved when that chain hired a fleet of buses to get them out. Patients in one hospital were saved when a doctor who knew Al Gore contacted the former Vice President, who was able to cut through government red tape and charter two planes that took them to safety. This is what is meant by the catch phrase "social capital," a resource most unevenly distributed by class and race.

Racial segregation has engineered a situation in which wealthier whites have secured homes in suburban areas, while black people have few if any options to live anywhere other than the inner city, where, in the case of New Orleans, the worst flooding occurred.[12]

Insofar as poor people and people of color are disproportionately dependent upon public services, including public transportation, the consequences of the failure of public services prior to and following Katrina were not "color blind" or impartial with regard to color and class. These groups had extremely inadequate private resources to draw from in times of chaos. This is not only true during catastrophic events like Katrina, but during times of personal trauma associated with sickness, physical impairment, and familial tragedy. Indeed, as James Carr, senior vice president of research for the Fannie Mae Foundation argued, if New Orleans had been a more inclusive community with regard to race and class, the city's population would have had the social and economic capital to improve its levee system well in advance.[13]

The point here is that although individual racist and classist acts endure with devastating effects, institutional malfeasance and dishonesty often born of racial and class-based stereotypes enabled the incompetence of FEMA and various public and private entities in Katrina's wake. These entities have proven themselves to be the most powerful forces in creating and maintaining racial disparities among the communities they are charged with serving. This "institutionalized racism," as it has been called, is all too familiar to people of color, yet generations of privilege have rendered it almost incomprehensible to many white people. It should come as no surprise then that Katrina's devastation fell hardest upon the city's poor people and persons of color. New Orleans, like most urban areas in America, has suffered and will continue to be marred by gross racial inequality as long as the effects of individual prejudice, institutional racism, concentrated poverty, and inequitable progress remain permanent features of the city's social psychology and sociopolitical order. If these forces are allowed to prosper unimpeded by progressive and concerted action, they will continue to encumber the repopulation and redevelopment of New Orleans and other American communities in which security and prosperity are desired by all their residents.[14]

Hurricane Katrina was not the first storm that unmasked blatant inequalities in America. The "Great Mississippi Flood of 1927," long before Hurricane Katrina, revealed the vulnerable and unequal status of African Americans in the United States. During the fall, winter, and spring of 1926–27, seasonal rains were so heavy that the tributaries of the Mississippi overflowed, causing devastating floods. On New Year's Day, 1927, the Cumberland River at Nashville topped levees at 56.2 feet. The Mississippi River levee system broke in 145 places and flooded 27,000 square miles or about 16,570,627 acres of land, an area equal to the combined size of Connecticut, Massachusetts, New Hampshire, and Vermont. In some areas the floodwater depth reached 30 feet. The flood caused over $400,000,000 in damages and killed upward of 246 people in seven states. The flood overran parts of Arkansas, Illinois, Kentucky, Louisiana, Mississippi, and Tennessee. Arkansas sustained the most damage as 14 percent of its territory was enveloped by floodwaters. On April 16, the main levee in southeastern Missouri broke, followed by breaches in 144 additional areas. The floodwaters engulfed millions of acres of land, impacting some 930,000 people in seven states. The waters smashed into 160,000 homes and decimated 41,487. By May of 1927, the Mississippi River south of Memphis, Tennessee, reached a width of 70 miles. By July 1, even as the flood began to recede, 1.5 million acres were under water.[15]

To help preserve and protect the people and the land affected by the flood, President Calvin Coolidge appointed Secretary of Commerce Herbert Hoover to organize and direct what became the Red Cross and the Army Corps of Engineers' turbulent and exploitive plan to raise the levee by stacking sand bags on top of it. Camps were erected throughout deluged areas. Many, such as the camps near Greeneville, Tennessee, housed the men who labored to protect the levees. The stations near Greeneville, atop an 8-foot-wide levee, trapped between the river and the flood, were stocked with field kitchens and tents for thousands of plantation workers—all African Americans—to live as black men filled sand bags and white men stacked them on the levee. Although most white authorities viewed African Americans as inferior people, they still viewed them as an indispensable cheap labor source at best, and as virtual property at worst. Despite the eminent flood threat, most whites conspired to undermine black people's ability to evacuate. Black men were forced to work on the levee, and those who attempted to escape were driven back at gunpoint by the National Guard. Indeed, preoccupied with losing "their" labor force, argues historian Robyn Spencer, white plantation owners and local relief officials fashioned relief camps "as holding pens designed to ensure the retention and preservation of the southern labor force." Such measures demonstrate that the individuals leading the recovery effort undertook to reestablish the racially unequal and unjust sharecropping system that welcomed them. Hoover addressed this issue specifically when he stated that "national agencies have no responsibility for the economic system which exists in the South." Hoover was slow to respond to the disaster, and when he did, he failed to involve the government in the rebuilding process in a substantive way. Furthermore, his deference to white supremacy curtailed his ability to orchestrate relief on an equal basis, thereby reinforcing white supremacy and racial inequality throughout the region for generations to come.[16]

The river near Greeneville broke on April 21, creating a massive 100-foot channel upriver from Greeneville, one half mile in width. In ten days it covered one million acres with water ten feet deep—and the crevasse continued to pour water for months. Water, more than twice the volume of Niagara Falls, roared out of the breach, ushering in one of the ugliest episodes in American history. Panic ensued, and hundreds of levee workers crawled onto a nearby barge to escape. The Red Cross, influenced by the economic and political power of local planters, however, abandoned and detained African Americans on the levee. Cotton, and the white planter barons who made a fortune on it, were kings in the Delta region. Cotton cultivation was labor intensive; cotton was planted, grown, and picked by hand by black laborers who earned $1.00 a day for twelve hours of work. White planters understood that if they helped black laborers evacuate, they might loose their cheap labor source. African American workers now had nothing to return to, and given the malevolent racial etiquette in the south, many believed that anyplace would be better than the Delta.[17]

The Great Mississippi Flood, like Hurricane Katina, did not simply ravage the landscape; it revealed the brutal and longstanding problems associated with systemic racism, political cowardice and corruption, and governmental malfeasance. Blacks were displaced from their homes; denied proper food and shelter; trapped in a dangerous disaster zone; accosted, abused, and detained unfairly by the authorities; and forced to work under dangerous circumstances for little or no pay. Like the recovery effort after Katrina, the Mississippi flood rescue, according to Spencer, "lacked any reforms that addressed the structural inequalities abundant in a land where the tenant farming and sharecropping systems kept blacks perpetually in a cycle of debt and dependence."[18] Not only did this concentration camp atmosphere smack of virtual slavery, but it undermined the future generational earning potential and asset acquisition of blacks in the area, who scattered about eventually as a part of the Great Migration of African Americans from rural to urban areas, and from the south to the north.[19]

Moreover, the Great Mississippi Flood serves as a powerful historical precedent; evidence that when racial and economic inequality and government malfeasance meet nature's wrath, the worst of human nature is exposed. Black people, poor people (who are disproportionately women of color), the sick, and the elderly across the Gulf Coast were in harm's way long before Katrina. No student of history can claim that the aftermath of Katrina was a surprise, given the socioeconomic status of the majority of Katrina's victims before the storm formed. The history of American chattel slavery, Jim Crow segregation, economic inequality, patriarchy, political apathy, gross disparities in educational opportunities, police brutality, and legal injustices loomed large before Katrina, and they continue to ensnare our hearts and challenge America's promise of freedom and democracy to its people.

This book examines the history and lives of African Americans in the Gulf Coast, their socioeconomic status prior to Hurricane Katrina, the impact of the storm on black people in the region, the response of the government and the private sector, the disaster's bearing on the health of African Americans, the various legal ramifications of the storm and its aftermath, and the nature and implications of massive dislocations associated with the hurricane. Although this book speaks of victims, it is about agency and resilience at its core. It emphasizes the inspiring deployment of African Americans' unique culture of struggle, resistance, and hope in the face of tragedy, squalor, and rejection. Key issues will include the legacy of chattel slavery and Jim Crow segregation in the Gulf Coast, economic inequality, the gendered nature of Katrina's impact and the various responses to it, the government and legal community's response (or lack thereof) to Katrina and its victims, the various ways in which those who were most affected by Katrina can rebuild their lives and communities, and the ways in which our society can ameliorate the kind of racialized poverty that was painfully exposed in Katrina's wake.

In chapter 1 Mitchell F. Crusto offers his personal account as a native of New Orleans as he and his family evacuated the city prior to Hurricane Katrina, and his reaction to the news of the devastation and the government's mishandling of the situation in the months, albeit now years, following the hurricane. He tells his story through letters written to his fictitious mother, the City of New Orleans herself. Crusto is a multigenerational descendant of enslaved blacks, free people of color, and white French and Spanish enslavers. He has written on the legal history of black women's struggles for property and wealth in the antebellum South with particular emphasis on Louisiana law, and he believes this history helps to explain the government's reaction to the Katrina situation in treating black people as discarded property.

In chapter 2 Bryan K. Fair explores the deep chasms in American life that rendered so many of New Orleans' black citizens trapped and under siege during and after Hurricane Katrina. He argues that America's longstanding discriminatory practices and caste-like socioeconomic structure have relegated millions of Americans to a permanent subordinate status by virtue of their birth, from which very few escape. He maintains that this heritage is powerful and repressive, and that pre- and post-Katrina New Orleans offers a window from which we can appraise and understand the impoverished lives of America's most vulnerable citizens. He contends that poverty is an international problem that begs for solutions, one that America and the world must face before the storm.

In chapter 3 Charles R. P. Pouncy challenges conventional economic analyses of the disaster. He examines the economic and financial policies that enabled the post-Katrina disaster. Pouncy critiques the poorly conceived and executed interventions that exacerbated the tragedy, and he evaluates the policies that have the potential to transform the legacy of the calamity into opportunities for more equitable distribution of resources for the wealthy and the truly disadvantaged. Pouncy makes a case for the adoption of alternative economic initiatives that minimize the influence of natural disasters and limit their impact to temporary socioeconomic disruptions rather than permanent dislocations.

In chapter 4 Andre L. Smith offers Katrina victims various strategies for empowering themselves and ameliorating the economic pain and suffering that they have endured. He proposes that a "good offense is the best defense" against future tragedies in the mold of Hurricane Katrina. Framing the potential empowerment of Katrina victims within the larger context of economic justice for disadvantaged groups, Smith argues that the reconstruction of New Orleans will offer opportunities for employment and investment in new businesses and real property if redevelopment is implemented efficiently and fairly.

In chapter 5 Phyllis W. Kotey examines the effects of Hurricane Katrina on the court system in New Orleans and other areas affected by the storm. She evaluates how the judicial system operated before and immediately after Katrina, and how its operation—and hence justice—was severely constrained by the hurricane. Kotey also explores Katrina's impact on the judiciary through the prism of three distinct perspectives: defendants, victims, and the court system. She considers how local and state government can better respond to the needs of defendants, victims, and the judiciary and justice system as a whole when faced with public emergencies.

In chapter 6 Alyssa G. Robillard investigates the relationship between race, socioeconomics, and health, particularly for African Americans who have had a long and problematic history with health care providers and the health care industry. Robillard contends that racism and the history of prejudice and discrimination toward Americans of African descent have contributed significantly to the health disparities experienced by black people in America. Additionally, and not surprisingly, she maintains, those with lower incomes do not fare nearly as well on health indexes as those with higher incomes. For people whose socioeconomic conditions and physical health were already compromised, Katrina made a bad situation worse. In the face of the trauma and tragedy Katrina wrought, the storm has afforded us an opportunity for lessons learned and improvement on many levels related to health. Robillard discusses the health of African Americans in the regions affected by Katrina, the public health response during and after the storm, the health care infrastructure as it exists now, and the notion of preparedness as it relates to inequalities and inequities in health.

In chapter 7 Carleton Waterhouse explores the findings of the Independent Levee Investigation Team. This group scrutinized the New Orleans levee system failures and described them as a typical example of the effects of environmental injustice that primarily affects people of color and the poor. Waterhouse's research matches several of the team's findings with existing complaints and studies. This is particularly true for the inferior quality of environmental protection provided to minority and poor white communities ranging from the design and implementation of Superfund cleanups to the issuance and enforcement of permits under the Clean Air and Clean Water Acts. Based on the correlation between the planning failures associated with the New Orleans levee system and those associated with federal, state, and local environmental protection for people of color and poor people, Waterhouse shows how the environmental injustices associated with Hurricane Katrina reflect the environmental injustices devastating other communities around the country.

In chapter 8 Kenneth B. Nunn argues that the loss of lives and property in New Orleans and the Gulf Coast was not the result of inadequate warnings but was, in part, the result of a failure to act on the part of local, state, and national authorities. Moreover, he considers whether the failure of authorities to prepare, warn, and rescue could be characterized as a crime. Nunn examines the appropriate legal standards for both civil and criminal liability in these cases and explores the events leading up to and in the aftermath of Katrina in light of these standards. He also analyzes Katrina-related events with an eye on the characteristics of the victims of this catastrophe, arguing that the failure to properly assist Katrina victims in the manner that U.S. citizens rightfully expect from their government was colored by race and class.

In chapter 9 Linda S. Greene reveals government knowledge of the possibility of Katrina-like floods in the Gulf Coast region and government failure to act on this knowledge in the face of eminent death and destruction. She examines the government's control and misuse of all measures necessary to protect the citizens of New Orleans against Katrina-like disasters and explores the legal, moral, and ethical claims of citizens to protection by the government from catastrophic disasters like Katrina. Greene's chapter assesses post-Katrina analyses of political and legal findings to determine whether any court or governmental body has acknowledged its duty to protect its citizens. She suggests that the scope of redress available to the citizens of New Orleans, as well as future efforts to prepare for catastrophic disasters, should be measured against this standard.

In chapter 10 Ruth Gordon argues not only that Hurricane Katrina wrought horrendous physical damage, but that the response of the U.S. government made a grave situation truly catastrophic. Images of mostly poor and mostly black people stranded on rooftops surrounded by water and in a "hellhole" that had been a football stadium were endlessly played on television screens, evoking true outrage from all quarters of the political spectrum. There was genuine disbelief that our government could be so hapless and incompetent. In the face of this ineptitude and the human suffering it wrought, reporters and commentators referred to Katrina victims as refugees and generated images reminiscent of the Third World to a world audience. Whether or not these unfortunate people came within the legal definition of refugees is a separate matter. What is striking, Gordon argues, is the notion that such terms as "Third World" and "refugees" were viewed as pejorative terms that describe the poor, the disenfranchised, the oppressed, and people of color. Indeed, Gordon maintains that some people from the Third World noted that it meant that perhaps they were not so incompetent and America was not all-powerful. It also demonstrated, as Gordon posits, that Americans of whatever class or status stand apart from these depths, and that Katrina presents an opportunity to pause and examine our assumptions and biases, even as we try to go beyond those limitations.

The book's final chapter, prepared by D. Marvin Jones, reminds us that civil rights laws presuppose that the majority guarantees equal justice to minority citizens. But what does that guarantee mean in this context? According to the debates during the era of Reconstruction (1868–77), it was not only a legal guarantee but a financial one as well. Yet because of the traditional imposition of a set of common law baselines, the "reparational" nature of civil rights laws is evident only from a reading of legislative history of these civil rights laws. This cannot, however, obscure the original definition and purpose of these laws, Jones maintains. His chapter argues that while common law legalisms are relevant to federal litigation, and perhaps foreclose litigation, they in no way limit the power or moral duty of the legislature to respond to government-imposed racial inequality. He argues, therefore, that civil rights laws presuppose that victims such as Hurricane Katrina evacuees would be made whole by the government for their losses, at least from the standpoint of the original understanding of civil rights laws. Thus, the question becomes not "why" to provide reparations based upon the aforementioned issues but, in light of the nation's original commitments during reconstruction, "why not."

All of the chapters in this book were prepared to offer a critical examination of the social, political, economic, and legal tempest before the storm, during it, and in its aftermath. Specifically, this text argues that the inequalities linked to race, class, gender, and other socially constructed indicators are not preordained and absolute. Rather, they manifest deliberate choices rendered by political and economic resolutions and executed by public and private institutions. In this sense, the book is ultimately about choices, and as we come to the end of the first decade of the new millennium, we pause to assess our history and the extent to which we can learn from our mistakes. Indeed, this book explores one of the biggest mistakes in the history of the United States, Katrina, America's unnatural disaster.

Notes

1. Brian Handwerk, "Eye on the Storm: Hurricane Katrina Fast Facts," *National Geographic News*, September 6, 2005, 1; Douglas Brinkley, *The Great Deluge: Hurricane Katrina, New Orleans, and the Mississippi Gulf Coast* (New York: William Morrow, 2006), 1–10; John McQuaid and Mark Schleifstein, *Path of Destruction: The Devastation of New Orleans and the Coming Age of Superstorms* (New York: Little, Brown, 2006), 151–307. Also, the term "Katrina" is often used as a quick reference to Hurricane Katrina and the physical, social, and economic chaos that arose as a result of the storm. Likewise, even though this book is concerned with the effects of Katrina on the Gulf Coast, "New Orleans" will be used as an inclusive term that will cover the greater Gulf Coast, including Louisiana, Mississippi, Alabama, and Texas.

2. Handwerk, "Eye on the Storm," 1; Brinkley, *Great Deluge*, 1–10; McQuaid and Schleifstein, *Path of Destruction*, 151–307.

3. Handwerk, "Eye on the Storm," 1; Michael Eric Dyson, *Come Hell or High Water: Hurricane Katrina and the Color of Disaster* (New York: Basic Books, 2006), 1–15; Chester Hartman and Gregory D. Squires, eds., *There Is No Such Thing as a Natural Disaster: Race, Class, and Hurricane Katrina* (New York: Routledge, 2006), 1–12. Also see David Dante Troutt and Charles Ogletree, eds., *After the Storm: Black Intellectuals Explore the Meaning of Hurricane Katrina* (New York: New Press, 2007).

4. Jennifer Lai Browne-Dianis, Marielena Hincapie, and Saket Soni, eds., *And Injustice for All: Workers' Lives in the Reconstruction of New Orleans* (Washington DC: Advancement Project, 2006), 50–54.

5. Henry Jenkins, "People from That Part of the World": The Politics of Dislocation," Culture at Large Forum with George Lipsitz, *Cultural Anthropology* 21, no. 3 (August 2006), 469–86; Browne-Dianis, Hincapie, and Soni, *And Injustice for All*, 9–14, 32–38, 50–54.

6. Hartman and Squires, *There Is No Such Thing*, 18; Dyson, *Come Hell or High Water*, 1–2.

7. Nancy Denton and Douglass S. Massey, *American Apartheid: Segregation and the Making of the Underclass* (Cambridge MA: Harvard University Press), 1–55; David Brooks, "Katrina's Silver Lining," *New York Times*, September 8, 2005, A-29; Hartman and Squires, *There Is No Such Thing*, 3; Dyson, *Come Hell or High Water*, 7; Gwendolyn Mildew Hall, *Africans in Colonial Louisiana: The Development of Afro-Creole Culture in the Eighteenth Century* (Baton Rouge: Louisiana State University Press, 1995), 1–118.

8. Dyson, *Come Hell or High Water*, 7–8; Brookings Institution, *New Orleans after the Storm: Lessons from the Past, a Plan for the Future* (Washington DC: Brookings Institution, 2005), 5–6.

9. Brookings Institution, *New Orleans after the Storm*, 5–6.

10. Thomas M. Shapiro, *The Hidden Cost of Being African American: How Wealth Perpetuates Inequality* (New York: Oxford University Press, 2003), 42–154.

11. Jack Balkin, *What Brown v. Board of Education Should Have Said: The Nation's Top Legal Experts Rewrite America's Landmark Civil Rights Decision* (New York: New York University Press, 2002), 3–28, 185–200; Marc Mauer, *Race to Incarcerate* (New York: New Press, 2006), 1–14, 118–41; Neil J. Smelser, William Julius Wilson, and Faith Mitchell, eds., *America Becoming: Racial Trends and Their Consequences*, vol. 2 (Washington DC: National Academy Press, 2001), 1–20, 222–52, 371–410; Alice O'Conner, Chris Tilly, and Lawrence D. Bobo, eds., *Urban Inequality: Evidence from Four Cities* New York: Russell Sage Foundation, 2006), 1–33, 89–303, 444–95; Denton and Massey, *American Apartheid*, 424.

12. Andrew Hacker, *Money: Who Has How Much and Why* (New York: Scribner, 1998), 57–72, 145–72; Hartman and Squires, *There Is No Such Thing*, 5.

13. June Manning Thomas, *Redevelopment and Race: Planning a Finer City in Postwar Detroit* (Baltimore: Johns Hopkins University Press, 1997), 179–202; James H. Carr, Comments on "Predatory Home Lending: Moving toward Legal and Policy Solutions," conference at John Marshall Law School, Chicago, September 9, 2005).

14. Peter Dreier, John Mollenkopf, and Todd Swanstrom, *Place Matters: Metropolitics for the Twenty-First Century* (Lawrence: University Press of Kansas, 2001), 1–75; Ronald, J. Daniels, Donald, F. Kettl, and Howard Kunreuther, eds., *On Risk and Disaster: Lessons from Hurricane Katrina* (Philadelphia: University of Pennsylvania Press, 2006), 1–14, 59–76, 243–62; Dyson, *Come Hell or High Water*, 203–12.

15. John M. Barry, *Rising Tide: The Great Mississippi Flood of 1927 and How It Changed America* (New York: Simon and Schuster, 1998), 399–411; Hartman and Squires, *There Is No Such Thing*, 18.

16. Barry, *Rising Tide*, 399–411; Robyn Spencer, "Contested Terrain: The Mississippi Flood of 1927 and the Struggle to Control Black Labor," *Journal of Negro History* 79, no. 2: 171.

17. Spencer, "Contested Terrain," 399–411.

18. Spencer, "Contested Terrain," 172.

19. Hartman and Squires, *There Is No Such Thing*, 19; Spencer, "Contested Terrain," 172.

ONE

Letters from a Native Son

Do You Know What It Means to Miss New Orleans?

MITCHELL F. CRUSTO

The following is a journal of a native son's experiences and reflections as he and his family evacuated the City of New Orleans prior to Hurricane Katrina. It also chronicles his reaction to the news of the devastation and the government's mishandling of the situation in the months, albeit now years, following the hurricane. Mitchell F. Crusto keeps his journal as if writing letters to his mother. But in this instance, his "mother" is the City of New Orleans herself.

Letter One, Katrina the Natural Disaster, Evacuation, and
Dodging the Bullet, the Morning of August 29, 2005

Dearest Mother Dear (City of New Orleans),

Friday, August 26, 2005, three days before Katrina hit you, Mother Dear New Orleans, and changed our lives forever, Cousin Nakia called today and asked where we were going to evacuate. I asked her why we were evacuating this time. She said Hurricane Katrina is in the Gulf, and the news said it is projected to hit New Orleans.

On Saturday, August 27, 2005, Lisa and I gathered our daughter

Theresa and some things, thinking this would be another brief holiday away from work, as had been the other evacuations each fall over the last several years. We didn't board up the windows. We didn't move previous personal belongings to higher levels on the second floor. We didn't even take our precious cat Autumn, as we would certainly be back in a week at the latest.

We called Honey, my mother, and told her to pack a bag, that she was coming with us. She said that would mean she would miss an important social engagement: the fiftieth anniversary party for one of her dearest friends. We told her to call them and apologize and blame her overprotective son for her missing the special event. We called Sister Deborah, who said she was boarding her house and would catch up. We called Brother Al, who said he might leave. We called Brother Rene, who said that he was going to ride it out in New Orleans. (Sister Kathy and her family were living in Arlington, Texas, and were ready as usual to greet unannounced visitors escaping pending disasters.)

So we packed the Suburban, thank God for a black man with a good job, and the family, and some gas, and some food, and armed with some cash and credit cards we ventured to face our Katrina destiny. We picked up Honey on the way and drove along the back roads outside the city to avoid the traffic jams. The newscasters were telling everyone to travel west along Interstate 10 toward Houston; we decided that it would be better to head north along Interstate 55, first to Jackson and then to Memphis. Eventually, we concluded our evacuation two days later with a visit to my children Eve and Mia, who were living with their mother in St. Louis.

So we left you, Mother Dear New Orleans, on Saturday, August 27, 2005, two days before Hurricane Katrina smashed into your lovely landscape and shattered your southern serenity. On Monday, August 29, 2005, we joined the world as we watched the Weather Channel, our steady diet for information over the last several days.

It showed scenes of the Gulf Coast and yes, you, our previous New Orleans, being battered with Category 5 winds, torrential rains, and 30-foot tidal waves. But we were greatly relieved when the news reported that you, our ancestral city of African American culture, jazz, creole cuisine, Zulu balls, and Mardi Gras Indians, had been spared as Katrina had at the last minute veered east and directly into Bay St. Louis, Mississippi, which was virtually wiped off the map. There were scenes of people cheering in the streets of New Orleans and thanking God for being spared, once again.

Letter Two, Katrina the Un-Natural Disaster, It's the
Levees, Stupid, the Evening of August 31, 2005

Dearest Mother Dear,

We are here at the Culpepper's Restaurant off Olive Street in suburban St. Louis, watching the international news coverage of the devastation of Hurricane Katrina. It was reported that you have been spared Katrina's direct hit, although your sister Gulf Coast cities of Pascagoula, Bay St. Louis, Biloxi, and Mobile were less fortunate. And then came the horrible news of your levees. Some say that there were explosions; that the levees were intentionally dynamited to relieve damage to the more affluent, tourist-significant sections of the city: the French Quarter, the Garden District, the Uptown, the Downtown, and the Tulane-Loyola University areas along the St. Charles streetcar line. The news cameras zoomed in on a street sign that, for your native sons and daughters, said it all. Flooded water reached up to the bottom of a street sign showing Frenchmen and Marigny Streets in the affluent African American neighborhood of Gentilly, which was a noted high elevation in the city. If water was at this level, the news reports were not showing and no one was saying something of greater significance. More than half of you, our beloved city, was under water! And so our teardrops rolled down our trembling faces. This would be the first time following Katrina that we cried for you, New Orleans, but it would not be the last.

Letter Three, Battered Homes, Shattered Lives,
September 1–December 31, 2005

Dearest Mother Dear,

The media was hailed for its coverage of Hurricane Katrina and its aftermath, especially for what happened to you, my Beloved City. Some of the coverage was helpful, but most of it exploited you and your family of citizens, and did not tell the truth. The truth was that Katrina was not about a hurricane or a nature disaster. Katrina is about the failures of the levee system around you and the failed politics before, during, and after Katrina. The truth is not about the "looting" of stores for food and shelter or the apparent civil insurrection by gangs of lawless people. It is about the failure of all levels of government, local, state, and federal, to take immediate action to comfort the survivors who were negatively impacted by Katrina. Katrina survivors number over a million people and were in various distressful circumstances. Katrina survivors include the people on the rooftops or in the attics of their home, stranded in the flood. Katrina survivors include the people at the Superdome and at the Convention Center. They include the people stranded on bridges and highways, surrounded by polluted, rising waters. They are the people who were shot at by police officers on the West Bank of the city, and the people who were prevented from evacuating from the flooded parts of the East Bank. Katrina survivors included most of our family, who now live elsewhere with or without other family members in Baton Rouge, in Atlanta, in Houston, in Dallas/Fort Worth, in Memphis, St. Louis, Chicago, and in every big city and small town throughout the country. Katrina survivors include people who were herded into airplanes and buses and shipped without permission to faraway places such as Oakland and Minneapolis, where they remain stranded today and unable to return to their homes.

There were the thousands of our loved ones who did not survive. Francis Robinette, or "Nanny," died along with hundreds of others in nursing homes that were either unprepared or negligent in their response to Katrina. And it might be easy to forget about the thousands of others who died after being evacuated from New Orleans of old age and heartbreak like Maurice Prevost. "Uncle Morris" died at the age of ninety-five in Indianapolis, where he had evacuated with his daughter Anne-Maureen.

Letter Four, the Matter of Race, September 1–December 31, 2005

Dearest Mother Dear,

All of your children, of all races, are debating whether race was a major factor in what happened to you following Katrina. Many African Americans believe that if you were a vanilla city, rather than a chocolate city, the Katrina story would have been different, less tragic. Many Anglo-American citizens of the City are offended by the notion that the disaster was about race, as if their misfortunes are less significant because they are not minorities in the traditional sense. It was apparent to me that there are seven reasons why race does not define Katrina. First, Anglo-Americans were equally impacted by Katrina. Second, President Bush is a fair-minded person and treats all American citizens equally. Third, Governor Blanco is racially blind and so is Mayor Nagin. Fourth, if race were a major factor, the media would have said so. Fifth, to say that race is a factor is contrary to our Nation's history. Sixth, Katina was really about ineffective levees and the environment. And seventh, it was about poverty and class, not about race.

All right, Mother New Orleans, I can lie to you; I am unconvinced that Katrina was not about race. Maybe I feel this way because my entire life had been molded by race as an African American, albeit a Fifth Ward creole, citizen of the city. Here is my take on the question of race and Katrina. First, African Americans were more likely to live in lower-lying sections of the city than Anglo-Americans because of the history of housing segregation in New Orleans. This does not mean that there were no African Americans living in the high and dry sections of the city, such as the French Quarter or the Garden District, or that no Anglo-Americans lived in low-lying and flooded-prone areas of the city, such as the Lower Ninth Ward. The greatest reality is that the entire City of New Orleans is below sea level and therefore subject to flood. The real question is whether race played a factor in the development and maintenance of the levee and water-pumping systems in New Orleans. I honestly cannot answer that question based on my current knowledge, but I can say that it would not surprise me if race played a fact in the underfunding of levees in the city over the years. Also, I am familiar with studies showing that environmental injustice in this country is connected to race and class, particularly when it comes to the level of protection against environmental harms that is afforded to African Americans and other impoverished minority communities.

Second, as to President Bush. It appears that there are many reasons to believe that President Bush does in fact like black people (contrary to Kanye West's statement). After all, he had placed many African Americans in leadership positions in his cabinet, from Colin Powell to Condoleezza Rice to Alphonse Jackson. But the question is not about personal racism. The question is, rather, are his policies racially biased against African Americans? It would appear that the evidence supports an affirmative answer. Clearly, President Bush and his party developed and promoted policies that negatively affect African Americans. These include substantial cuts in social safety net programs. Third, as to Governor Blanco and Mayor Nagin, there isn't enough ink to analyze these two players, so I won't try. Fourth, the popular broadcast media is inadequate to cover a story as big as Katrina. Apparently popular journalists did not think it in their best interest to cover Katrina through a race lens. Fifth, race has been a determinate factor throughout our Nation's history, so why not use it to define Katrina? Would the national government hesitate to provide substantial disaster relief had the city's residents been affluent, Anglo-American Republicans? I guess we will just have to see when we have the next major disaster in a different part of the country, like Sacramento, California. Sixth, was race a factor in the design, funding, construction, and maintenance of the levee system? And seventh, perhaps Katrina had more to do with poverty, class, and party politics than with race. I suspect that a comparative study of the national government's response to Katrina's effects on the Mississippi Gulf Coast, versus its response to the storm's effects on New Orleans, will reveal any differences or similarities.

Letter Five, President Bush, Governor Blanco, Major C. Ray Nagin, and the Irresponsibility of the Government at All Levels, and Federalism

Dearest Mother Dear,

The disclosure of America's Dirty Secrets, the existence of communities in distress, leads to another thought: the relationship between federalism and racial equality. I want to challenge us with a renewed vision of American federalism, one that repairs the vestiges of our nation's legacy of the enslavement of African American people and of legally treating people as property. One of the guiding principles of our nation is federalism. Most legal scholars today seem focused on the structural aspects of federalism; that is, the balance of political power between state governments and the federal government. But "true" federalism, President Abraham Lincoln federalism, I believe, is much, much more. It is the belief in the integrity of the individual, in what today might be called human rights. It is my thesis that federalism is about the constitutional rights of every American to be guaranteed human dignity. I believe that all levels of government have the legal and moral responsibility to protect the integrity of each and every individual.

What about federalism and race? Hurricane Katrina showed the world that we have failed to remediate our past of slavery. We are continuing to live a conflicted legacy. It is a legacy of tremendous respect for the integrity of the individual's rights, liberty, and pursuit of happiness, but unfortunately also a legacy of the enslavement of people because of their race. Our legal history of treating people as property leads us to treat people on the fringe of society as rubbish, abandoned or discarded trash.

This year is the 150th anniversary of the Dred Scott decision, wherein the United States Supreme Court pronounced that enslaved African American people were legal property of their owners and that all African Americans lacked the basic rights of American citizenship under the U.S. Constitution. Isn't it time for us to amend our conflicted past? But I have spoken too long about too many depressing things.

What next? What hope? What dream? There is a legal movement at all levels of government to erase race from policy debate and policy considerations. Recently, the State of Michigan has joined other states in passing a referendum to erase race from public policy. In some ways this movement is commendable, as it could reflect the progress we have made as a nation. Unfortunately, removing race from policy criteria does not, and in my view will not, eradicate racism.

In order to protect the rights of all American citizens, my vision of the federalist ideal is that we must continue to support inclusion strategies to maintain open markets and open doors. We must also engage, when we can, in greater consciousness and positive debate to challenge those who hold the view that "affirmative action" has reached its zenith. We must continue to work at all levels to protect the constitutional rights of each and every American, regardless of her or his race, ethnicity, religion, sexual preference, or other social-dividing criteria. Racism of all kinds can be eradicated with courage, leadership, and example, but not by eliminating "race" as a policy criterion. Furthermore, we must become devoted to remedying the needs of our communities in distress.

Letter Six, Katrina, Communities in Distress, and Unveiling America's Social Disaster

Dearest Mother Dear,

As a recent survivor of the ravages of Hurricane Katrina, I want to share some observations of what I previously referred to as "America's Dirty Secrets." Hurricane Katrina was a worldwide media event that unveiled these secrets to the world. What are these secrets? Before I share them with you, I want to reflect on Dr. Martin Luther King Jr.'s vision, his Dream.

Has this Dream been realized? It would appear to me, after growing up in a racially segregated, impoverished New Orleans neighborhood in the 1950s and 1960s, that today there are many examples to indicate that America is living "The Dream." Our people are cabinet secretaries, governors, senators, congresswomen, and yes, presidential contenders. We are CEOs of major corporations, we lead our military forces, and we teach at the most cherished institutions of higher learning.

But The Dream is not just about opening doors for African American leadership. It is about brotherhood and sisterhood among all of God's people, regardless of racial divides. It is my belief that in

31

America today there is more harmony and fellowship among our people than at any other time in our nation's history. And so there is hope. Dr. Martin Luther King Jr. would be proud.

So why did I mention despair, when there is cause for hope? Hurricane Katrina was more than a natural disaster; it exposed America's social disaster, or our Dirty Secrets. What are America's Dirty Secrets? The worldwide media coverage of Katrina showed that despite the successes of many African Americans, there are many among us who live in what I refer to as "communities in distress."

You know what communities in distress are, because to most of us they are no secret. Many of us, of many backgrounds, come from them, and many of us still live within them. They are not just within the City of New Orleans; they are throughout this country, in the South, the North, the West, and the East.

Communities in distress, much like my beloved New Orleans, are deceptive. On the surface, they are thriving economically and socially. Their downtowns have tall, shining, new buildings. They feature new, publicly funded stadiums and parks. They often have shiny airports that serve businesspeople and tourists. But behind the glamour, not unlike that of New Orleans, distressed communities suffer. They need our help. Not unlike abandoned Katrina survivors, the majority of residents in distressed communities are impoverished African Americans.

A recently published Harvard University study shows that African Americans, especially those who reside in urban areas, have a quality of life that is lower than all other ethnic groups nationwide. Researchers at Harvard University's Initiative for Global Health and School of Public Health examined the U.S. Census and various health studies produced between 1982 and 2001. They found that the nation is divided into "eight Americas." Not surprising, African Americans in "high risk" cities nationwide and in rural areas of the Deep South are at the bottom of the social ladder. These communities in distress suffer from high unemployment, poor schools, chronic health effects, illicit drug abuse, inadequate housing, and high levels of crime, murder, and suicide.

Katrina represents America's social disaster as an example of the local, state, and federal governments' failure to aid people in crisis. The people of New Orleans, and all people in distressed communities, illustrate Katrina, the Social Disaster.

Letter Seven, Katrina and beyond Private Insurers and Federal Flood Coverage

Dearest Mother Dear,

Many of your citizens had homeowners' insurance, although a great number were renters or recipients of public housing. Even those with private homeowners' insurance did not expect the effect of the flood exemption in their homeowners' policies. These exemptions generally mean that homeowners will not be covered for property damage, content damages, and loss of use (additional living expenses) if their homes are damaged as a result of flooding. They are required to purchase federal flood insurance if they want to be compensated for flood damages. Some had flood coverage through insurance, others did not, and many who had insurance had insufficient coverage.

Letter Eight, Eulogy, Do You Know What It Means to Miss New Orleans? March 29, 2007 (18 Months Later)

Dearest Mother Dear,

This is my last letter to you, and it is your eulogy. Sure, some will say that your demise is greatly exaggerated and claim that you are still with us, and they present some convincing evidence. The Superdome has been renovated, but the spirit of betrayal still permeates the place. Mardi Gras is still celebrated in great splendor, but the small sizes of the public school bands tell a story of a public school system virtually destroyed and grossly abandoned. America's port of New Orleans is still thriving as it continues to deliver goods, including oil and gas, to citizens of the world. You are still a tourist destination with rich food, jazz, and Afro-centric culture.

Yet something has died in this tale of two cities, the City That Care Forgot and the City of Mardi Gras Affluence. The latter is indeed alive and will continue to live in good health. The former, the city that I know and love, is dead and gone forever. The African American middle class that was the stabilizing feature of a city with sharp racial and economic divisions is gone. Gone too are the neighborhood-based public school system and its African American teachers' union. Gone is the upper class of African American professionals, doctors, lawyers, and professors who have found it easier to stay displaced in their new home communities than to fight to be returned to their old, damaged communities. Gone is a generation of older African Americans who did not survive the Katrina ordeal, as well as those who have chosen not to relive their memories of Katrina by returning to New Orleans.

Perhaps there will be a resurrection of the City That Care Forgot. And if the Chocolate part of New Orleans survives, perhaps it can be reconstructed better than before. Perhaps in this new city, we can eradicate poverty, erase social, economic, and racial barriers, and eliminate social ills such as AIDS. Perhaps we can build new schools and replace crumbling infrastructure. And perhaps we can beat the odds against African American political empowerment.

So what are the lessons from Katrina for all Americans? Every community in America, from Sacramento, California, to St. Louis, Missouri, to New York City, is subject to catastrophic loss due to man-made or natural disasters such as hurricanes, earthquakes, tornados, mudslides, tidal waves, levee breaches, toxic releases, or acts of terror. When it happens to you, will you feel betrayed? By incompetence or by design?

TWO

After Katrina

Laying Bare the Anatomy of American Caste

BRYAN K. FAIR

Speaking Truth to Power and to Ourselves

Like hundreds of thousands of others, I visited New Orleans several times in the spring and summer of 2005. On the one hand, I always considered New Orleans to be one of the great American cities. It was an outstanding convention and conference center, a cultural haven for artists and musicians, an educational center boasting outstanding colleges and universities, and a wondrous place for diverse cuisines. I enjoyed everything: the spectacular meals, the melodious jazz and blues scenes, the educational excellence, and the great walking and festive shopping venues throughout the Big Easy. New Orleans was always an exciting getaway!

On the other hand, despite all its scintillating pleasures, I also always experienced a deep uneasiness, a disturbing sense of local division, decay, and despair all around New Orleans. Something palpably pungent always laced the New Orleans air.

I was keenly aware of the vexing, concentrated poverty, which relegated many of the mostly black residents of New Orleans to desperate lives in the shadows of the city's historic grandeur. I knew that just outside of the French Quarter or just north of the Garden District, many New Orleans residents who had been left out of the city's wealth and opulence made a life, legal or extra-legal, out of almost nothing.

Certain zones in the city were havens for violent crime; unwitting tourists might easily fall victim to street muggings or worse. I knew that some considered New Orleans to be the homicide capital of the country. I actively avoided especially isolated spaces, but I could never escape the many signposts of caste throughout the city. There were obvious pockets of privilege and abundance in various quarters, but many residents who were barely able to afford basic food and shelter were only a stone's throw away. New Orleans always seemed combustible, a powder keg of haves and have-nots waiting to explode.

I was less aware of the growing political crisis and the neglect of local, state, and federal policymakers, especially regarding the preparation of the city for the increasingly frequent and more severe hurricanes and storms along the Gulf Coast. New Orleans was one of the nation's most vulnerable cities, but no emergency plan was in place to protect or evacuate its poorest residents from storms or flooding. I also had no idea that the city's all-important levee system had not been properly maintained for years, creating even more of a risk of crisis for the most vulnerable and least mobile New Orleans residents.

Then, Hurricane Katrina's storm surge caused the old, decaying levee system to fail. In its wake, Katrina laid bare for the world that America, too, has its own castes. This nation includes people who live on the margins of U.S. society, unequally protected and often abandoned, who, because of an intersection of color, class, and history, are permanently excluded from equal citizenship and equal opportunity. Katrina's victims were and are America's poor, black and nonblack; they were and are America's huddled masses yearning to be free from danger, but with no place to go and no one to render basic, timely assistance.

The post-Katrina images from New Orleans seemed surreal, leaving observers from around the world to ask: how could such human devastation, chaos, and despair occur in the United States? It was inconceivable that neither local, state, nor national officials could immediately aid the residents of New Orleans or other parts of the Gulf Coast. The images on CNN reminded me of Soweto and the worst abuses and neglect under South African apartheid. Yet this was New Orleans, not Soweto, and I was forced to consider parallels and whether apartheid was the appropriate lens for critiquing what I observed or read about New Orleans and other cities in Alabama and Mississippi.

The Katrina story is about the intersection of history, race, space, law, and politics. It is about the history and traditions in the U.S. that have relegated so many American citizens to second-caste status. It is about the social construction of racial identities, which privileges a white majority as the superior race and deems all other racial groups inferior. The story is about segregation's legacy, which traps America's most vulnerable citizens in its poorest, most dangerous land areas. And the story is about a political and legal tradition of grand compromises, built on the exploitation of many so that a few might live lavishly.

After the loss of so many precious lives, after the tragic images of human suffering, and after all the chaos and despair, I am forced to look beneath the Big Easy's veneer. I am also forced to look more closely at myself and my country to try to comprehend how such a terrible event could occur, why so many people were stranded in harm's way, and what we must do to protect people from the next great storm.

Katrina is a personal wake-up call. It is a reminder that each of us can and must do more each day to turn back all forms of caste.

It is a call to arms for me personally to do more, say more, write more, and demand more from myself and my country.

The purpose of this essay is to expose the deep racial chasms in American life that rendered so many of New Orleans' black citizens beleaguered and trapped in such wretched conditions. I argue that a central legacy of America's longstanding discriminatory practices is racial caste: the relegation of many Americans with darker skin to a permanent subordinate status in society by virtue of their birth or descent, from which very few escape. New Orleans after Katrina is a window from which to analyze the legally sanctioned caste of America's most vulnerable citizens.

Our Unequal Past

I often wonder if African Americans have any rights that white Americans are bound to respect. Do Americans with darker skin have the same rights to life, liberty, and the pursuit of happiness as are presumed for whites? Do African Americans have a right to due process and to equal protection under the law on the same basis as whites in the United States? Do Americans with darker skin have a fundamental right to equal educational opportunity, a right to equal employment opportunity, a right to equal political participation, or a right to equal application of the criminal laws? Do African Americans have a right to stand before the government as equals to whites, or have the state and federal governments rendered Americans with darker skin second-caste citizens?

Despite constitutional guarantees and federal civil rights legislation dating back fifteen decades, I think the answer to the above questions must be no. Whether one examines U.S. history, Supreme Court precedent, the practices in the states, or enforcement of the law, one might well conclude that despite an end to slavery, to Jim Crow segregation, and to other forms of explicit discrimination on the basis of color, legal reforms have done little to eliminate black caste or other forms of caste in the United States. Since Charles Sumner said that the chief aim of the Fourteenth Amendment was to eliminate black caste, it would appear the amendment's purpose has been thwarted.[1]

If, as Justice Holmes admonished, "a page of history is worth a volume of logic," then several hundred years of historical practices must be instructive about questions regarding the legal status of people of color in the United States.[2] Even the most cursory glance at the Supreme Court's pronouncement of the law leaves no doubt about the inferior legal status of Americans with darker skin relative to whites.[3]

In my research and writing I assert repeatedly that discrimination in the United States has produced multiple forms of caste throughout the country. I use the term "caste" intentionally, because I think there is significant evidence that the principal goal of the Fourteenth Amendment's sponsors was to eliminate black caste. I argue we have yet to eliminate black caste because we have not adopted an anti-caste principle in accordance with the central meaning of the Equal Protection Clause; we lost the anti-caste moorings of the Fourteenth Amendment. We have not imposed on government an affirmative duty to dismantle all racial caste. Until we do so, the equality guarantee of American law will remain a hollow promise.[4]

Racial caste is America's apartheid. We see it in every aspect of American life today: in education, employment, housing, political representation, and wealth accumulation. By each benchmark, many people of color trail significantly behind their white counterparts.

Modern racial caste in the United States generally, and in New Orleans specifically, is not an accidental byproduct of a few bad actors or a few poor policy choices. American racial caste today rests on four centuries of legal practices and judgments. Modern racial caste is the legacy of slavery, as well as racial inequality after slavery. It is the consequence of a nation's declaration that some of its citizens were a superior, dominant group entitled to exercise control over others.[5]

When I look for the origins of modern racial caste, I begin in Europe six centuries ago with people who declared that native indigenous peoples across the globe had no rights that the English, French, Dutch, Spanish, Italian, and other peoples of Europe were bound to respect. Year after year, decade after decade, those Europeans made war against humans with darker skin, raping, pillaging, and robbing native peoples of their human dignity and human rights as well as their natural resources and wealth.[6]

Today half of the world's population lives mired in caste, with no effective means of escape. According to the United Nations, more than one billion people in the world live on less than $1 a day. Nearly 3 billion humans on our planet live on less than $2 per day. For almost half the world's population, poverty confines their lives to hardship and despair, to diseases that have been preventable or treatable for decades, to illiteracy, to violence, and to myriad forms of exploitation.[7]

The UN also reports that every year 6 million children die from malnutrition before their fifth birthday. Every 30 seconds an African child dies of malaria. More than 800 million people go to bed hungry every day, 300 million of them children. Many of them are in the United States. Every 3.6 seconds another person dies of starvation. Most of them are children under five years old. More than 40 percent of the world population, 2.6 billion people, do not have basic sanitation. One billion people have no access to safe drinking water. Five million people, mostly children, die each year from water-borne diseases.[8]

According to CARE, more than 30 million children are not immunized against preventable diseases. Two million children are believed exploited through the commercial sex trade. Over 130 million children have never been to a school. Some countries still give educational preferences to boys over girls. Nearly a quarter of a billion children are forced to work to survive.[9]

I am convinced that the images from New Orleans after Katrina are a small microcosm of various types of caste from across the globe. Much more must be done to reduce each form of caste in and outside of the United States. Although racial caste is an international phenomenon and present on each continent, it has particular salience in the United States, the land of the free, the home of the equal citizenship principle. African American caste and exploitation have deep roots in the United States. For nearly 235 years, blacks had no rights that white Americans were bound to respect. This was also true, albeit to a different degree and extent, for other Americans with darker skin: for native American Indians, Mexicans, Asians, and to an even more limited extent, some European immigrants, especially from Eastern and Southern Europe, until they became "white."[10]

Blacks were condemned to the status of slaves for life. That status extended to each new generation, and it appears that blacks are still relegated to inferior caste today. Thus, it seems reasonable to conclude that constitutional caste for blacks ended in form but not in substance.[11]

Slavery was a symptom of a much broader disease that has yet to be cured. The real culprit in the creation of racial caste, then and now, is the belief by some that they are entitled, by God, talent, or race, to declare what rights other people should have; racial caste is created when some believe that they have the right to declare through the law that other humans are a subordinate and inferior class of beings. This is what the founders did in the U.S. Constitution when they declared for purposes of taxation that black slaves were equivalent to three-fifths of a person; this is what Chief Justice Roger B. Taney did when he declared that persons of African ancestry, whether slave or free, were not U.S. citizens; this is what Justice Samuel F. Miller did when he declared that the Privileges and Immunities Clause of the Fourteenth Amendment provided no federal protection of civil rights to former slaves; this is what the Supreme Court did when it declared that Congress lacked the power under sections 1 or 5 of the Fourteenth Amendment to forbid racial discrimination in public accommodations. Each of these actions legalized black caste. In each case the Court sacrificed the human rights of blacks and elevated the unfair privileges of whites.[12]

The Court declared in *Dred Scott* that blacks had no rights that whites were bound to respect. Taney wrote:

> [Blacks] were at that time considered as a subordinate and inferior class of beings, who had been subjugated by the dominant race, and, whether emancipated or not, yet remained subject to their authority, and had no rights or privileges but such as those who held the power and the Government might choose to grant them. . . . [Blacks] had for more than a century before been regarded as beings of an inferior order, and altogether unfit to associate with the white race, either in social or political relations; and so far inferior, that they had no rights which the white man was bound to respect; and that [blacks] might justly and lawfully be reduced to slavery for [their] benefit.[13]

Taney's critique and conclusion have been significant in law and practice ever since.

The Court continued its assault on the human rights of blacks in *Plessy v. Ferguson* by declaring that Jim Crow segregation was not unconstitutional; instead the doctrine of separate but equal did not violate the constitutional rights of blacks. Justice Brown wrote:

> It is claimed by [Plessy] in error that, in any mixed community, the reputation of belonging to the dominant race, in this instance

the white race, is "property," in the same sense that a right of action or of inheritance is property. Conceding this to be so, for the purposes of this case, we are unable to see how this statute [requiring segregation in railway cars] deprives him of . . . such property. If he be a white man, and assigned to a colored coach, he may have his action for damages against the company for being deprived of his so-called "property." Upon the other hand, if he be a colored man, and be so assigned, he has been deprived of no property, *since he is not lawfully entitled to the reputation of being a white man.*[14]

The doctrine of separate but equal was little more than slavery in disguise, leaving blacks inferior to whites socially, politically, economically, and civilly.

The Court failed to prevent extensive discrimination or protect the political, economic, and social rights of blacks. For too many years, the Court accommodated racial discrimination in the criminal justice system, racially restrictive housing covenants, discrimination in graduation and professional education, discrimination in voting rights, discrimination in public accommodations, and discrimination in employment.[15]

Even in *Brown v. Board of Education* and its progeny, the Court did little to change the caste conditions of most blacks. In *Brown*, Chief Justice Warren relied on findings from the lower courts to conclude:

Segregation of white and colored children in public schools has a detrimental effect upon the colored children. The impact is greater when it has the sanction of the law; for the policy of separating the races is usually interpreted as denoting the inferiority of the [black] group. A sense of inferiority affects the motivation of a child to learn. Segregation with the sanction of law, therefore, has a tendency to [retard] the educational and mental development of [black] children and to deprive them of some of the benefit they would receive in a racially integrated school system.[16]

The Court acknowledged the stigma imposed on colored children by segregation, but it did not acknowledge the white privilege inherent in an educational policy that allocated ten-to-one resources to white schools versus black schools. Again, as before, the Court did not admit that the real disease was not segregation but rather whites' assumption of the power to deny equal human rights to blacks and other colored people seeking equal education.[17]

Our Present Caste

Racial caste in the United States today, as well as in New Orleans, is derivative and consequential. Many African Americans across the country are patently vulnerable in all aspects of their lives. They are generally under-educated, under-employed, and economically insecure. They live in high-risk areas, their lives are shorter and more prone to disease, and they live in urban ghettos or rural pockets of despair where there are few economic opportunities for escape or betterment. Millions live from paycheck to paycheck or subsidy to subsidy, with insufficient resources to adequately provide food, clothing, or shelter for themselves or their families. They have old transportation, no transportation, or insufficient funds for limited public transportation. They live separately from whites, even from those who share their poverty. It seems very little has changed.

Ten years ago, Andrew Hacker cogently described America as two nations: one black, one white, separate and unequal. The entrenched racialized poverty laid bare by Hacker is apparent in many American cities, including New Orleans. There, in a city over two-thirds African American, whites appeared to any outside observer to be the dominant, ruling class. Whites had higher educational attainment, higher median incomes, higher property values, and better access to employment. They lived in safer communities, with less poverty, less violence, and less crime. They attended better schools and received better basic public and private services.[18]

According to Bruce Katz, 34 percent of black New Orleans residents lived below the poverty line prior to Katrina. Indeed, extreme concentrations of poverty in New Orleans left nearly 40 percent of its residents without sufficient educational skills, employment opportunities, or incomes to support themselves. In some communities in the city, 80 percent of black children are raised in single-parent, mostly female-headed households. In the poorest neighborhoods six of ten working-age residents were part of the labor force, and only one in twelve adults had a college degree. These staggering statistics suggest that the United States has made almost no progress toward eliminating extreme poverty. Indeed, Juan Williams has written that poverty in the United States has been on the rise for the past several years.[19]

I agree with Williams that blacks in New Orleans could take some steps to reduce their disproportionate poverty. They could stay in school, delay marriage and families, and seek and find gainful employment. All people, black or nonblack, must do everything in their power to help lift themselves out of extreme poverty. I do not agree that such anti-poverty strategies will significantly alter extreme concentrations of black poverty in New Orleans or the United States generally. I certainly do not believe that present racial caste in New Orleans is unrelated to local, state, and national history. Moreover, any real anti-poverty program must improve black schools, black housing, public transportation, and employment, and reduce segregation. Government must eliminate the political and legal structures that reinforce black poverty.

As long as black children attend inferior schools, most will remain in caste. As long as they lack access to early literacy programs and safe, educationally effective schools where they learn to read and write above grade level, and where math and science instruction is extensive, they will never be able to compete fairly with affluent whites. Likewise, as long as blacks live in squalid, dense ghettos, or in dilapidated, overcrowded housing with little or no resale value, which is segregated from middle- and upper-class housing, most will never escape their caste. We must each demand these things, and those of us with real economic and political power must see that it is done. In the United States that means, significantly, that whites must do much of this work.

Blacks in New Orleans and elsewhere in the United States need a Newer Deal, another comprehensive anti-poverty effort to counter their persistent disadvantage. We need a new series of initiatives designed to help Americans at home to eliminate extreme poverty, improve reading and math literacy among children aged three to eight, expand public educational opportunities and aid for all students who maintain passing grades, and upgrade public housing and expand home ownership. These programs brought white America back from the brink of economic death in the 1930s, before the end of official segregation. Now our nation must do for its poor colored people what it once did for its millions of poor whites.

Where Do We Go from Here?

Increasingly I am convinced that the history of racial caste in the United States costs the nation billions of dollars each year, both in lost revenue and in higher costs. We who pay various taxes, sometimes even on food, bear the brunt of all such costs. In our history, every time we cheated black people of their political, economic, or social rights, we have imposed enormous costs on others in the society who must pay for despair and poverty. We pay for more police and jails and courts. We pay for health care costs for those who become sick from their poverty. When some citizens are under-educated and under-employed, we pay for welfare. These costs are almost never measured, but I suspect the amount is staggering. Again, it seems we have a simple choice: do we pay now to improve the lives of all Americans or do we pay the staggering costs of neglect later? Surely it makes more sense to build schools, houses, and community centers than to construct even more prisons and jails.

The horrid aftermath of Hurricane Katrina makes me think that government agents simply did not understand how bad conditions were, and they didn't care enough about the victims to respond swiftly when they understand these conditions. Hurricane Katrina left devastation in its wake throughout the Gulf Coast. It left death and destruction, but it also left survivors who still need help to improve their status and their lives. It has left people with nothing from their pasts. Even more, it made visible the extensive, intergenerational racial caste of many American cities. For me, it laid bare racial caste here and in many parts of the world, where colored people have little material wealth and virtually no protection from all kinds of catastrophes. It has made me see that I must personally do more.

More than rebuilding New Orleans and returning its residents from throughout the country, I see a much bigger project and challenge facing the United States; we have yet to face our national disease and shame. We as a nation still appear to tell African Americans that they do not belong, their lives do not matter, their suffering is not a national concern, and they are not full citizens. We still seem to believe that a small political class has the right to deny basic human rights to some Americans with darker skin.

Despite the myth of the American Dream, pledges of equal treatment before the law, and political movements to free Americans from slave-like castes, we do not yet honor the social contract for African Americans. We are not committed to their equality, to their equal rights to food, clothing, and shelter, or to their equal rights to education, employment, and political and economic participation.

The United States must reverse its legacy of racial caste before the next great storm.

As people committed to the human dignity of every person and as social justice advocates, we must develop new ways to combat human poverty. Rather than a war on terror, we need a global war on poverty to lift up the billions of people and millions of children who deserve what most of us take for granted: a real chance at life. We must fight this war on poverty with even greater vigor and resources, and with the cooperation of many other wealthy countries, because to do otherwise dishonors each one of us and threatens the peace of much of the world.

We must care more about the least among us, in New Orleans and throughout the world. Each one of us can do at least one thing to make a difference in our world each day. We cannot wait on presidents. We must take responsibility by touching another person's life each day.

Notes

1. Bryan K. Fair, "The Anatomy of American Caste," *St. Louis University Public Law Review* 18, no. 2 (1999): 381.

2. *New York Trust Co. v. Eisner*, 256 U.S. 345, 349 (1991).

3. See Bryan K. Fair, *Notes of a Racial Caste Baby: Color Blindness and the End of Affirmative Action* (New York: New York University Press, 1997); John Hope Franklin, *Mirror to America* (New York: Farrar, Straus and Giroux, 2005); John Hope Franklin and Alfred A. Moss Jr., *From Slavery to Freedom: A History of African Americans*, 8th ed. (New York: Knopf, 2000); A. Leon Higginbotham Jr., *Shades of Freedom: Racial Politics and Presumptions of the American Legal Process* (New York: Oxford University Press, 1996); A. Leon Higginbotham Jr., *In the Matter of Color: Race and the American Legal Process: The Colonial Period* (New York: Oxford University Press, 1978); *Plessy v. Ferguson*, 163 U.S. 537 (1896); *Dred Scott v. Sandford*, 60 U.S. (19 How.) 393 (1856).

4. See Fair, *Notes of a Racial Caste Baby*; Bryan K. Fair, "Re(caste)ing Equality Theory: Will *Grutter* Survive Itself by 2028?" in symposium, "Race Jurisprudence and the Supreme Court: Where Do We Go from Here?" *University of Pennsylvania Journal of Constitutional Law* 7 (2005): 721, 722; Bryan K. Fair, "The Darker Face of *Brown*: The Promise and Reality of the Decision's Anticaste Moorings Remain

Unreconciled," *Judicature* 88 (September–October 2004): 80; Bryan K. Fair, "Taking Educational Caste Seriously: Why *Grutter* Will Help Very Little," *Tulane Law Review* 78 (2004): 1843; Fair, "Anatomy of American Caste"; Bryan K. Fair, Review of *Black Trials: Citizenship from the Beginnings of Slavery to the End of Caste*, by Mark. S. Weiner, *Washington Post*, January 5, 2005, C04; Cass R. Sunstein, "The Anti-Caste Principle," *Michigan Law Review* 92 (1994): 2410.

5. "The white race deems itself the dominant race." *Plessy v. Ferguson*, (Harlan, dissenting).

6. Juan F. Perea et al., *Race and Races: Cases and Resources for a Multiracial America* (St. Paul MN: West Group, 2000), 173–75.

7. United Nations Millennium Project on World Poverty, "Investing in Development," Final Report (2005), http://www.unmillenniumproject.org/.

8. United Nations Millennium Project, "Investing in Development."

9. "Facts about Children and Poverty," CARE (2007), http://www.care.org/campaigns/childrenpoverty/facts.asp.

10. *Dred Scott v. Sandford*, 60 U.S. (19 How.) 393 (1856); Perea, *Race and Races*, 91, 173, 246, 367, 429.

11. Perea, *Race and Races*, 103–30, 165–72.

12. *Plessy v. Ferguson*; *Dred Scott v. Sandford*, 404–5, 417–20; U.S. Const. art. 1, § 2, para. 3; *Slaughter-House Cases*, 83 U.S. 36 (1872); *Civil Rights Cases*, 109 U.S. 3 (1883).

13. *Dred Scott v. Sandford*, 60 U.S. (19 How.) 404–7.

14. *Plessy v. Ferguson*, 549 (emphasis added).

15. *Plessy v. Ferguson*, 549; *McCleskey v. Kemp*, 481 U.S. 279 (1987); *Shelley v. Kramer*, 334 U.S. 1 (1948); *McLaurin v. Oklahoma State Regents*, 339 U.S. 637 (1950); *Sweatt v. Painter*, 339 U.S. 629 (1950); *Sipuel v. Board of Regents*, 332 U.S. 631 (1948); *Missouri ex rel. Gaines v. Canada*, 305 U.S. 337 (1938); *Smith v. Allright*, 321 U.S. 649 (1944); *Heart of Atlanta Motel, Inc. v. U.S.*, 379 U.S. 241 (1964); *United Steelworkers of America*, AFL-CIO-CLC *v. Weber*, 443 U.S. 193 (1979).

16. *United Steelworkers of America*, AFL-CIO-CLC *v. Weber* at 494.

17. *Brown v. Board of Education*, 347 U.S. 483 (1954); Fair, "Darker Face of Brown."

18. Andrew Hacker, *Two Nations: Black and White, Separate, Hostile, Unequal* (New York: Scribner's, 1992).

19. Bruce Katz, "Concentrated Poverty in New Orleans and Other American Cities," *Chronicle of Higher Education*, August 4, 2006, http://www.brookings.edu/views/op-ed/katz/20060804.htm; Juan Williams, "Getting Past Katrina," *New York Times*, September 1, 2006; Juan Williams, *Enough: The Phony Leaders, Dead-End Movements, and Culture of Failure That Are Undermining Black America—and What We Can Do about It* (New York: Crown, 2006).

THREE

Hurricane Katrina and the "Market" for Survival

The Role of Economic Theory in the Construction and Maintenance of Disaster

CHARLES R. P. POUNCY

Prologue

Uncle Bob sat on the porch, reading the Sunday paper as the children played nearby. The younger ones were on the porch working intently with their crayons and coloring books. The older ones played in the yard tossing a ball. The front of the newspaper was plastered with pictures of people fleeing from the Katrina disaster, languishing in the Astrodome and floating lifeless in brown, littered water.

"Why doesn't anybody help those people?" Dorie asked. Although there had been a Dorethea in every generation of the family for as long as anyone could remember, Bob's sister called herself Dorothy, and now the most recent Dorethea calls herself Dorie.

"They need help, right?" she continued. "Jesus told us to help people. I gave my whole allowance in the missionary collection at church to help, but the pictures don't look any better than they did last week. We are supposed to be a blessed nation—"

"A blessed but sinful nation," Bob interrupted. "We have put our faith in the gods of this world, and they are false gods." Bob thought about "the free market," capitalism, globalization. "Yes, they are false gods indeed."

The story of Hurricane Katrina and the devastation that followed in her wake is, of course, a story of man's inhumanity to man. It is a story of neglect and incompetence. It is a story of greed and avarice. But it is also a story that bears witness to the efforts of our leaders and the institutions that they direct to fashion our world into one moved by the invisible hand of a very false god, the so-called free market. Any examination of the Katrina disaster would be incomplete without an appreciation of the ways in which mainstream economic theory created the foundation upon which this tragedy was constructed.

This discussion is particularly important in light of the economic claims made by mainstream economists and those who believe in that perspective. The Katrina disaster was blamed on the victims. It has been argued that the victims made choices, both in terms of the way they lived their lives and in the ways they responded to the event that resulted in their suffering. The Katrina disaster was blamed on Ray Nagin Jr., the mayor of New Orleans, Kathleen Blanco, the governor of Louisiana, the Federal Emergency Management Agency (FEMA), and individuals and organizations that, again, were judged to have made choices motivated by their personal political self-interests that resulted in or amplified the disaster. The tragedy was blamed on the belief that the public sector, primarily federal, state, and local governments, was in the best position to prevent and correct the problems Katrina caused. These economic thinkers, politicians, and commentators claimed that reliance on the "market" would have better served the interests of all concerned and argue that we should look to businesses like Wal-Mart for guidance on how we should prevent and respond to catastrophe.[1]

Although these opinions claim to be based on economic theory, this claim is misleading. Neoclassical economic theory is just one of many of the theories used to understand economic processes and relationships. Neoclassical economic theory presents itself as the only way to understand the economy, or the true explanation for economic events, but neither claim is justified. What has become mainstream economics in the United States is not science, or even a genuine craft. It is a belief system that disguises itself as science so that its work of impoverishing those without money and power, and redistributing available wealth, resources, and opportunities to those with money and power, does not seem wicked and perverse, but instead natural and in the public good. It relies on the language of mathematics to express its positions in ways that mystify economic processes and relationships. Neoclassical economic theory's reliance on mathematical models also limits the number of people who can critically assess the claims advanced by this theory and converts economists from ordinary people with opinions into scientists who have discovered the "the truth," which they claim to pass on to the rest of us. It is a belief system that convinces the rich that they deserve to be rich. This system also teaches the rich that the well-being of their poor neighbors is not their concern. It convinces poor people that they deserve to be poor, and that they should spend their efforts and energy on acquiring money and material possessions at whatever cost.[2]

In the United States the economics profession is dominated by neoclassical economic theory, or what I refer to as mainstream economics. Neoclassical economics is descended from the classical economics of Adam Smith and others working in the first half of the 1800s. Their thinking was greatly influenced by the times in which they lived: by the rise of the Industrial Revolution and by the developing need for a person to have "a job" in order to meet their needs and the needs of their families. Their attempts to

understand the economy and economic relationships were also influenced by the discovery of scientific explanations for the behavior of matter (physics) and by the ability of the European countries in which they lived to use force and power to dominate the
peoples of the world.[3]

Classical economists took a broad view of the way the economy
functions, looking at the economy as a whole in what is referred to
as the macro economy. Its descendant, neoclassical economics, focuses on the economic actions of individual people, individual families, and individual businesses: the micro economy. Neoclassical
economists believe that the economy is best understood by adding
together all the decisions of individuals and ignoring the actions
and influences of groups, classes, and ideas.[4]

Neoclassical economic theory teaches that altering conditions in
the market can control the economy. The policies that are based on
this theory, however, frequently result in taking from low-income
and poor people to give to the rich. Therefore, we encourage the
economy to grow by providing massive tax cuts to the rich and pay
for these cuts by reducing basic services to low-income Americans.
Similarly, neoclassical economic theory supports the view that an
economy that is growing too quickly can be forced to slow down by
raising the price of money, by changing interest rates, for example,
with the express goal of increasing unemployment. Increasing unemployment will, in turn, reduce consumer spending and prevent
inflation. Policies based on neoclassical theory often affect change
by making it easier or harder for low-income people to live their
lives. By claiming to be "the only" or "the true" understanding of
economics, this theory allows politicians who subscribe to these
policies to benefit the wealthy while burdening low-income people and then to throw up their hands and claim, "It's not our fault,
it's the market, and the market knows best."[5]

This chapter examines and challenges the understandings of the

Katrina disaster expressed by advocates of neoclassical economic theory. It does so by examining one fundamental question: What is the economy? It explains why this question is important to understand the failings of neoclassical economic theory. It then examines how this theory blinds itself to the concerns of most people by making very unrealistic assumptions about the way the economy operates. Next, this chapter critiques the conclusions neoclassical economy theory has made about the Katrina disaster. Finally, the chapter argues that a more realistic understanding of what the economy is and how it works, along with the adoption of values that promote the well-being of all people, would lessen the pain and suffering that Katrina victims have experienced and continue to experience. It also seeks to describe the development of the so-called free market economy to enable the reader to appreciate the other ways in which mainstream economic theory impacts life in contemporary U.S. culture.

What Is the Economy?

Human beings have a variety of needs. Some of our needs are material; for example, we need food, water, and shelter in order to survive. We also have social needs, including the need for companionship, for self-appreciation, and for recreation. We also have spiritual needs, such as the need for contentment and for joy. Most economic theories define the economy as the way in which the material needs of human beings are satisfied. In traditional human societies, which existed before towns and cities developed, people satisfied their material needs by searching their local environment, collecting plants, and hunting animals for food, clothing, and building materials for their homes. As societies became more complex, labor became more specialized. Many people began spending time engaged in activities that did not meet all of their material needs.

It became important to obtain one's material needs by using specialized products or services that one individual, family, or group of individuals might create or provide. Patterns of exchange developed in which the people living near rivers might exchange some of the fish they catch for the fruits and root vegetables collected by people living closer to forests. With increasingly specialized labor, including farming, tool production, and fabric weaving, people began to agree upon marketplaces, or specific locations and specific times, where they could meet to engage in the exchanges necessary to supply their material needs. Some of these locations developed into towns or villages and later into cities. As the exchange activities became more complex, financial goods and services evolved. Money, for example, developed to facilitate transactions that would be difficult to accomplish by relying only on the exchange of one product or service for another. Additionally, as societies became more complex, the ability to exercise power over things and people played an increasingly important role in the way human needs were met and in the ways that the needs of some would come to be viewed as more important than the needs of others.[6]

This much-abbreviated description of economies, or the ways that human beings' material needs have been met over time, allows us to make some very important observations. First, the economy has changed over time. Therefore, the rules governing the way one economy operates at a particular time may not be relevant to the ways other economies function at other times. Many economists would say that, historically, there have been a large number of different economies. Many economists would also describe the economy as evolving. Second, the economy is a part, and only a part, of the way that all human beings live: the part that involves the way they meet their material needs. The way those human beings engage in activities to meet their other needs, including their social and spiritual needs, influences the way that economic activity takes place. So, for example, practices and behaviors concerning the ways in which people meet their spiritual needs may influence when and where exchanges of products and services take place. A society's practices and behaviors may influence, for example, which families or clans can engage in exchanges of products and services with one another. Finally, if the function of an economy is to meet the material needs of the members of society, then an individual economy can be viewed as more or less effective based on how well it is able to meet those needs.[7]

The Development of Neoclassical Economic Theory

An examination of the development of neoclassical theory provides additional reason to question its validity as an analytical tool and, therefore, to question the reliability of its policy proposals. Early neoclassical economists, who analogized economics to physics, argued that there were universal laws, like the law of gravity, that could be used to describe and explain observations of the ways in which human beings behaved. Therefore, it was believed that the economy could be described and explained using scientific principles and mathematical expressions. These early economists understood that an ability to describe experiences and observations using mathematical terms would bolster their claim that economics is a science. They also understood that describing economic processes and relationships in a language that few people would understand, in the language of higher mathematics and differential calculus, would give economics a power and prestige that rarely was provided to philosophers. Philosophers merely state opinions, but scientists possess "the truth" about things. Opinions can be ignored, but "the truth" cannot be ignored so easily. In order to develop mathematical models of the economy, however, it would be necessary to describe it differently. Economics changed from being the way that a society provides for the needs of its members to "the science of allocating scarce resources to unlimited wants." This view of the economy and its operation encouraged the belief that people should compete with each other to obtain the things they need for survival. This model created winners and losers.[8]

According to this economic theory, the wins and losses of an individual resulted not from selfishness or a lack of compassion but from the "natural" operation of the market. Everything from lumber to wheat to human beings became viewed as commodities subject to the laws of supply and demand: things that properly could be bought and sold. In the marketplace, people with the best combination of money and power are able to obtain everything they need as well as many things they do not need but merely desire. People without money and power, in contrast, are not able to obtain anything, including the basic things that they need to survive.[9]

The Assumptions Made by Neoclassical Economic Theory

Neoclassical economic theory and the policies it supports become even more questionable when we recognize that the theory requires the adoption of several very unrealistic assumptions. These assumptions about the way people make decisions and about the operation of the market were necessary in order to make their formulas work. Real scientists, of course, do not use assumptions in this way. Nevertheless, over time these economists convinced themselves and others that they were scientists and that their views should be respected as scientific truths.[10]

First, they assumed that the economy could be best understood by looking at the behaviors of individual participants in the economy, or economic actors. Economic actors make decisions about the way property, money, and opportunities are used. An economic actor could be an individual person, an individual family, or an individual company. That individual is assumed to act to obtain his or her particular goals and preferences by making decisions that are believed to provide the result desired. Economists also assumed that the goal motivating all human behavior was the desire for profit or material gain, and that this desire was "natural" to all people. These economists argued that without such a desire, society would collapse because people will not work simply because work is interesting, or fun, or helps their neighbors. Neoclassical economists call such decisions, made on the basis of self-interest, rational. They consequently endow decisions made on the basis of selfishness and greed with the aura of reasonableness.[11]

Neoclassical economists also made assumptions about the "market" and about the ways people behaved in "the market." The "market" became a place or method for people to come together to buy, sell, or exchange in an effort to obtain profit. Neoclassical economists claimed that the "market," therefore, was a "natural" practice that came into being as a result of human beings' "natural" tendency to seek profit and personal gain. The "market" was given a central but undeserved role in human culture and society. It was assumed to be the way that all societies regulate the way goods and services are produced and distributed.[12]

Although they made other incorrect and unrealistic assumptions, the remaining one that is most connected to this analysis is the assumption that people seek, in all of their activities, to behave efficiently. In other words, people "naturally" strive to do as little as possible in their efforts to supply their material needs. Efficiency was viewed as a natural part of the economic process, and the market's presumed efficiency became a reason to rely on market processes in the allocation of societal resources.[13]

The problem with this perspective is that using efficiency as the favored value premise treats people and their lives in much the same way that we treat machines and the activities for which we use them.

The efficient worker was the one who produced as much as possible for as little pay as possible. Mainstream economic theory supports the view that workers ideally should receive only as much as they need to survive, and the value they create through the things they produce should be captured by the business owners. Neoclassical economic theory encourages the view that workers need not be viewed as complete people with a range of human needs and desires, but only as part of a machine-based process designed to make business owners as wealthy as possible. After nearly two hundred years of being taught that only the efficient is valuable, people have accepted that belief and allow themselves to be treated as replaceable, disposable things rather than as human beings with value and worth independent of what they are able to produce. Thus, mainstream economic theory argues that the "market" should be responsible for regulating as much of human life as possible because market-based decisions are best for society.[14]

All of these assumptions are fundamentally wrong. Although they make it possible to describe some of the activities we see in the market using mathematical terms, they produce an understanding of the economy, and the way people should act in the economy, that is both deceptive and harmful. Trying to understand the economy based on the way an individual acts or is presumed to act is very unrealistic. Individuals are members of groups, communities, and societies and frequently make decisions based on the ways that they interact with these groups. Groups, communities, and societies each have histories, values, and perspectives that may influence how individual members act and may result in the groups, communities, and societies behaving in ways that serve their combined or collective interests, even though such actions may not be in the best interests of any one individual member. Therefore, trying to understand an individual person's behavior, based exclusively on what we would assume that person wants or desires, will provide a very incomplete understanding of that person, his or her behavior, and the operation of the economy. In some ways, it would be similar to removing one ant from an ant colony, studying it and making conclusions about the life of the entire colony based on the observations of one ant. Of course, human beings are not ants, but social beings who live in communities and who make the decisions about the way they will or will not behave based on a large number of considerations.

Traditionally, people did not focus their efforts and energies around making money or acquiring material possessions. Instead, people concentrated on obtaining social standing in the community. A person's relationships, social interactions, and performance of expected religious behavior, among other things, were believed to be more important than a person's wealth and material possessions. Wealth and material possessions could be valuable in improving a person's or a family's or a group's social standing, however, because they could be used to demonstrate generosity and commitment to the community. Moral and ethical members of traditional societies did not view the acquisition of wealth or material possessions as appropriate goals.

Before the creation of classical and neoclassical economic theories, markets were controlled by the society's ethical, moral, and spiritual beliefs. As markets grew larger and provided a wider array of goods and services, and therefore less subject to control, they were regulated to prevent marketplace practices from interfering with the economic organization of the rest of society. It was only when governments recognized that they could use markets to enhance their political power that markets were permitted to develop into the complex, sophisticated structures in operation today. Nonetheless, neoclassical economic theory's view of the market as natural and desirable has become firmly embedded in the thinking of most U.S. residents and has been exported by the processes of globalization into the lives of people around the world. So, today, decisions about who does and does not have a job are made by the marketplace, the decision about who has food and who does not is made by the marketplace, and often decisions about who has health care and will live, and who does not have health care and will die, also are made by the marketplace.[15]

The Acceptance of Neoclassical Economic Theory

If neoclassical economic theory misuses mathematics and relies on inappropriate assumptions, then why is it so popular in the United States? One of the things that make us human is our ability to learn. Unfortunately it is just as easy to learn false information, or to learn to take a wrong path, as it is to learn correct information, or to learn to take a proper path. In other words, when people are taught by neoclassical economic theory to be selfish or are shown that their personal well-being is more important than the well-being of their neighbors, people often will behave selfishly. People, as individuals and as members of society, come to expect the things that the economic theory in which they believe tells them to expect. As "economic science" and the ways of looking at the world that it supports have intruded into other areas of human life, "waste not want not" has been transformed from a statement about being careful into an ethical and moral value. "Greed is good" has become a statement of an economic "truth."[16]

Generally people try to be fair and cooperative. Generally they do not value selfishness or taking unfair advantage of others. When people are taught that markets are the natural and proper ways to make decisions about who lives a comfortable life and who lives an impoverished life, many of the people living a comfortable life will find it preferable to believe that their well-being is the result of a "natural" market process and not a consequence of unearned privilege. For such people, it is comforting to believe that the market knows best. Believing that the people who live in poverty have chosen to do so minimizes the guilt of the privileged. Impoverished people recognize that their poverty is not simply the result of decisions that they make, however; they understand that their poverty also involves decisions made by others over which they have no control. A person whose parents are rich has an entirely different set of choices, or life options, than a person whose parents are poor. In this country a person who is female or is a member of a racial or ethnic minority is valued differently by the marketplace than a white male. According to mainstream economic theory, however, such discrimination should not occur. The market should make decisions based only on a person's value as a worker, and race and gender should be irrelevant. The fact that race, gender, and ethnicity are not irrelevant demonstrates that the market is influenced by the prejudices and biases of the participants in the market who hold the most power. The fact that this society must enact and enforce laws that prohibit discrimination based on race, gender, and ethnicity is further evidence that the economy and the markets that guide it do not follow natural laws, but instead are governed by the power and prejudices of wealthy people and are designed to serve and promote their interests. All of the talk about the wisdom of the marketplace, supply and demand, and all of the mathematical formulas that are supposed to explain the way the economy works are largely ways to convince people to accept manufactured ideas that common sense would tell them are not true or, assuming they are true, simply should not be permitted in a civilized society.[17]

Katrina and Free Market Economics

Mainstream economic theory claims that things work best when we let the "market" determine how society's resources are distributed. This belief is directly related to the way the Katrina catastrophe originated and developed. The people most severely impacted by Katrina are usually described as poor. To be poor means that one lacks the resources to participate in the marketplace and to satisfy one's material needs. If people do not have the financial resources to participate, then the "market," politicians, and the policy makers who promote this as the way to determine society's needs and desires can easily ignore them. The "market" decides that people with resources are "normal" people and that the people without resources are not.[18]

Poor people are viewed as "the other." Instead of being viewed as internally displaced people, they are treated as refugees in their own country. They become presumptive criminals; the people who are paid to serve and protect them view themselves as responsible for protecting the rest of society instead. Property, which is valued by the market, becomes more important than people. These market-driven perceptions create the foundation upon which the response to the victims of Katrina was formulated. Neoclassical economic theory creates the mechanisms by which victims of Katrina are blamed for their situation; the theory allows this opinion to appear to be a "truth." This "truth" conveniently allows neoclassical economists, and the policy makers who rely on their theories, to ignore the role that race and class played in the development and maintenance of this crisis.[19]

Survival and the Housing Market

The ability to participate in the housing market, to buy or sell a home, and to rent or lease an apartment, requires money or financial resources. Katrina's victims suffered because their limited ability to participate in the housing market forced them to live in sensitive areas that were likely to be most heavily impacted by a hurricane or flood. U.S. residential housing patterns are influenced by longstanding and continuing patterns of racial segregation and housing discrimination. Approximately 33 percent of the people living in areas impacted by Katrina were African American. Decisions about which areas received the best protection from potentially catastrophic events were not based on the local risk of each area, but on the residents' political influence. Further, the decisions about which areas in New Orleans will be rebuilt also are based on the desire to "whiten" the city by building new housing that will be out of the financial reach of people displaced by Katrina, or transforming former residential areas into recreation facilities for the rich. In this sense, housing decisions do not occur in a "free market," but instead in a market contaminated by racism and class prejudice.[20]

Neoclassical economic theory focuses on the individual and concludes that the fact that a particular individual is denied the ability to rent a particular apartment in a particular part of town is the result of inadequacies on the part of the individual. Mainstream theory avoids recognizing race, ethnicity, or class-based discrimination by focusing on the individual. It ignores the history of the groups or communities to which the individual belongs, and fails to acknowledge the patterns of oppression and exploitation to which the individual's group or community has been subjected.[21]

The neoclassical perspective argues that oppression and exploitation either do not exist or should be viewed as rational. The rational—that is, self-interested—economic actor judges individuals based on, for example, their ability to be effective employees or good renters. The rational economic actor would not discriminate against someone who would be a good employee or a good renter because of the individual's race; this would be irrational. So, if a rational economic actor will not hire or rent to an individual of a certain race, or if the rational actor chooses to pay such an individual less salary or charge such an individual more rent than others, then those decisions must reflect the market's conclusions about the value of that individual as an employee or the risks that the individual presents as a renter. Anything else would be inconsistent with the assumption that individuals always act to increase their profit or gain. So rather than reject the assumption of self-interest as the force motivating human behavior, neoclassical economic theory insists on interpreting this situation in a way that defies common knowledge and the lived experience of most of the people in this country. Thus, ignoring the impact of race in the distribution of societal resources eliminates their ability to address such discrimination. Members of the favored race will benefit, and members of disfavored races and ethnic groups will be burdened. The blame for this unequal treatment, however, will be placed on those whose race is disfavored because blaming racism is inconsistent with neoclassical economic theory. Therefore, the fact that certain people chose to live in housing vulnerable to the impact of storms and floods is not the result of their preference or choices they made in their lives, but the result of economic policies and perspectives that argue that poverty is the result of individual choice rather than the interaction of a variety of factors over which low-income people have no control, including discrimination.

Neoclassical economic theory avoids the more fundamental question of whether decisions about who has quality housing should be made by "the market." The market makes housing a commodity, or a thing that landlords and sellers bring to the market in order to profit. The market does not view housing as a basic human need or as a fundamental right, but only as a commodity that can be used to create profit. And in this country, the ability to profit in the housing market is not enough. It is clear that business can profit by building affordable housing, however they can profit more by building housing for the affluent. The market allows housing developers to make the decision to choose projects that result in high profits and to reject ventures that merely provide a reasonable profit. This demonstrates an internal inconsistency in neoclassical economic theory. The theory argues that if there is a demand in the market that can create a profit, such as the demand for affordable housing, then businesses will enter the market to supply the demand and earn the available profits. When this does not happen, neoclassical economic theory declares the existence of a market failure that permits a government intervention, such as public housing, to fill the gap. This will occur only if government has the resources and desire to do so, however. Public housing has been disfavored by government due to the belief that the market is the best way to distribute housing, and because the market has taught them to ignore the needs of the people who need public housing. Additionally, the neoclassically inspired aversion to "big government" has bled away the resources government could use to provide for needs like affordable housing. The role that the "market" played with respect to housing in New Orleans was to ensure that poor people would have access to the least-protected housing; the role it now attempts to play is to prevent poor people from returning to the city by ensuring that little new, affordable housing will be built. This will be particularly damaging to renters, who have fewer options and less power in the housing market than buyers.[22]

Transportation and the Market for Survival

Analysis of the Katrina disaster inspired by neoclassical economic theory claims that the victims of Katrina suffered because they lacked the resources to access the transportation market. They did not have personal automobiles or the ability to pay for transportation out of the disaster area. Yet this perspective does not look at the way that "the transportation market" has been abused to make most people in the U.S. dependent on private automobiles as their primary means of transportation. The automobile industry in this country used its wealth and power to have its agents purchase public transportation systems across the country, particularly light rail systems. They initially replaced these systems with buses and gradually decreased the services provided to force more and more people to buy automobiles. The people who could not afford personal automobiles became irrelevant because they were no longer able to participate in the personal transportation market that the automobile industry was permitted to create. The automobile industry also led the effort to expand the nation's highway system and influence public opinion against mass transportation. As a result, the United States is the only industrial power that does not have a national rail system. Despite the claim that the market promotes efficiency and avoids wasting societal resources, the U.S. transportation market encourages the most inefficient mode of transportation and one method that is very harmful to the environment.[23]

The nation's transportation system, like other critical sectors in our economy, also has been influenced by racism. The development of highways responded to white flight and suburbanization. Highways were essential to the new suburban housing market, as these areas were constructed with government complicity to be "white only" communities. Public transportation to and from these communities was disfavored because it could enable the wrong people to access the suburbs. The victims of Katrina did not suffer because they lacked transportation; they suffered because of the decision the "market" made about the "best" way to provide personal transportation services in this society. This was not a decision made by a "free" market; this decision was made in a market corrupted and manipulated by the automobile industry. As a result, public monies have been used to focus the transportation system on the needs of white suburban communities at the expense of urban communities.[24]

The "Government" and the Market for Survival

Much neoclassically inspired commentary has focused on the role of the government at all levels in the development and the perpetuation of the Katrina catastrophe. The victims of Katrina suffered because of the inability of federal, state, and local governments to respond quickly and effectively to the risk of natural disasters and to the disasters themselves. Democratically elected governments are viewed as too complicated to prevent or respond effectively to Katrina-like events because of their need to balance the interests of many different groups. William Shughart, for example, blames the inadequate prevention and response of government on four primary factors. First, politicians are self-interested economic actors who will postpone investment in infrastructure, like levees, in the hope that disaster is not likely to strike on their watch. Second, when politicians invest in infrastructure, public works projects invariably result in poor construction and do not receive adequate maintenance. Third, in the face of a crisis, politicians are likely to do nothing rather than risk the possibility of making a decision that is later viewed as incorrect. Finally, corruption and waste absorb the minimal financial resources that are committed to prevention and response. Instead, it is argued that the private sector provides the best model for disaster planning and prevention. According to this argument, the victims of Karina suffered because they placed their faith in the government and not in the private sector.[25]

It is important to recognize that this argument is structured in a way to prevent comparisons between the U.S. government's response to Katrina and the Cuban government's response to Hurricane Ivan in September 2004. Although Hurricane Ivan resulted in 27 deaths in Florida, there was no loss of life in Cuba despite very heavy storm damage resulting in the destruction of approximately 20,000 homes. Similarly, in September 1998, 5 people died when

Hurricane Georges hit Cuba, compared to 4 deaths in the United States, 210 deaths in the Dominican Republic, and 167 deaths in Haiti. In 2004 Hurricane Charley killed 30 people in Florida and 4 in Cuba. In Cuba, disaster preparedness is emphasized at every level of education and in the workplace.

> Everyone knows how to interpret the information given by the Cuban Institute of Meteorology. Television and radio play a vital role in informing the public as the level of alert rises. All institutions are mobilized 48 hours before the hurricane is foreseen to hit the island, to implement the emergency plan, and measures such as massive evacuation are taken. Every individual has a role to play at the community level. Local authorities know who needs special care and how to assist the most vulnerable. Schools and hospitals are converted into shelters and transport is immediately organized.[26]

In contrast to the response of U.S. federal officials, Cuban leaders immediately took charge and mobilized the population. Three days after Katrina made landfall, U.S. president George W. Bush was playing golf. When he eventually visited the devastated areas, the *New York Times* observed that "nothing about the president's demeanor yesterday—which seemed casual to the point of carelessness—suggested that he understood the depth of the current crisis."[27] Indeed, the U.S. response to Katrina, particularly when compared to the Cuban response, seems utterly careless.[28]

Cuba serves as a model for disaster management because its government has accepted primary responsibility for the welfare of its people. This response to disaster focuses on the needs of communities and the coordination of available resources and services to meet those needs. In the United States people are instructed, among other things, to prepare a personal evacuation plan, purchase the supplies recommended for a personal or family disaster kit, and fill their automobile's gas tank. Responsibility for disaster preparation is treated as a personal rather than as community or a governmental responsibility. In the United States people are provided with the level of protection that they personally can afford to finance, even though such policies will leave many vulnerable and unprotected. As the United Nations Office for the Coordination of Humanitarian Affairs noted, the knowledge to reduce risk and hazard is widely available. Without specific programs and the political will to implement the necessary policies, vulnerabilities will continue to exist, however.[29]

Therefore, despite the existence of effective models for risk reduction, little will change without the will to put aside economic ideology. In fact, the lessons that could be learned from Cuba are rejected for ideological reasons, because the Cuban government is not "democratically" elected and the Cuban economy does not subscribe to U.S.-style capitalism. Neoclassical economics instead suggests that we should emulate the model provided by Wal-Mart.

> Based on detailed information about customer's buying patterns in hurricane-prone areas, Wal-Mart began pre-positioning supplies it knew would be in high demand: bottled water, flashlights, batteries, generators and tarps, before the storm hit; mops, chainsaws and Strawberry Pop-Tarts afterwards.[30]

Although Katrina resulted in the closing of 126 Wal-Mart stores, within two weeks all but 15 stores had reopened. Although Shughart acknowledges that opening a store is not quite the same thing as evacuating a city, he nonetheless argues that the incentives provided by the market enabled Wal-Mart and other private firms to accomplish what the Federal Emergency Management Agency (FEMA) and the Red Cross, a nonprofit organization, could not. Lost in this analysis is the fact that Wal-Mart's efforts were inspired by its interest in making a profit, and it is unlikely that Wal-Mart would have devoted the resources to re-establishing its operations if it believed that doing so would not be profitable.[31]

Cuba provides another interesting counterpoint to analyses of profit interest. Following Hurricanes Georges and Mitch, Cuba established the Latin American School of Medical Sciences in Havana and provided full scholarships to young people from poor rural areas in eighteen Latin American and Caribbean countries. The Cuban government made the decision to mitigate the health consequences of natural disasters, among other things, by educating a new generation of medical professionals to provide medical care in communities across the region where it was unavailable or prohibitively expensive. Without the opportunity to generate profit, markets are unlikely to produce a comparable response to the needs of people who require but are unable to pay for services.[32]

The application of neoclassical economic theory in the arena of governmental activity relies on the same assumptions that attempt to convert human beings into perpetual calculators of personal wealth and advantage. It is generally true that politicians in this society are interested in being seen as successful and correct, but this is not the issue. The issue is whether the agencies and authorities that these politicians lead are committed to meeting the needs of people rather than business. Is the government structured to act with compassion, or is it structured to act like a market? Neoclassical economic theory attempts to distract us from the way it has enabled politicians to ignore low-income and powerless people and has encouraged government actions. By focusing analysis on the behavior of individual politicians rather than on the values that animate government policy, neoclassical theory suggests that inadequate governmental response to disaster is inevitable. Additionally, if decision makers were in closer communication with all people, they would be less fearful of the possibility of making a "bad" decision because their decisions would be informed by public sentiment. Unfortunately "the people" and their collective interests and perspectives are not a part of the neoclassical economic analysis. It consequently is to be expected that politicians will be more responsive to their personal self interests and the interests of their largest campaign contributors than to the interests of the people they are elected to represent.

Neoclassical economic theory assumes that in the absence of direct personal financial self-interest, government workers will do a poor job in constructing and maintaining government facilities. This reasoning assumes people have been convinced that the only value of work is financial compensation. Nevertheless, craftsmen still take pride in their workmanship, scientists would still be motivated by intellectual curiosity even if patents were not available, and many people identify as members of "the public" and view public service as a privilege, rather than as an opportunity to enrich themselves. It is true that waste and corruption exist. There is a difference between waste and a mistake, however. Mistakes can be interpreted as wastes of resources, or they can be interpreted as valuable learning experiences and as opportunities to evaluate potential solutions and develop courses of action based on learned experience rather than on theoretical models. Finally, it is ironic that an economic theory that preaches the value of self-interested decision making would point to corruption, a prime example of self-interested decision making, as a consequence of the government's attempt to provide services. By advancing self-interest as the explanation for human motivation and action, neoclassical economic theory encourages the self-interested corruption that it blames on government processes. What is surprising is that in spite of the justifications provided by this economic theory for self-interested behavior, there is far less corruption than one might anticipate.

It is clear that the governmental response to Katrina was inadequate and ineffective at all levels. Nevertheless, there is ample reason to believe that a public sector response is preferable to one that relies on market processes. Enron, WorldCom, and Adelphia, among others, demonstrate that the private sector is dominated by individuals who are willing to put their self-interest ahead of the legal responsibilities they owe to their corporate constituents and to society. The neoclassically inspired preference for the private sector is based on the recognition that governments can be forced to respond to the needs and interests of the people. Should that happen, the wealthy and powerful will find themselves without the protection of the power and privilege that their wealth can buy, and the world might change. Therefore, neoclassical economic theory attempts to minimize the role of government and increase the power of the private sector in order to limit the ability of democratically elected governments to change the current distribution of societal resources. By draining the government of resources and diminishing public confidence in the ability of government to address their needs, the theory promotes a self-fulfilling prophecy of government failure.

Conclusion

A just society could have prevented the devastation wrought by Katrina, and a just society certainly would not have allowed the event to devastate the lives of so many for so long. Neoclassical economic theory has encouraged our society to be blind to issues of justice, both in the economy and in the operation of society in general. Neoclassical economic theory does not see the world in terms of the weak and the strong; instead the world is divided into suppliers and demanders, producers and consumers. Those without the ability to participate in the production of consumables, or who lack the financial resources to consume, simply do not count. Neoclassically inspired thinking has so permeated our culture that it has achieved the goal of many of its advocates. It preserves this society's current distribution of assets, resources, and opportunities to the greatest extent possible.[33]

Nevertheless, the desire to obtain money and material possessions in excess of what we need to survive is not "natural," but rather taught and learned. If it were not impressed upon us by the corporate media, schools, and even churches, people would be less willing to trust in the "market" and less fearful of one another. Survival in a society that can afford to sustain everyone is not a commodity that should be distributed by "the market"; it is a right.[34]

Afterword

Two years have passed. Dorie is now reading the Sunday paper to Uncle Bob:

> Over a year and a half later, there are 64,000 people still sleeping in trailers in Louisiana and far too many communities without schools, hospitals and other basics. These are unacceptable failures. At least part of the problem is a law that requires states to contribute 10 percent of the cost of most federally-financed reconstruction projects. Mr. Bush waived that requirement after the Sept. 11 attacks (as his father did after Hurricanes Andrew and Iniki) but he refuses to do so for the Gulf Coast.[35]

She shakes her head and sighs deeply, "I guess they really just don't care, do they?"

Notes

1. For example, Roger D. Congleton reports, "Interviews conducted after the flood suggest that most of those who chose to stay behind did so after a rational assessment of their own circumstances," Roger D. Congleton, "The Story of Katrina: New Orleans and the Political Economy of Catastrophe," *Public Choice* 127 (2006): 5, 15. Choice, in the way the term is used in mainstream economic theory, is largely an illusion: "World views, mores, taboos, and sanctions are among the social influences that shape and guide our behavior, so much so that characterizing

our activities as 'choice' and 'decision making' is often inappropriate." John T. Harvey, "Heuristic Judgment Theory," *Journal of Economic Issues* 32 (1998): 47; William F. Shughart II, "Katrinanomics: The Politics and Economics of Disaster Relief," *Public Choice* 127 (2006): 31; Walter Block, "Government and the Katrina Crises," *Free Market*, October 2005, http://www.mises.org/freemarket_de tail.asp?control=565&sortorder=articledate ("In the weeks following the hurricane, it became clear that most of the destruction was not the work of Mother Nature but those who are charged with preventing precisely such disasters as this.") See, for example, the Cato Institute, a think tank advocating libertarian philosophies and policies, "Did Big Government Return with Katrina?" *Cato Policy Report*, November/December 2005, http://www.cato.org/pubs/policy_report/v27n6/ cpr-27n6-2.pdf; Russell S. Sobel and Peter T. Leeson, "Flirting with Disaster: The Inherent Problems with FEMA," *Policy Analysis* (Cato Institute) 573 (2006): 1, 9.

2. There are many schools of economic thought that reject the neoclassical view of the economy and the way it is supposed to work. The heterodox schools of economic thought, including institutional economics, post-Keynesian economics, and anti-essentialist Marxian theory, are often more sensitive to both the limits of markets and to the cycles of instability that they generate. Additionally, the heterodox schools of economic thought recognize the influence of institutional factors embedded, for example, in history, racial subordination, and domestic income inequality that continue to interact in contemporary economic processes to limit access to assets, resources, and opportunities to those with wealth and power. Charles R. P. Pouncy, "The Rational Rogue: Neoclassical Economic Ideology in the Regulation of the Financial Professional," *Vermont Law Review* 26 (2002): 267–68, n 12.

3. Jurg Niehans, *A History of Economic Theory: Classic Contributions, 1720–1980* (Baltimore: Johns Hopkins University Press, 1990), 60–69. These early economists, including David Ricardo, Jean Baptiste Say, John Stuart Mill, and Karl Marx, among others, elaborated on the work of Adam Smith. Ricardo developed the theory of comparative advantage, which, among other things, argues that countries should produce those goods and products that it can export most profitably and import those goods and products that are prohibitively expensive for it to produce domestically. This theory would later be used to justify the economic relationships between the European colonial powers and their colonial subjects in which the colonies produced raw materials for export to the colonizers and imported manufactured goods from the colonizers. Say's law can be paraphrased as "supply creates it on demand," i.e., producers will always be able to find demand for their products because the market will adjust the price of such products to achieve that result. Paul Davidson, *Post Keynesian Macroeconomic Theory* (Northampton UK: Edward Elgar, 1994), 14–15; Marx's work focused on the consequences of the economic structures that accompanied the industrial revolution on workers and

society, arguing that economic relationships justified by the work of Smith, Ricardo, Say, and others resulted in the exploitation of workers by business owners and colonies by imperialists. Charles A. Barone, *Radical Political Economy* (Armonk NY: M. E. Sharpe, 2004), 10–15.

4. Paul Robeson Jr., *A Black Way of Seeing* (New York: Seven Stories Press 2006), 36, 83–84. Robeson argues that contemporary conservatives are the heirs of the Confederacy and have adopted free market principles because they are consistent with their Confederate values.

5. Richard W. Stevenson, "The President's Budget Proposal: The Overview; President Submits $2 Trillion Budget That Raises Deficit," *New York Times*, February 5, 2002, A1. The Federal Reserve uses its ability to influence interest rates as a policy instrument to either increase or decrease employment, believing that such actions will enhance economic performance. Also see Federal Reserve Board, "Monetary Policy Report to the Congress," *Federal Reserve Bulletin* (2000): 161.

6. "The economic process is not a natural one, shaped by forces beyond human discretion. Instead, the economic process is an artificial one, shaped by human action through the exercise of power." William Dugger, *Underground Economics* (Armonk NY: M. E. Sharpe 1992), xxii.

7. This conflicts with one of the assumptions of neoclassical economic theory, i.e., that the economy seeks to achieve equilibrium, at which, for example, supply equals demand. E. Ray Canterbery, *The Making of Economics* (Belmont CA: Wadsworth, 1976): 92–95. Therefore, it is often said by economists who do not rely on neoclassical theory that the economy is embedded in the way a society works; it is not separate from the society's culture, history, and social structure as neoclassical economic theory maintains. Geoffrey M. Hodgson, "What Is the Essence of Institutional Economics?" *Journal of Economic Issues* 34 (2000): 317, 323. The story from the Christian tradition of Jesus of Nazareth overthrowing the tables of the money changers and dove merchants provides an example of the ways in which various societal practices, including religious and economic transactions, can influence each other. For corresponding Bible verse, see Matthew 21:12, *Holy Bible, King James Version*, 1227. In that situation, the business of merchants interacted with religious practices in ways that can be viewed as limiting access to religion to people with the resources to purchase sacrificial animals, a view inconsistent with the views espoused by Jesus.

8. Canterbery, *Making of Economics*, 30–34, 95; Philip Mirowski, *More Light Than Heat: Economics as Social Physics, Physics as Nature's Economics* (Cambridge: Cambridge University Press, 1989): 107–8; Niehans, *History of Economic Theory*, 160–61.

9. "When the individual believes that the proper and scientifically-sanctioned goal of her existence is to maximize her utility, then rationality serves to encourage

the commoditization of all aspects of her experience. Once that has occurred, the individual can reduce all aspects of her experience to preference functions that can be prioritized to maximize her ability to consume both the outcome of production and "nature objectified." Pouncy, "Rational Rogue," 290.

10. "The term 'science' can be used in at least two different ways. First, the term is used by Kuhn to describe an overarching paradigm at whose center is a set of generally held core concepts to which most practitioners subscribe and that establishes the parameters of the 'natural science' they investigate. . . . The term 'science' also can be used in the logical-positivist sense of 'knowledge-claims' being tested against experience, of the various propositions not yet falsified constituting a logically coherent whole, and of the theory's explanatory power steadily increasing over time." Pouncy, "Contemporary Financial Innovation: Orthodoxy and Alternatives," *Southern Methodist University Law Review* 51 (1998): 505, n. 202 (citing Thomas S. Kuhn, *The Structure of Scientific Revolutions* (Chicago: University of Chicago Press, 1970), 10–12); E. Ray Canterbery and Robert J. Burkhardt, "What Do We Mean by Asking Whether Economics Is a Science?" in *Why Economics Is Not Yet a Science,* ed. Alfred S. Eichner (Armonk NY: M. E. Sharpe, 1983), 15–22.

11. "Methodological individualism posits the individual as the appropriate unit of economic analysis and argues that all social phenomena result from the aggregation of the behavior of individuals. In opposition to methodological individualism is methodological collectivism, which argues that individual behavior is meaningful only in the context of the cultural whole. The neoclassical assumption of methodological individualism contrasts with the approaches taken by other economic disciplines. For example, institutional economics views the transaction as the appropriate unit of analysis and methodological collectivism as a way to understand the individual by reference to how he or she relates to the relevant cultural whole. Marxian economics uses the process as its basic unit of analysis and views the aggregation of all designatable processes as reality." Pouncy, "Rational Rogue," 272–73 (citations omitted). Economic rationality is the decisional heuristic traditionally used to explain human decision making by classical and neoclassical economists. It conceptualizes human decision making as motivated primarily by the individual actor's efforts to maximize her personal utility as she understands it.

12. George Dalton, *Primitive, Archaic and Modern Economies: Essays of Karl Polanyi* (Garden City NY: Anchor Books, 1968), 3–5.

13. "Neoclassical economics describes the economy as a state of equilibrium, in which the forces of supply and demand interact to achieve optimal allocation of society's resources. The focus of neoclassical economics is on the decision-making activity of entrepreneurs, households and firms. It assumes that economic decision-making is voluntary, informed and rational (i.e., utility maximizing). The

models used in neoclassical economics are based on transactions occurring in exchange (i.e., barter) markets, in which perfect competition prevails. In these markets, goods are exchanged for goods, with money serving only as a neutral intermediary in the exchange. Economic models based on exchange markets also assume gross substitution effects. The axiom of gross substitution states that the demand for good A will change only in response to a pricing differential between good A and a substitute product. Exchange transactions also are envisioned as being costlessly reversible, and as occurring in an ergodic environment, in which there are no financial institutions. The market becomes the instrument of allocation, and individual self-interested economic decisions collectively achieve an optimal societal equilibrium." Pouncy, "Contemporary Financial Innovation," 540–41.

14. Jason DeParle, "Liberal Hopes Ebb in Post-Storm Debate," *New York Times*, October 11, 2005, A1. For example, Judge Richard Posner has argued that the adoption process should be viewed as a market and that children should be rationed for adoption based on the wealth of the potential parents. Richard A. Posner, "Adoption and Market Theory: The Regulation of the Market in Adoptions," *Boston University Law Review* 67 (1987): 59, 61.

15. Karl Polanyi, *The Great Transformation* (Boston: Beacon Press, 2001), 65–70. Charles R. P. Pouncy, "Stock Markets in Sub-Saharan Africa: Western Legal Institutions as a Component of the Neo-Colonial Project," *University of Pennsylvania Journal of International Economic Law* 23 (2002): 85, 97–98.

16. Gerald Marwell and Ruth E. Ames, "Economists Free Ride, Does Anyone Else? Experiments on the Provision of Public Goods, IV," *Journal of Public Economics* 15 (1981): 295, 296; Pouncy, "Rational Rogue," 274, 296.

17. In 2005 the median annual salary for women was $31,858; for men it was $41,386. On average women make approximately 77 cents for every dollar earned by men. Black households had a median income of $30,858 compared to white households with a median income of $50,784. U.S. Census Bureau News, "Income Climbs, Poverty Stabilizes, Uninsured Rate Increases" (Washington DC: Government Printing Office, August 29, 2006). Gary S. Becker, *The Economics of Discrimination* (Chicago: University of Chicago Press, 1957), 5; Milton Friedman, *Capitalism and Freedom* (Chicago: University of Chicago Press, 1962), 108–12.

18. In 2004 19 percent of Louisianans were poor and 28 percent of the residents of New Orleans were poor; 21.6 percent of Mississippians were poor, and 16.1 percent of the residents of Alabama were poor. The national poverty rate during the same period was 13 percent. Arloc Sherman and Issac Shapiro, *Essential Facts about the Victims of Hurricane Katrina*, Center on Budget and Policy Priorities, September 19, 2005, http://www.cbpp.org/9-19-05pov.htm. Former First Lady Barbara Bush toured the Louisiana Superdome in New Orleans on September 6, 2005. During a radio interview conducted by the American Public Media

program "Marketplace," she commented, "What I'm hearing, which is sort of scary, is they all want to stay in Texas. Everyone is so overwhelmed by the hospitality. And so many of the people in the arena here, you know, were underprivileged anyway, so this is working very well for them." "Mrs. Bush Remarks Were 'Observation,'" *Boston Globe*, September 8, 2005, http://www.boston.com/news/weather/articles/2005/09/08/mrs_bush_remarks_were_observation/; "The Former First Lady, Barbara Bush Calls Evacuees Better Off," *New York Times*, September 7, 2005.

19. Eric Lipton, "FEMA Is Set to Stop Paying Hotel Cost for Storm Victims," *New York Times*, November 16, 2005, A20. Police officers in the suburbs of New Orleans forcibly prevented New Orleans residents from leaving the city, and some confiscated the food and water of residents who had made an encampment near the bridge approaching Gretna, Louisiana. Gardiner Harris, "Storm and Crisis: Battling the Storm; Police in Suburbs Blocked Evacuees, Witnesses Report," *New York Times*, September 10, 2005, A13.

20. See for example, Janny Scott, "Report Alleges Bias by a Real Estate Giant," *New York Times*, October 11, 2006, B6 (one of New York City's largest real estate agents alleged to engage in discriminatory sales practices); Marcelle S. Fischler, "Pushing the Fight against Racial Segregation," *New York Times*, March 25, 2007, 14LI (Levittown, the nation's first post–World War II suburb enforced racially restrictive covenants preventing African Americans from buying or renting property in the area). While claiming to steer anti-terrorism funds to the cities with the highest risk in 2006 the Department of Homeland Security slashed funds to New York City and Washington DC while increasing funds to Omaha, Nebraska, and Louisville, Kentucky. "Security Cuts for New York and Washington," *New York Times*, June 1, 2006, A18.

21. Howard J. Sherman, "A Holistic-Evolutionary View of Racism, Sexism, and Class Inequality," in *Inequality: Radical Institutionalist Views on Race, Gender, Class, and Nation,* ed. William M. Dugger (Wesport CT: Greenwood Press, 1996), 39, 41.

22. Niehans, *History of Economic Theory*, 321. "Representative Richard Baker, a white Republican from Baton Rouge, did little for the cause of racial trust when he was overheard thanking God for the projects' destruction. "We finally cleaned up public housing," he said. "We couldn't do it, but God did." Now the federal government wants to knock down about 4,500 of the remaining 7,900 apartments and replace them with mixed-income sites." "Orphaned," *New York Times*, August 27, 2006, 2006 WLNR 14835392.

23. A. Sherman and Shapiro, *Essential Facts about the Victims.* Over 33 percent of African American households in New Orleans did not own a personal vehicle. If the focus is shifted to poor African American households, then the number rises to

59 percent. Cliff Slater, "General Motors and the Demise of Street Cars," *Transportation Quarterly* 51 (1997): 45; Matthew L. Wald, "Transportation Chief Predicts Rejection of Airline Merger," *New York Times*, June 6, 2001, at C10.

24. See, for example, Fischler, "Pushing the Fight," 14LI.

25. Shughart, "Katrinanomics," 32.

26. United Nations Office for the Coordination of Humanitarian Affairs, "Cuba: A Model in Hurricane Risk Management," press release, IHA/943 (September 14, 2004) http://www.un.org/News/Press/docs/2004/iha943.doc.htm.

27. Nancy Cohn, "Cuba's Hurricane Response Far Superior," *truthout Perspective*, September 3, 2005, http://www.truthout.org/docs_2005/090305Y.shtml; "Waiting for a Leader," editorial, *New York Times*, September 1, 2005, A22.

28. Neil Smith, "There's No Such Thing as a Natural Disaster," *Understanding Katrina: Perspectives from the Social Sciences*," http://understandingkatrina.ssrc .org/Smith/; Cohn, "Cuba's Hurricane Response Far Superior"; Associated Press, "Hurricane Georges' Damage Reports," http://www.usatoday.com/weather/hur ricane/1998/wgrgedmg.htm; "Cuba: A Model."

29. American Red Cross, "Hurricane," http://www.redcross.org/services/ disaster/0,1082,0_587_,00.html#Plan. FEMA's suggested hurricane preparation includes building a safe room and determining how and where to secure one's boat. See Federal Emergency Management Agency, "Before a Hurricane," http://www .fema.gov/hazard/hurricane/hu_before.shtm; United Nations Office for the Coordination of Humanitarian Affairs, "Cuba: A Model."

30. Shughart, "Katrinanomics," 42.

31. Shughart, "Katrinanomics," 42.

32. David Gonzalez, "Havana Journal; To Latin Neighbors, Cuba Plays the Good Doctor," *New York Times*, February 17, 2000, A4.

33. See, generally, Charles R. P. Pouncy, "Institutional Economics and Critical Race/LatCrit Theory: The Need for a Critical 'Raced' Economics," *Rutgers Law Review* 54 (2002): 841.

34. Although Jesus of Nazareth taught, "It is easier for a camel to go through the eye of a needle, than for a rich man to enter into the kingdom of God" (Mark 10:25, *Holy Bible, King James Version*, 1261), contemporary Christian prosperity theology teaches that "God wants you to prosper financially, and rewards generosity, often to the church, generously." Tara Dooley, "Fervent Followers," *Houston Chronicle*, May 26, 2007, 1. According to this perspective, material possessions are viewed as an indication of righteousness and poverty as divine disfavor. Alan P. Stanley, "The Rich Young Ruler and Salvation," *Bibliotheca Sacra* 163 (2006): 46, 48–51.

35. "Broken Promises to a Broken Gulf," *New York Times*, April 17, 2007, A26.

FOUR

The Internal Revenue Code Don't Care about Poor, Black People

ANDRE L. SMITH

The federal government's immediate response to Hurricane Ka-trina was itself a disaster. The government was caught unaware, it claimed. Then Hurricane Rita hit. One is hard pressed not to wince and cringe when glimpsing at the spectacularly sad video images of both disasters. To its credit, the U.S. Congress responded to both disasters in several ways, in part by providing income tax relief. Yet the type of tax relief made available to the disaster victims has also made some tax experts wince and cringe.[1]

In response to Hurricane Katrina, Congress passed the Katrina Emergency Tax Relief Act (KETRA). One feature of KETRA allowed Katrina victims to file their tax returns late without penalty. An-other feature allowed disaster victims to make early withdraw-als from their retirement accounts without penalty. Impoverished people, however, generally do not have retirement accounts from which to draw. They may, however, benefit from having a longer time to file for a tax refund.[2]

KETRA is more beneficial to wealthier folks. Wealthier people are more likely to have retirement accounts and, thus, would receive a greater benefit from this provision of KETRA than would poor people. KETRA also eliminates a restriction on losses attributable to the destruction of property, which is more beneficial to those victims who owned the most property. Plus, if a bank forgives the mortgage of someone whose property was destroyed, KETRA prevents the Internal Revenue Service from taxing the gain attributable to the cancellation of debt. These laws primarily benefit those who own real estate.[3]

In response to Hurricane Rita, Congress provided more tax relief in the Gulf Opportunity Zone Act (GOZA). GOZA was directed primarily toward commercial interests that might engage in redevelopment. For instance, GOZA permits an extraordinary depreciation deduction for those who hold property for use in a trade or business or for the production of income. Those who will take advantage of this legislation include anyone who owns real estate for business use or who rents real estate to others. For local governments seeking to raise money to subsidize home ownership in their area, GOZA allows local governments to issue tax-free bonds for the purpose of subsidizing housing construction. Subsidized housing construction benefits the purchasers of bonds and real estate developers. It also helps poor people, to the extent that Congress requires that housing projects developed using these bonds dedicate a portion of the project to low-income housing stock. Ellen Aprill and Richard Schmalbeck analyzed the provisions of GOZA and found that it includes subsidies for utility companies, timber interests, and oil and gas producers.[4]

Predictably, KETRA and GOZA favored those least in need of aid. KETRA extends tax-filing deadlines, a benefit equally available to all. Even this provision has no real value to those who did not earn income the previous year, however. True, encouraging low-income housing is part of one provision in GOZA. The remaining provisions, though, offer relatively little to no value to those most in need.

Instead of providing tax subsidies to the propertied, Congress should use those same amounts to fund other programs designed to help all victims on an equal basis. Since they are unlikely to stop enacting legislation that inequitably benefits the propertied, it then becomes incumbent upon the poor and the institutions representing them to encourage home ownership as a means of escaping poverty and gaining equal entitlement to governmental resources. Placing the blame and the burden of this tragedy on Congress may have its moral value. As it comes to Katrina and Rita, the federal government has much for which to answer. Increasing home ownership is, I believe, strategically superior.

KETRA and GOZA Provide Inequitable Tax Subsidies

When Congress reduces someone's tax debt, it gives them money. If a solvent taxpayer owes the government $100, it makes no material difference whether the government gives the taxpayer $20 or reduces the tax debt by $20. When Congress enacts tax legislation providing extraordinary deductions or other relief from taxes to Katrina victims, then, it gives them money. Not only that, it gives them money that can no longer be used for the benefit of the rest of the country.[5]

Poorer Katrina victims will not receive these subsidies, however, for two reasons. First, extraordinary tax relief like that provided for in GOZA and KETRA has no real value for those who have not earned income and, for that reason, do not owe taxes. Second, even for those Gulf Coast residents with earned income, extraordinary tax deductions relating to property ownership have no value for residents who do not own real estate.

Tax relief is a subsidy only if someone owes taxes. If a taxpayer owes nothing to the government, it makes no difference if the government provides $1 or $1,000,000 in tax relief. The disaster victim with no tax liability receives no aid from KETRA or GOZA. Among those Katrina victims with tax liabilities, KETRA and GOZA primarily aid those who own real estate. By enacting these two bills, Congress directed more of the peoples' resources to those who earn higher incomes and own property than to those least able to fend for themselves in a time of crisis.

Concerns over the equitability of tax legislation are not new. Long before Hurricane Katrina, Beverly Moran and Bill Whitford asked whether the Internal Revenue Code was racist. They found that the Internal Revenue Code disadvantaged blacks, but not in a way that was intentional. The code heavily subsidizes the private ownership of real estate. These same subsidies are not available to renters. Since poor people are more likely to rent real estate than own it, the code favors the wealthy. To the extent that blacks represent a disproportionate number of the poor, the code discriminates against blacks. KETRA and GOZA follow the same pattern. Its provisions benefit the wealthy to the disadvantage of poor people. Since blacks represent a disproportionate number of poor Katrina victims, KETRA and GOZA represent another inequitable racial circumstance.[6]

Congress should not provide relief to one group of Katrina victims to the exclusion of another, and it certainly should not help those least in need of relief at the expense of those who need the most support. This problem becomes racially charged when blacks disproportionately represent those most in need. For these reasons, Congress should discontinue using federal taxes to help disaster victims. Instead, financial relief should be provided to victims directly and indiscriminately.[7]

Trickle-Down Theory Supports Tax Breaks to the Propertied

Tax subsidies to property owners may offend some senses of justice, but Congress latches onto the argument that they are useful because they alleviate the suffering of poor people, especially in a disaster area. After a disaster of the scale of Katrina, some real estate owners may abandon the area. Others may decide not to invest in the area because of doubts that it can be rebuilt. Still others may decide not to invest in real estate located in disaster areas, period. If commercial and residential housing stock in the Gulf South drops dramatically, its recovery may be prolonged or permanently suppressed.

Extraordinary tax subsidies relating to real estate ownership in disaster areas address these issues, but do so badly. This "trickledown" approach relies on the controversial notion that poor people need rich people in order to escape poverty. Tax subsidies for real estate ownership encourage rich people to stay in the Gulf. They encourage others from outside the Gulf to invest new monies into the area. In the same way, they indirectly encourage real estate investment in other potential disaster areas, such as earthquake zones.

Other critics oppose these tax subsidies because they only compensate the victims of certain disasters. Ellen Aprill and Richard Schmalbeck oppose tax subsidies to real estate owners in disaster areas because these subsidies are not available to all property owners who suffer from any unexpected disasters. They question the wisdom and fairness of subsidizing property owners who suffer publicly recognized disasters, but not property owners who suffer nonpublicized, local disasters, such as tornadoes.[8]

Defending subsidies to the rich on the basis that they help poor people has never been very persuasive, however. The financial benefits inuring to the rich do not in fact "trickle" down to the poor; they are retained by the rich. The wealthiest Americans get richer from subsidies while the poor become worse off. Besides, rich people do not need government incentives to invest in the Gulf Coast region. Disasters in commercially exploitable areas like the mouth of the Mississippi provide tremendous "buy low" opportunities for so-called corporate carpetbaggers, vultures, and scavengers. The tax code is hardly necessary to encourage such behavior.[9]

Trickle-down theory suggests, "A rising tide lifts all boats." This metaphor is often used to justify concentration on gross national product (GNP) rather than on direct alleviation of the pain and suffering of poor people. It suggests that as long as the United States as a whole is progressing technologically, economically poor people will be better off. Though they fall further behind the richest in our society, this argument insists that poor people in the United States have it easier than poor people in other countries. The aftermath of Hurricane Katrina shattered this delusion. Media coverage did not show all of the death, destruction, and despair, but what it did show strongly suggested that poor people in the United States are not much better off than poor people elsewhere. The trickle-down theory was put asunder on every TV screen in vivid color.

Still, KETRA and GOZA passed overwhelmingly. Congress was pressured to do something, almost anything. Since most, if not all, congressional representatives are property owners, and since most already respond more to property owners than to the nonpropertied, it is no surprise that their legislation following Katrina favored real estate holders. And make no mistake, property owners were severely affected by Hurricane Katrina. Thanks to State Farm and other national insurance companies, which sought to abdicate their contractual responsibilities, property owners shared some of the collective pain in the aftermath of Katrina. It is no mere coincidence that legislation passed in response to Katrina favored the relatively wealthy. In fact, it is likely to happen again. Yet the question remains: What should be done in the face of this inequitable legislation?[10]

Katrina Victims, Strategies, and Tax Subsidies

Poor people and those who care about them have three reasonable, non-exclusive options in the face of inequitable legislation such as KETRA and GOZA. First, those poor and working-class people who hold real estate need to be aware and take advantage of the subsidies available to them. Second, the less wealthy can lobby Congress against passing legislation of this type. Third, poor people should place a higher priority on acquiring real estate. Given current circumstances, this last option, though difficult, is probably most effective.

Some poor people own their own homes. Owning one's home has been the "American Dream" and can be the most effective route out of poverty. Many poor people take this to heart and succeed in acquiring real property, despite the obstacles. Working folk who own homes must take advantage of extraordinary tax subsidies for real estate when they are made available.

Most poor people do not own real estate, however. Those who do own real estate typically own only their own home. Very few own real estate that is rented to others. Poor people should not support tax relief that favors property owners, since relief acts like KETRA and GOZA favor those who own real estate, and especially those who use real estate in business activities. Poor people and the institutions that represent them should lobby Congress not to pass inequitable tax subsidies. Those who agree that the federal government's disaster-related relief should not subsidize property owners at the expense of non-property owners must mobilize politically. Property owners receive special tax breaks because they have the political resources (votes and money) to do it. They are aided by the fact that congressional representatives are property owners themselves. There are more people who do not hold real property than there are property owners. Most of the people who do not own property can vote. There will be less of a chance that future bills such as KETRA and GOZA are enacted with the same provisions if the nonpropertied vote in greater numbers. Poor people are also represented by nongovernmental organizations. These organizations must better recognize and fight inequities latent in the tax code.

The third strategy available to poor people may be the least palatable, yet most effective. Poor people must place greater emphasis on home ownership. Escaping poverty involves hard choices and sacrifice; it is not easy, and the odds may be stacked against many. Some strategies for escaping poverty are more effective than others, however. Some among the less fortunate are enamored with quick ways to escape poverty, even if the escape is temporary. Illicit drug dealing and get-rich-quick schemes of all types exemplify this strategy. Home ownership, on the other hand, is a slower method to maintain and gain wealth, but one that is relatively safe. It is also the anti-poverty technique most subsidized by the federal government.

The home ownership strategy is even more attractive after considering that Congress is likely to continue doling out tax subsidies for real estate ownership. The Constitution itself, since 1791, has specially protected the private ownership of property. As an example of our commitment to the hoarding of real property, Congress has created Fannie Mae and Freddie Mac, quasi-public corporations that protect the value of real estate holdings. In addition, institutions already exist to assist people with this third strategy. There are no national organizations focused on preventing inequitable tax subsidies that favor the rich as part of congressional disaster relief. There are, however, national organizations that already fight vigorously to provide more opportunities for less fortunate to own their own homes. Since there is little reason to believe that significantly greater political mobilization will prevent tax breaks like those included in KETRA and GOZA, the second strategy may in fact waste valuable public and private resources; these resources could be better used to subsidize low-income housing and loan programs.

Take Advantage of Current Disaster Relief Provisions

Low- and middle-class property owners must be aware of and take advantage of all the tax breaks offered by KETRA and GOZA. By criticizing KETRA and GOZA's preference for property owners, I do not suggest in any way that low- and middle-income property owners boycott the legislation. Disaster victims should take advantage of what is provided to them in disaster relief. KETRA's and GOZA's aid to low- and middle-income Gulf Coast residents may be slight, but we must take advantage of aid to the extent we can. Use the extended deadlines to file for your tax refund, no matter the refund's size. If you own property that suffered damage, fully utilize the extraordinary deductions that KETRA provides. Any little bit not owed to the federal government and every amount that the federal government must refund help one's personal rebuilding process as well as the local economy.

Awareness is key. Oftentimes poor people are not familiar with government programs that can help them. The federal government has numerous programs with respect to education, small businesses, and home ownership. Those who are best informed get to take advantage of these programs. Funds available in government programs tend to be distributed to those who are most informed and strategic. It is not laziness that prevents poor people from taking advantage of these programs, because laziness requires one to know about such programs in the first place and then fail to utilize them. It is about awareness and access to information, both of which must become more widely available to poor people in order for them to operate effectively in both the political and economic arenas.[11]

Do not be misinformed; go directly to the source. Scam artists on the Internet and elsewhere sometimes convince poor people to demand things to which they are not entitled. A few years ago, many black people wanted to believe that the federal government was providing reparations to former slaves in the form of a "Black Tax Credit." This was an Internet con. Instead of saving money on their taxes or receiving funds from the U.S. Treasury, many who claimed the fake credit were audited by the IRS and hit with large penalties.[12]

Many people use tax preparation software. Those who do should make sure that the software incorporates benefits available to Katrina's and Rita's victims. Those who use a tax preparation service and have relocated temporarily or permanently to another part of the country, as a result of either Hurricane Katrina or Rita, must make their preparer aware that they were residents of the Gulf Coast and entitled to specific, extraordinary tax relief.

Mobilize against Inequitable Tax Subsidies

A second strategy for responding to inequitable legislation is for nonpropertied Gulf Coast residents to mobilize politically against the type of subsidies that KETRA and GOZA provide to property owners. Extraordinary tax subsidies provided only to property owners violate principles of fairness. Since providing tax relief is the same as taking money out of the U.S. Treasury and giving it to specific beneficiaries, a fairer policy would provide relief equally to all disaster victims. If relief cannot be provided through taxation, then taxation should not be used to relieve disaster areas. Instead, those funds from the Treasury should be used in programs that provide direct aid to all, through the Federal Emergency Management Agency (FEMA) or the Red Cross, for example. This second strategy may not be suitable, however, since Congress will likely continue to provide tax relief to property owners or because FEMA is an unsavory alternative.

Voting for or against candidates based on the type of disaster relief they would support is part of this second strategy of political mobilization. Lobbying those congressional representatives who are elected could also influence the types of disaster relief that will be made available after future disasters. Voting and lobbying are activities one can do on either an individual or collective basis; almost every adult has a vote to exercise. Individuals may also form or join existing organizations seeking to lobby against lopsided tax relief.[13]

With respect to ending inequitable tax relief, however, political mobilization expends substantial amounts of time and resources toward benefits that may never be realized. Politicians do not often respond to the threat of losing an individual vote. Though political victory by way of extraordinary personal involvement is the stuff of television movies and other types of feel-good stories, it is highly time-consuming, frustrating, and sometimes very expensive. Donating the same personal time or resources to a national or grassroots organization may be a more efficient way to pool resources toward a common goal.

This author is aware of no national organizations dedicated to ending inequitable tax subsidies to the propertied, however. To convince a national organization to put this issue on their agenda would itself entail considerable effort. Control over the temper and shape of the issue would be determined by the national organization, once one did change and prioritize this issue; those most affected by inequitable subsidies would not control the agenda set by the national organization. In negotiations with congressional leadership, the organization may trade away this issue in order to acquire something else on their agenda.

Political mobilization might not be the best strategy for attacking tax subsidies to the propertied as a distinct issue. Poor people must spend considerable time and resources trying to make ends meet. Any time, money, or energy left over would then be divided between escaping poverty and political mobilization toward the end of preferential tax subsidies. Clearly, escaping poverty altogether is of a higher priority than preventing inequitable tax subsidies. This may be especially true considering the formidable opposition this mobilization would meet, including millions of U.S. property owners who benefit from the type of tax subsidies already in the Internal Revenue Code and the extraordinary ones provided for in KETRA and GOZA. Though the nonpropertied easily outnumber the propertied, those who own real estate have substantially greater resources to draw upon than the nonpropertied in order to remain entrenched as legislative favorites.

Typically politicians representing the poorer districts, as well as leaders of grassroots and national organizations, are property owners themselves. This is true irrespective of race and ethnicity. To ask these individuals to fight against extraordinary tax subsidies for the propertied is to ask them to fight against their own interests. Even if leaders agree verbally, their actions may lack the intensity of their words. Consider that many influential African Americans adopt a more conservative ideology. Presidential hopeful Barack Obama, for example, espouses traditionally conservative rhetoric, such as "personal responsibility." To these "leaders," poor people are either personally responsible for their own poverty or the only people who can be expected to respond to it. To them, no one has a duty or obligation to another; demanding assistance is evidence of personal or cultural weakness.

Those espousing personal responsibility believe it is not the government's role to help people in need. They ignore the fact that rich people depend on poor people's adherence to the "game." After all, the social order would disintegrate if poor people decided that the system was set up to guarantee their failure, while ensuring the success of others. Unfortunately for ultra-conservatives, there are enough decent Americans who understand the interdependence of our social structure. The mainstream of America does accept that tragedy can befall good and decent people; they offer help to others, either out of pure charity, the expectation that they will receive similar aid if found in a similar situation, or perhaps simply because charity helps maintain law and order.

Yet convincing the government to do something is not the same as getting the government to do something well. Some believe that the bureaucratic nature of government prevents it from doing things efficiently. Even if congressional leaders were convinced not to provide extraordinary tax subsidies to the propertied at the expense of the nonpropertied, if they were indeed convinced to respond to disasters by providing aid to all in equal fashion, the federal government might still provide aid badly. FEMA's performance in the Gulf Coast is an all too saddening example of this.

Though the government can do things somewhat efficiently, not all citizens support government-sponsored aid. Some in our society actively seek to prevent the government from working for the benefit of its citizens; some ultra-conservatives have adopted a strategy that includes sabotaging those governmental agencies they don't like. If conservatives do not like a government program and cannot eliminate it, they prefer that it perform poorly. For instance, the Bush administration appointed John Bolton to the position of undersecretary for arms control, even though the appointee does not believe in arms control. He was later appointed U.S. ambassador to the United Nations, even though he does not believe in the mission of the UN. In terms of taxation, this is called "Starving the Beast." Conservatives give tax breaks to the wealthy so that the U.S. Treasury does not have enough money to fund programs they do not support; this action is nearly as effective as scuttling the government programs from the start. In terms of Katrina, this political strategy was on display for the world to witness.

Specifically the Bush administration appointed to the head of FEMA someone who never managed an agency through an emergency. Former FEMA director Michael Brown had no experience in disaster relief. He was appointed to the position as a political reward for his activities in support of the Republican Party generally and the Bush administration specifically. Strangely, as FEMA's response to Katrina and Rita became more and more embarrassing, some in the media focused on Mr. Brown's attitude toward his job rather than on his lack of qualifications to lead. Until the ultra-conservative ideology is substantially undone, the result for poor people will likely remain inadequate and sad, even if Congress were convinced to provide disaster relief more equitably. Given the chances that political mobilization will not succeed, perhaps a third strategy is more appropriate.

Increase Housing Opportunities for Low- and Middle-Class People

Nonpropertied Gulf Coast residents should dedicate their time and resources toward commercial mobilization. In other words, since Congress will continue to favor property owners, and because even-handed approaches to disaster relief have proved inadequate, low- and middle-income people must acquire and hold real property in order to fully enjoy the benefits of our government. Providing greater opportunities for home ownership has both political and social components. Increasing the number of homeowners in the country is a goal Congress has traditionally supported. Greater demand for homes drives up the market price for housing, which benefits those who already own property. Thus, Congress can be convinced to encourage low- to moderate-priced housing stock and to support Fannie Mae and Freddie Mac as a means of ensuring affordable mortgage financing. In fact, the most laudable provision included in either GOZA or KETRA encouraged the creation of affordable housing in the Gulf Coast.

There is also a social component to this strategy; greater home ownership will change attitudes toward commerce. Commerce will become an activity in which poor people must engage to escape poverty, rather than an institution that rich people use to oppress poor people. There are many short-term escapes from poverty. For example, spending time and money on one's personal entertainment, or in pursuit of an illicit trade, can sometimes bring temporary relief and perhaps even joy to someone who is otherwise deprived. Time and money have a much more lasting effect, however, when directed toward the acquisition and maintenance of one's home. Once in possession of a home, or several, Congress will provide you with many ordinary and extraordinary preferences, as described throughout this chapter.

To this end we must encourage in the nonpropertied a stronger ethos toward savings, credit, and partnerships. Without jobs in the local economy, of course, it is difficult to save and keep good credit. Without the proper information, of course, it is difficult to earn, save, and borrow effectively. Lack of jobs and information do not foreclose the home ownership option, however.

For those without the highest-paying jobs, who have less relative business sophistication than their wealthier counterparts, partnering with others is the way to acquire and maintain wealth through property ownership. Families, friends, and colleagues of modest means must combine their time and resources toward wealth maximization. Acquiring and maintaining real estate is a daunting task for an impoverished individual. It is more effective when the work, risks, and rewards are shared with others. General partnerships, limited partnerships, small corporations, real estate investment trusts, cooperatives, and perhaps even nonprofit associations are all vehicles the nonpropertied can use to acquire, maintain, and exploit home ownership. In fact, these organizations are also vehicles in which the propertied and nonpropertied can join forces for the betterment of all America.

Lobbying Congress for Programs That Increase Home Ownership

The best strategy, then, is for the poor and their allies to develop strategies that increase the number of homeowners so that more people can take advantage of disaster-based tax relief like that offered in KETRA and GOZA. As property owners, rather than renters, they will have more influence politically, and political decisions will more likely favor them. What makes this third strategy more effective than the first two is that individuals and small groups of individuals can cooperate and succeed without depending on very many others. At the same time, the success of these new homeowners indirectly, economically, and symbolically helps those who have yet to succeed.

One might bristle initially at my recommendations. Admittedly, it seems somewhat heartless to suggest to poor people that the best way to fend for themselves in times of emergency or disaster is not to be poor anymore. In functional terms this argument is hardly different from those of ultra-conservatives who advocate openly for government to ignore the least endowed. However, I wish to conclude by showing that my suggestions "come from a different place" and are in fact different from ultra-conservative arguments. In other words, I want to prove to victims of Katrina and Rita that I make these cold and calculated recommendations because I care.

To that end, I must make clear three things that I am not suggesting, and one additional thing that I am. I am not suggesting that those more fortunate in our society have no moral duty to help those who are less fortunate. I am also not suggesting that poor people abandon political mobilization altogether. Probably more importantly, I am not suggesting that poor people are poor because they are in some way morally derelict. One can easily mischaracterize what I have written to suggest these things, so I want to be proactive in preventing misconceptions. What I do suggest, as a pragmatic and commercial approach to resolve inequitable circumstances, requires an attitude adjustment; this attitude adjustment applies equally to the poorer Gulf Coast victims of Katrina and Rita and to poorer black victims of America's legacy of racial subordination.

Those More Fortunate Have a Duty to Help Those Less Fortunate

Those more fortunate have a duty to help those less fortunate; I do not care if this duty is described as moral, civic, or selfish. Principles of justice and fairness, and the tenets of most religions, require those who have to help those who lack. This suggests a moral duty. By contrast, calling this duty a civic one emphasizes that the social order, on which we all rely to some degree to bring some semblance of peace and safety to our daily lives, depends on the consent of poor people. Our social system, which very much resembles a cruel game or "rat" race, does not work if poor people stop playing or running. To the extent that those more fortunate depend on the existing social system to maintain what they have, it is their civic and personal duty to help those less fortunate so that they too will accept the existing social system. Whether moral, civic, or selfish, the wealthy have a duty to help those in need.

The problem in enforcing this duty through disaster relief is that disasters like Katrina and Rita jeopardize the moderately wealthy almost as badly as the poor. It is unrealistic to expect the middle class to ignore their own needs at such a time. Thus, it is unrealistic to expect the middle class to oppose extraordinary tax subsidies relating to property ownership that are offered as disaster relief. As we have seen in the Gulf Coast, the middle class around the country help others during disasters in many ways, including financial assistance. Yet they will not help others by eliminating their own advantages relating to home ownership.

Poor People Are Not Morally Derelict

Poor people are not poor because they "choose" to be poor, or "choose" not to escape poverty. Poor people are not poor because they, as a group, lack fortitude or moral agency. Poor people are poor because resources are scarce, and our system allows people to hoard more than they need. Our system promotes competition, which in turn produces winners, middlers, and losers. Most of us accept the system for what it is, though our rhetoric suggests that we as a society would like to see fewer losers and winners, and more middlers. Our economic system guarantees losers, however. The economists who run our country universally accept that there is a point where the national economy reaches "full employment." You would think full employment means that everyone who wants a job has one. This is not true. Most economists believe that if less than three percent of Americans seeking a job cannot find one, then the government should do things to *prevent* more people from being hired. Economists say that full employment will bring about higher prices; to keep prices down for the more fortunate, we sacrifice our own fortunes. The concept of full employment means that there will never be a time when everyone who wants a job will have one, and that if we came close to it those in power would actively prevent full employment. The "system" we have ensures poverty.

Similarly, I am not suggesting that poor people must work harder. I am already convinced that poor people, especially those who would take these suggestions seriously, work as hard as the middle class and rich, and probably more if we account for the stress and strain that deprivation adds to our bustling lives. Yet this begs the question: How do poor people who already work their tails off focus more on home ownership? Aren't I suggesting that they are too ig-norant or lazy to have done so before?

Poor people need neither to be more moral nor to work harder. Instead, poor people must work smarter. The same resources al-ready devoted to other activities should be directed toward home ownership. The same energies spent on political activism generally should be spent on political activism that specifically promotes low- and middle-class housing stock and financing. The same friends and family members with whom one associates for entertainment purposes might be the people with whom one should partner re-sources and energies.

Political Organizations and Mortgage Financing

The whole point of associations, unions, and such is to allow sim-ilar-minded people to coalesce efficiently and to be heard louder and stronger than they would be as individuals. The reason I do not support coalescing around the specific issue of inequitable tax subsidies to disaster victims is simply because, for reasons previ-ously detailed, I do not think it will work. Too few politicians, and few of their supporters, care enough about inequitable tax subsi-dies. They do care about increasing the housing stock and creating greater access to mortgage financing, however. The benefits of these two programs "trickle up" from the poor to the wealthy. Demand-ing opportunities for home ownership, secured through national and grassroots political organizations that advocate for low and moderate-income households, is much more likely to be effective.

While there are no organizations that focus on ending inequita-ble tax subsidies in times of disaster, several grassroots organiza-tions already focus on increased home ownership. One of the most successful of these organizations is called the Neighborhood Assis-tance Corporation of America (NACA). NACA "was established in 1988 as a non-profit community advocacy and home ownership organization" and claims to be the first nonprofit organization to fight against predatory lending. NACA includes "more than 30 offices across the country [from Oakland to Boston] and an unmatched home ownership program."[14] The Association of Community Organizations for Reform Now (ACORN) also advocates for greater home ownership.[15]

Shifting Attitudes toward Home Ownership

The strategy I outline requires an attitude shift toward greater acceptance of commercial competition. I do not in any way suggest that capitalism is a morally just system, or even that it is a better system than any other. I do suggest, however, that it is not going anywhere anytime soon, and that poor people have to deal effectively with it. This essay concerns itself not with how the system ought to be, but how it is in order to most practically help those affected by Katrina and Rita, as well as those most vulnerable to future disasters. Sure, Congress ought to provide disaster relief on an equal basis. Certainly people of every economic strata should support this principle. Yet they will not. They will continue to question why poor people are not prepared for disasters, and ask why so many poor people did not leave before the hurricanes hit. They will ask why the poor didn't have insurance for these types of situations. Essentially, they ask, "Why didn't you do what I would have done if I were in your shoes?"

The answer to this question is obvious, I think. I doubt whether these critics would have been prepared if they were Gulf Coast residents without the wherewithal to satisfy all of their urgent needs. Victims of Katrina would have prepared themselves if they were in the financial shoes of those who do the criticizing. Had the shoes of Katrina's victims been bought at Macy's or the like, I am willing to bet they would have had the resources to adequately prepare for the storm, or to leave the area before it hit, or to always have insurance sufficient to cover any and all disasters. Of course, the point about having insurance is mitigated by the failure of State Farm and others to honor Katrina- and Rita-related claims.

Yet to the extent that people temporarily escape poverty by purchasing nondurable luxury items, attitudes must adjust. The temporary fix must be exchanged for something more lasting. Far from being a personal responsibility issue, this is a collective mentality thing. Our value and esteem systems must change.

One's esteem and value are derived from two sources: self and others. Individuals and their peers must increase the esteem associated with the acquisition of real property, property that appreciates instead of depreciates, and property that produces income rather than drains resources. Esteem relating to the acquisition of real estate should pervade our music, be important to our relationships, and even be a weapon in the beefs in which we engage. It will be a happier day when hip-hop artists aggrandize themselves or denigrate others based on their ownership and wise commercial exploitation of real estate. To the extent the "hustler" mentality prevalent in the current era of hip-hop comports with this notion, I support Jay-Z, Mike Jones, and Rick Ross.

Of course, a culture of inferiority is very hard to reverse. While most critics of black culture focus on hip-hop, I want to take note of black comedians. It frightens me that they get tremendous applause from black audiences when they state, "You know, black people ain't gonna boycott no Wal-Mart," or, "You know, black people can't run no business." Even if there were no evidence one way or another, this statement would offend me. People hold boycotts, and people run businesses. So if black people can't do these things, then we are inferior. Second, rather than "know" that black people can do those things, we know black people have boycotted and have run businesses. In fact, in the past we created businesses for ourselves while and because we were boycotting others.

Those applauses made out of ignorance ingrain a massively disgusting untruth.

On the other hand, I was recently heartened by the way black people responded to the Don Imus situation. After he made racially incendiary statements about black women on his radio show, black people did not rely solely on marching, nor did we request government intervention. CBS Radio and MSNBC fired Don Imus strictly because of the commercial repercussions threatened by the black community. To my mind this exemplified a more sophisticated civil rights strategy then we have employed in the past. Our response, and their response to our response, were entirely predicated on recognition of African American market power.

The disaster that was Don Imus certainly pales in comparison to the disaster brought by those major hurricanes. Yet the larger principle is at work. The best way to defend oneself or one's group against attack from natural or manmade forces is to acquire the resources and the market wherewithal to fight back in the commercial context. This country's attachment to private property ownership is so far ingrained in the people and our institutions that it would be foolhardy to swim against that stream. Instead, let's ride it out through the seas of deprivation and into the oceans of prosperity.

Conclusion

When addressing the aftermath of a natural disaster like Hurricane Katrina, Congress should not aid the wealthy at the expense of the poor. Yet this is exactly what KETRA does; it provides substantial material support to property owners and hardly any to those who do not own property. In fact, KETRA provides material support to property owners in a disaster area without giving the same benefits to property owners who suffer smaller local disasters. The act violates principles of both horizontal and vertical equity.

Unfortunately, the situation is unlikely to change, and Congress is likely to respond similarly in the future. Property owners enjoy a special place in our Constitution and in the minds and hearts of most federal legislators. Despite the obvious obstacles preventing it, poor and middle-class peoples must dedicate themselves even further to the acquisition of real property. Those with real property must be keenly aware of the tax benefits to which they are entitled, normally and with respect to disaster relief. Those without property should spend their time and money not on convincing Congress to stop passing such lopsided legislation, but instead on placing themselves in a position to take advantage of it.

Notes

1. Ellen P. Aprill and Richard Schmalbeck, "Post-Disaster Tax Legislation: A Series of Unfortunate Events," *Duke Law Journal* 56 (2006): 51, 58. "The provisions of [KETRA and GOZA] are, with only a few exceptions, a sad combination of ineffective disaster relief and poor tax policy."

2. Katrina Emergency Tax Relief Act (KETRA) of 2005, Pub. L. No. 109–73, 119 Stat. 2016 (2005).

3. Internal Revenue Code § 165 ordinarily disallows these types of losses to the extent they do not exceed 10 percent of the taxpayer's adjusted gross income. KETRA suspends this provision for Katrina victims. A loan is not income and not taxable because it must be paid back. If the debt is forgiven and not paid back, the taxpayer has income subject to federal taxes. Internal Revenue Code §§ 61 and 108.

4. Gulf Opportunity Zone Act (GOZA), Pub. L. No. 109-135, 119 Stat. 2577 (2005); Aprill and Schmalbeck, "Post-Disaster Tax Legislation," 51, 65.

5. Stanley S. Surrey and Paul R. McDaniel, *Tax Expenditures* (Cambridge MA: Harvard University Press, 1985). "Special income tax provisions are referred to as tax expenditures because they may be considered to be analogous to direct outlay programs, and the two can be considered as alternative means of accomplishing similar budget policy objectives." U.S. Congress, Joint Committee on Taxation, "Estimates of Federal Tax Expenditures for Fiscal Years 2006–2010," 109th Cong. (Washington DC: Government Printing Office, January 12, 2005), 2.

6. Beverly I. Moran and William Whitford, "A Black Critique of the Internal Revenue Code," *Wisconsin Law Review* 1996 (1996): 751.

7. Two essential features of "good" or "sound" tax policy are horizontal equity

and vertical equity. Horizontal equity stands for the proposition that similarly situated taxpayers should be taxed similarly. Vertical equity requires the wealthy to contribute more to the Treasury than the poor. See Michael J. Graetz and Deborah H. Schenk, *Federal Income Taxation: Principles and Policies*, 5th ed. (Washington DC: Foundation Press, 2005).

8. Aprill and Schmalbeck, "Post-Disaster Tax Legislation," 61–68.

9. Scholars questioned whether Congress needed to encourage investment in an area for which businesses typically needed no incentive. Aprill and Schmalbeck, "Post-Disaster Tax Legislation," 88.

10. KETRA was passed unanimously. 151 *Congressional Record* H8197, daily ed. (September 21, 2005); 151 *Congressional Record* S10320, daily ed. (September 21, 2005).

11. For details about KETRA or GOZA, or any tax relief under any circumstance, go to the Internal Revenue Service's website, at www.irs.gov.

12. An Internal Revenue Bulletin, IRB 2004-12, declares that "No law, including the Internal Revenue Code, allows taxpayers to claim a reparations tax credit or any other similarly-named credit." Courts repeatedly have rejected reparations tax credit claims as frivolous and penalized taxpayers making these claims and promoters and return preparers who assist taxpayer in making these frivolous claims. See, e.g., *United States v. Bridges*, 86 A.F.T.R.2d (RIA) 5280 (4th Cir. 2000) (rejecting as frivolous the non-existent "Black Tax Credit" and upholding conviction for aiding and assisting the preparation of false tax returns); *United States v. Haugabook*, 2002 U.S. Dist. LEXIS 25314 (M.D. Ga. 2002) (ordering a permanent injunction against a promoter prohibiting the preparation of returns or other documents claiming a tax credit for slavery reparations or other similar frivolous credits and requiring that the promoter place an advertisement in the local newspaper declaring that there are no such tax credits); United States v. Mims, 2002 U.S. Dist. LEXIS 25291 (S.D. Ga. 2002) (ordering a permanent injunction against a promoter prohibiting the preparation of returns or other documents claiming a tax credit for slavery reparations or other similar frivolous credits); *United States v. Foster*, 2002-2 U.S.T.C. (CCH) ¶ 50,785 (E.D. Va. 2002) (holding "no provision of the Internal Revenue Code allows for a tax credit for slavery reparations" and ordering a permanent injunction prohibiting the preparation of returns or refund claims based on a "fabricated tax credit for slavery reparations").

13. For better effectiveness, ending the disenfranchisement of ex-convicts should be part of the political mobilization strategy.

14. See http://www.naca.com.

15. See http://www.acorn.com.

FIVE

Judging under Disaster

The Effect of Hurricane Katrina on the Criminal Justice System

PHYLLIS KOTEY

A year and a half after Katrina flooded New Orleans, the city's legal system continues to limp along with understaffed courts, a poorly funded public defense system and temporary prison accommodations.—VESNA JAKSIC, "A Fresh Start: The Stories of Those Who Left," *National Law Journal*, February 13, 2007

As the Parish of Orleans struggles to rebuild after a disaster of monumental proportion, the criminal justice system continues to hemorrhage. The prison, the courts, and the participants in each of these institutions grapple with difficulty of fashioning a remedy for problems that existed prior to Hurricane Katrina. These problems were exacerbated by the storm, creating a chaotic and morose state in every aspect of the criminal justice system. Hurricane Katrina revealed the significant racial divisions that have long existed in New Orleans. The U.S. prison system has a long history of cruelty and neglect rooted in the high rate of incarceration of African Americans. In addition, the court system seemed impervious to the need to be proactive in preventing the continued incarceration of those held illegally following Katrina. The public defender system of criminal representation for the indigent collapsed due to severe underfunding and work overload—problems that were already characteristically embedded in the system prior to Katrina.

The imprisoned, poor, and unrepresented became the most visible victims of Hurricane Katrina in the criminal justice system. The federal government failed to immediately step in to mandate order in a system that was in obvious disorder. The basic constitutional protections guaranteed to all citizens of the United States were absent, while only marginal efforts to defend the Constitution and citizens were instituted. The problems in the criminal justice system became magnified by the enormity and severity of the storm and its effects. In commenting on the problems confronting the Gulf Coast in rebuilding after the storm, President Bush vowed to end "the legacy of racial discrimination and social inequality that has compounded poverty."[1] Specific comments regarding the criminal justice system of the city, however, were not forthcoming.

How was this legacy of racial discrimination and social inequality allowed to become so firmly rooted in the prison and criminal justice systems in a city, in a state, and in a country that boast guarantees of equal protection to all under the law? Why does this legacy of racial discrimination and social inequality persist: as a result of continued lack of funding and work overload in the system of indigent representation? Racial discrimination and social inequality prevail as the most obvious explanation for the state of affairs in the criminal justice system in the Orleans parish. This legacy remains unabated and exposed in the prisons, the courts, and the system of indigent representation.

The evacuation of people, the destruction of buildings and their contents, and the chaos and breakdown of the criminal justice system combined to create an unnatural disaster within a disaster zone. The stories of survival echoing throughout the criminal justice system exemplify the struggles that continue while the city tries to return to normalcy. The prisons, the courts, and our indigent defense systems crumbled under the pressure of a disaster of unnatural proportion. While the city of New Orleans was not the only area affected by Hurricane Katrina, it provides a suitable snapshot and a sufficient example of the devastation that was inflicted upon African Americans before, during, and after the disaster. Ironically, despite the time that has passed since Hurricane Katrina, the New Orleans criminal district still limps along with temporary prison accommodations, understaffed courts, and a poorly funded public defense system.[2]

The Prison System

There are no disaster exemptions to a person's constitutional rights. —PAMELA METZGER, in Peter Whoriskey, "In New Orleans, Justice on Trial: Katrina Strains Public Defender's Office," *Washington Post*, April 16, 2006

The prison system of New Orleans was the subject of criticism long before Katrina hit. Complaints of neglect and cruelty more than once resulted in examination and scrutiny by the federal court. New Orleans is one of the most segregated metropolitan areas in the country; its criminal justice system reflects this fact, from "the disproportionate targeting of African American residents by its police department to the over-incarceration of African Americans in its jail."[3] The city's criminal justice system reveals the legacy of racism.[4]

The New Orleans Police Department has a history of racial animosity that continues today. In 1990 a prisoner accused of killing a police officer was beaten to death by officers at the hospital where he was taken for treatment. The officers involved were neither administratively nor criminally sanctioned. In April 2006 the American

Civil Liberties Union (ACLU) of Louisiana filed a public records request with the New Orleans Police Department in response to numerous complaints of police misconduct. The organization's advocacy led to a call for systematic reform of the department.[5]

African Americans comprise a majority of the city of New Orleans. They make up 12 percent of the population of the United States, and 66.66 percent of the population of New Orleans. The New Orleans Parish prison population is 90 percent African American, compared to the U.S. prison population, which is 43.7 percent African American. The rate of incarceration of African Americans in New Orleans on the day that the city was hit by Hurricane Katrina creates an overwhelming picture. The city had the highest incarceration rate of any large city, which was double the rate of the U.S. average. For every 100,000 residents of New Orleans, 1,480 prisoners were incarcerated.[6]

It was estimated that approximately 8,000 prisoners were housed in the Orleans Parish Prison system (OPP) on the day that Hurricane Katrina landed. According to statistics produced by the sheriff's office, however, there were 6,375 prisoners in OPP. The sheriff's numbers included 354 juveniles from Youth Study Center (YSC) but did not include the approximately 300 adults and juveniles who had been evacuated to New Orleans from St. Bernard Parish. What is known is that the inmates held when Katrina landed included men, women, and children ranging in age from ten to seventy-three.[7]

OPP includes the entire prison system in New Orleans. It comprises twelve facilities, the oldest of which, the Old Parish Prison, was built in 1929. The twelve buildings are located in downtown New Orleans and routinely house nearly 6,500 prisoners a day. In fact, OPP houses more prisoners than the Louisiana State Penitentiary at Angola, which is the largest prison in the United States according to the U.S. Department of Justice, Bureau of Justice Statistics. Only after the storm arrived were the thousands of prisoners housed in OPP evacuated; they were scattered without adequate records into thirty-four facilities across the state. One is left to wonder why an effective, efficient, and orderly method of evacuation would not have been a principle subject of discussion as government officials made plans to prepare for the impending storm.[8]

While local, state, and federal officials took steps to evacuate the Gulf Coast in anticipation of Katrina's landfall, New Orleans Parish sheriff Marlin Gusman proclaimed, "We've been working with the police department—so we're going to keep our prisoners where they belong."[9] Consideration and planning for the safety of the city's animals was greater than the safety of the prisoners in OPP. Ironically, the Louisiana Society for the Prevention of Cruelty to Animals made the decision to evacuate the stray pets left in their care prior to the hurricane. After photographing each pet and ensuring that identification collars and paperwork were in order, the animals were evacuated. Surely the implementation of these minimal efforts would be a foreseeable necessity for an institution such as the OPP.[10]

Inadequate Planning and Preparation

Racial considerations pervade every aspect of the account of OPP and Hurricane Katrina: from the failure to plan, to prepare, and to evacuate to the premature repopulation of the prison over the objections of local authorities. While an overview of the ordeal at OPP would allow a glimpse of the effect of Katrina, a sampling of individuals' stories of survival present a more compelling view of the lack of responsible planning, preparation, and leadership that defined the OPP's response to Katrina.[11]

Rhonda Ducre was a deputy sheriff working at the House of Detention (HOD) for four years when Katrina struck. Like others, she was obligated to come to work during the storm and was allowed to bring family with her. She explained, "In my four years

there has never been a plan for what to do when hurricanes hit . . .
there was no preparation for this storm."[12] Ducre reported that the
food for inmates was in the kitchen of the Community Correctional
Center (CCC), which flooded when the levees broke on the Monday after Katrina landed. The prisoners had no food available to
eat. Why did OPP officials not plan to ensure that food was available for the inmates? Was it unforeseeable that flooding might occur? The prisoners became victims of the prison system that failed
to plan for the storm.[13]

At the time of the storm, deputies were allowed to bring family
and close friends to the prison, and a place was provided for them.
By the third day following the storm, the deputies and their families pooled their food for rationing, while supervisors barbequed
and kept fifty cases of water to themselves. The State Department
of Corrections initiated efforts to evacuate the prisoners, though
the federal authorities did not participate or assist in the operations.
Ironically, deputies and their families were left to fend for themselves, with no plan for their own evacuation and no idea about
what to do. Obviously, even the safety and security of those who
are directly responsible for safety and security of the prisoners did
not merit the importance of planning and preparation.[14]

Prior to the evacuation of the prisoners, lack of planning, preparation, and leadership seriously jeopardized the safety of the prisoners and the deputies. Brady Richard, a medical supply officer at
CCC, was instructed to report to work the day before the hurricane
landed. About 200 deputies and their families took refuge there.
According to Richard, the situation at the jail deteriorated as the
water level rose. The inmates became volatile and were left in the
dark for days with no food, no water, and little information. The
prisoners broke the interior walls of the first floor and gained full
access to all areas of the prison, forcing deputies and their families
to huddle together for safety behind the sole barrier that separated
them from the prisoners.[15]

Neither the sheriff nor the administration issued any directives to the deputies after the storm hit. Richard was sent to deliver medical supplies to HOD on Tuesday, the day after the levees broke. He traveled there by boat but had to wade through chest deep water full of feces, dead rats, and other garbage to get inside the facility. As he waited for a boat to travel back to CCC, he observed prisoners jumping into the water and heard civilians crying for help. He explained, "No one, including the deputies, seemed to know when and whether help was going to arrive."[16] Instead, staff and inmates were abandoned by the institutions that might have provided assistance.[17]

Inmates took their safety into their own hands at one OPP facility after deputies quit and refused to report to duty. Deputy Renard Reed said: "There was never any special training for us deputies about storm preparation, emergency evacuation, nothing. We didn't have fire drills or any other emergency drills that I can remember."[18] A deputy since 1998, Reed evacuated his family but reported to work at HOD the Sunday before the storm as required by his supervisor. From his stationed assignment on the tenth floor, Reed reported that he felt the entire brick building sway in the wind. After the levees broke the next day, he watched the water overtake his truck. Reed noted, "That's when it started to sink in: we're trapped."[19] Both prisoners and deputies were trapped, without the benefit of adequate planning, preparation, or leadership. Reed indicated that the deputies began quitting after the power went out, and the inmates became agitated and upset because no one told them anything. From his vantage point as a sniper on the roof of HOD, he said that he had enough. He saw inmates jumping from Templeton III through a hole knocked in the wall. They were "getting picked off and falling in the water. . . . It was almost like the Third World."[20] Reed witnessed spectacles at the prison that he never imagined would occur in his own country.[21]

An inmate from Templeton III validated Reed's accounts and provided an even more dire portrait of what transpired in the prison. The inmate reported that those left on the first floor after the evacuation of some inmates were forced to break the wall on the first tier and burn a hole in it, because the tier "had the airlock in the hall shut."[22] All OPP facilities except HOD are sealed without ventilation, so inmates soon found themselves in life-threatening situations. Surely the emergent possibility that a power outage could occur during a storm and create panic and danger in an airtight facility required little foresight. Minimal planning and preparation might have protected the inmates from this possibility.[23]

HOD was the last facility to be evacuated because unlike the other facilities that were sealed, it had ventilation. After the prisoners were evacuated from this final facility, the deputies were left stranded. No more boats arrived. Even the employees of the prison did not escape officials' careless indifference or failure to plan, prepare, and provide effective leadership. A deputy at HOD and Templeton III reported early failure of the generators, which failed to produce power sufficient to power the cell doors: prisoners were left trapped inside. Sheriff Gusman admitted, "We started to have power failures because the generators were not placed high enough when flood waters came."[24] Some deputies were not trained to operate the generators, and it was later found that even when generators were positioned safely above the floodwaters, the fuel to power them was stored on the first floor and was submerged.[25]

Questions still remain unanswered regarding the sheriff's failure to plan, prepare, and provide adequate leadership. His rank disregard for the safety and security of his prisoners and deputies serves as an example of infinite magnitude. What was the sheriff's plan? After repeated unsuccessful attempts to obtain a copy of the prison's emergency evacuation plan, the American Civil Liberties Union (ACLU) filed a public records request with the sheriff. When these efforts did not yield information, a lawsuit was filed. The sheriff finally responded to the requests, noting, "All documents re[garding] evacuation plans were underwater."[26] The OPP was ill-prepared for the storm, especially in light of the sheriff's decision not to evacuate. In a meeting on August 28, 2005, in the face of the impending storm, it is reported that the sheriff was told that there was insufficient water, flashlights, batteries, and food in his facilities. Gusman reportedly responded, "Those are incidentals and we'll deal with them later."[27] The sheriff failed to provide even basic necessities to inmates, despite his decision not to evacuate them.[28]

Doing "Katrina Time"

Expectedly, the inadequacy of a preparation plan, the loss of records, and the relocation of inmates created a logistical nightmare that resulted in a total breakdown of communication, record keeping, and identification. These deficiencies combined to create a phenomenon called "Katrina Time." "Katrina Time" was and continues to be used to describe those prisoners (known and unknown) being held illegally past the release date or statutory maximum for their sentences, without a hearing or without the benefit of counsel. Their detentions range from offenses as minor as reading tarot cards without a permit to the more serious charge of murder.[29]

OPP's South White Street Facility in the Conchetta Youth Center housed a number of juveniles. Fifteen-year-old Corey Stevenson was held in the juvenile section of the OPP prior to the storm. He was transferred to another facility after Katrina, but his mother could not locate him for over a month and a half because he was incorrectly identified as an adult. Even after correcting his status to juvenile, authorities continued to house him with the adults, saying, "You came in with adults, you stay with adults."[30] At this facility, two adult inmates beat Stevenson, splitting his jaw and giving him a black eye. He was again transferred; his new facility was located over three hundred miles from New Orleans. Meanwhile, in New Orleans, his case was on the docket to be handled and was continued three times. For his next court date, Corey was transferred back to New Orleans to Central Lock-up. However, authorities failed to transport him to court. Corey, now sixteen, has been locked up for over a year, doing time: "Katrina Time."[31]

Given the deficiencies in the system, the exact number of those doing "Katrina Time" is unknown. Typically, OPP's population is composed of individuals arrested on "orders to pick up," commonly called "attachments."[32] Generally, these arrests arise out of failure to comply with noncriminal court orders. Additionally, the population of OPP consists of felons and misdemeanants who face traffic violations and municipal ordinances. Men, women, and children were kept in OPP facilities prior to the storm. Eventually, many of those who were transferred throughout the state began serving "Katrina Time." Many of those doing "Katrina Time" were arrested on sworn affidavits by the police for petty offenses that included the previously mentioned reading of tarot cards without a permit, public drunkenness, traffic offenses, and other similar minor offenses.[33]

The experiences of those who did "Katrina Time" present a revealing depiction of the travesty of this phenomenon. For example, Tammy Sims was arrested in early August for public drunkenness. She was also held on a charge of solicitation of prostitution. Both of these relatively minor misdemeanor charges resulted in her incarceration at OPP. On August 18, 2005, she was found incompetent to stand trial and ordered to be transferred to Feliciana Forensic Facility.[34] Katrina wrought devastation in New Orleans, however, and she was never transferred to Feliciana. Ten months later, Sims remained at OPP until a "chance encounter" with a Tulane law student led to her release.[35] It is estimated that eight thousand people languished in prison while serving "Katrina Time" as the jail and courts struggled to identify those who had served long past their legal sentences. While many of those being held were still legally confined, others should have been released but had to wait for legal intervention to gain freedom.[36]

By October 2005 Sheriff Gusman reopened HOD amid criticism for his hastiness to repopulate a jail that was already filling up with new arrestees. Though city and other authorities were still assessing whether civilians could safely return to flood-ravaged areas, Gusman boasted that he "just ignored the city."[37] In moving back into the jail, the sheriff circumvented the city's safety procedures. His sidestepping of procedures designed to ensure the safety of inmates and of those working at the prison characteristically exemplifies his continued disregard for preparation and planning, as well as his haphazard leadership.[38]

Prisoners' constitutional rights appeared to have been granted a "disaster exemption" that has no expiration date. Pamela Metzger, a professor at Tulane University Law School, aptly captured both the spirit and letter of the law when she noted, "I understand that Hurricane Katrina upset everyone's lives. But as far as I know, there are no disaster exemptions to a person's constitutional rights."[39] The storm and its effects have presented a high-stakes constitutional standoff of monumental proportion as the criminal justice system is besieged on all sides.[40]

The Court System

The Supreme Court should have a system in place that allows for law, for civilization to continue in the face of a disaster. . . . We literally had no system of law for at least two weeks after the hurricane. —PHYLLIS MANN, "Hurricane Relief Aid," *Advocate*, Fall 2005

The storm gravely impaired the city of New Orleans and its institutions. Indeed, "Hurricane Katrina washed away the New Orleans criminal justice system."[41] The courts were no exception. The entire criminal justice system came to a grinding halt as there were no prisoners, witnesses, or lawyers due to the displacement of the city's population. There were no criminal trials from September 2005 to June 2006. As a consequence, in addition to dealing with the immediate disruption to the courts caused by the storm, the mass departure of residents created a ripple effect that broke down other parts of the criminal justice system. The displacement of the jail, the courthouse, and the lawyers involved in every aspect of the court continues to have a devastating effect on the city. Yet a significant and emphatic response from the federal courts to ensure the very basic constitutional rights guaranteed under the law has not taken place.[42]

Immediately after the storm, a temporary jail, powered by a locomotive, was set up at the Greyhound bus station and train terminal. The location was coined "Camp Greyhound," much to the chagrin of bus line officials. After the eventual evacuation of OPP, many prisoners were taken to an outdoor football field at the Elayn Hunt Correctional Facility in St. Gabriel, Louisiana. On September 6, 2005, Governor Kathleen Blanco issued an executive order suspending all deadlines in legal proceedings until September 25, 2005. Subsequent to the order, the Louisiana Supreme Court declared a "court holiday" until October 25, 2005. The state Supreme Court has been criticized for providing little assistance to the New Orleans court system, other than issuing this declaration. These orders offered some relief but provided no resolution for those doing "Katrina Time."[43]

The criminal court focused on the more than two hundred arrests that were made from August 30 to September 8, 2005, ignoring those already in custody. The displaced inmates from New

Orleans who were now held in custody outside of the city, and who appeared in state or federal court in their new jurisdictions, found that judges set extremely high bonds, when they were given a hearing, in order to prevent their release into the new city. Additionally, judges set high bonds in these hearings to avoid the need to provide the inmate with transportation back to New Orleans. Even if prisoners were released, many jails held displaced inmates past their release dates to allow New Orleans authorities time to pick up the inmate during scheduled, weekly pickups. This time schedule for pickup was sped up by the New Orleans sheriff's office only after a motion was filed to hold the deputy warden in contempt for failure to release inmates who were held past their release dates.[44]

Opening the Courts

New Orleans had essentially no court or system in place to seek relief for approximately two months following Katrina. Phyllis Mann, past president of the Louisiana Association of Criminal Defense Lawyers (LACDL), noted, "They [the courts] were just not functioning."[45] Even after these two months, the functioning of the court was neither efficient nor orderly. Justice was not just delayed but nonexistent when the courts that were created to ensure fundamental constitutional rights remained unavailable. Mann was allegedly told by some judges that the court of appeals was closed. She responded, "Where are you going to go?"[46] The state Supreme Court was forced to relocate to Baton Rouge and has attracted criticisms as well for its failure to take an active role in ensuring the orderly administration of the court system; the court might have made provisions to open, set hearings or, at the very least, accepted filings.[47]

In an attempt to seek relief when the courts closed after Hurricane Katrina, Motions to Re-Open the Supreme Court of Louisiana were filed in three unrelated noncriminal actions in the Louisiana

Supreme Court on September 27, 2005. The court denied the motions filed in each case that sought to consider a writ application. Two weeks later, on October 13, the Supreme Court granted the motion to open court but denied the relief sought. This case also sought relief in a noncriminal matter and, like the previous cases, was summarily denied without the issuance of an opinion.[48]

Eventually, applications for relief were filed in direct response to prison incarcerations in the aftermath of Katrina. Also on October 13, 2005, Mann filed a Motion to Re-Open the Court to seek habeas relief on behalf of Ansari and other detainees being held around the state following Katrina. The motions sought not only to open the court for the habeas proceeding but also to streamline the habeas process for the detainees by designating one clerk of the court and one judge to hear all the cases. This request for an opportunity to be heard for emergency relief was simply denied by the Supreme Court. It should be noted that three justices dissented in the denial of emergency relief, however.[49]

Judges began attempting to reestablish the criminal justice system by holding bond hearings at Hunt, the temporary jail, but the process proved difficult without records and other necessary paperwork. Temporarily, the Hunt facility and the jail established at the Greyhound bus terminal and train station became sites of the courthouse in New Orleans. Judge Terry Alarcon of the Orleans Parish Criminal District Court reported that until the courthouse was able to reopen, the criminal judges "took turns sitting at Hunt and the Greyhound jail."[50] Thereafter, they moved to borrowed courtrooms in the federal courthouse until December. The temporary courtrooms provided little opportunity for meaningful court disposition: the public was barred from attendance, and attorneys, clients, and witnesses were many times unavailable because of displacement. The first nonjury trial was held in criminal court on March 31, 2006. On June 1 the New Orleans Criminal Courthouse reopened at two locations.[51]

In December 2005 criminal court judges made plans to build a temporary courthouse in Algiers, which they would use until the Federal Emergency Management Agency (FEMA) verified that the Tulane and Broad courthouses were ready to be reoccupied. After the courthouse opened, the first jury trial was held five days later on June 5, 2006. While it was predicted that jury trials would be held nonstop in the reopened courthouse to alleviate the backlog, only fifteen jury trials were held from July to October 2006.[52]

Releasing from Custody

As late as December 2005 inmates continued to languish in custody with no release, no hearing, and no lawyer. In September 2005 the fight began in earnest to seek the release of inmates held across the state in prisons to which they were relocated after the storm. After failing to persuade the Supreme Court to adopt a streamlined procedure for handling the habeas process, Phyllis Mann launched into action, sending an appeal to criminal defense attorneys across the state to call their local sheriff's offices to obtain a list of inmates. On September 8, 2005, Sheriff Gusman produced a list of prisoners and the dates of their release. Mann and a team of volunteer defense attorneys struggled to ensure that the court provided the constitutional protections guaranteed under the law. Early efforts to secure the release of detainees were thwarted, but Mann and other attorneys were eventually successful in as many as 100 of the 120 cases heard three months later in December.[53]

The volunteer defense attorneys identified four categories of detainees from the list that was produced to secure their release: category one, those who already served their sentence or in excess of the statutory maximum sentence; category two, those held for minor offenses, but who were unable to post a bond or never had a bond set; category three, those who were never screened for appointment

119

of an attorney; category four, those being held or serving sentences for more serious charges.[54] Mann and other volunteers prepared to file habeas petitions for those in categories one and two, assuming that the hemorrhaging system would welcome the opportunity to relieve some of its overcrowding. A municipal court judge from New Orleans signed release orders in the municipal misdemeanor cases. Several months passed, however, without action on the other categories of cases. Petitions were filed throughout the state because the venue or place where the case was to be heard was dictated by the locale in which the inmate was being held.[55]

The initial focus of these motions was to obtain the release of inmates who were held without charges. Calvin Johnson, chief judge of the Criminal District Court, ordered the release of those who had not been formally charged. A stay was issued by the state Supreme Court on November 18, 2005, but was finally lifted, giving the state until 5 p.m. on January 6, 2006, to "file a bill of information or indictment."[56] Throughout the process of attempting to secure the release of persons who had served their sentences or who could or should be otherwise released, the prosecutor's office maintained that its job was not to secure the release of defendants. The task of properly and formally charging those held did, however, fall fully within its responsibilities with the issuance of this order. Finally, in an attempt to comply with the law and the order of the court, the district attorney filed charges against 1,140 defendants.[57]

This order only provided relief to those against whom no charges had been filed. Countless others were still held on charges for minor offenses. By April 15, 2006, Judge Calvin Johnson lamented that he and his staff were still finding "Katrina Time" victims, explaining, "We can't have people in jail indeterminately."[58] After several months of delay, Judge Johnson issued an order on May 17 to provide immediate relief for those inmates who continued to be held on most municipal or traffic offenses. The order called for, within seventy-two hours after receipt of the order, the release of any and all inmates who were charged with municipal or traffic violations with the issuance of a notice to appear for the next court appearance. The judge further ordered no detention for individuals charged for municipal or traffic violations, unless the charge was a violation of a charge against persons including, but not limited to, domestic violence, battery, and driving while intoxicated.[59]

As the first anniversary of Hurricane Katrina approached, Judge Arthur Hunter of the New Orleans criminal court noted the ineffectiveness of the offices of the district attorney and public defender, as some pre-Katrina inmates still remained incarcerated without talking to an attorney or appearing in court. District Attorney Jordan replied, "Simply releasing all defendants because the public defender's office is not fully functional is an injustice and undermines public safety."[60] An October 31, 2006, headline announced an improvement in the city's functionality, however: "Criminal Courthouse Bounces Back."[61] The day marked the first time that the Criminal District Court was fully operational. The opening of all twelve divisions eliminated the need for cases to be heard in weekly shifts. Yet all is still not well; although buildings are fully operational, the people are not. The entire criminal court system remains "hobbled by people problems, including lack of enough people to serve on juries and lawyers to represent poor defendants."[62] The New Orleans criminal court system is still in recovery.[63]

The Public Defender System

Hurricane Katrina is no longer an excuse. . . . Indigent defense in New Orleans is unbelievable, unconstitutional, totally lacking the basic professional standards of legal representation and a mockery of what a criminal justice system should be in a Western civilized nation. — JUDGE ARTHUR HUNTER, in "Doing Katrina Time," *San Francisco Bayview National Black Newspaper*, June 19, 2007

Even if one could find any of the thousands of individuals doing "Katrina Time" and secure a "temporary" courtroom in which to hear the pending case, the greatest obstacle would be finding court-appointed counsel to provide representation to the individual. Prior to Katrina, 85 percent of the defendants in criminal court were indigent and qualified for the services of a public defender. The funding scheme for funding indigent defense was successfully challenged in *State v. Pert*. The Louisiana Supreme Court warned that it may be forced to employ "more intrusive and specific measures it has thus far avoided to ensure that indigent defendants receive reasonable effective assistance of counsel."[64] Indigent defendants in New Orleans had difficulty accessing their constitutionally protected right to court-appointed counsel.[65]

Prior to Katrina in 2005, the Louisiana Supreme Court was again forced to address the issue of indigent defense programs and the failure of the legislature to provide adequate funding. In a unanimous decision, the court found that the legislature has enacted legislation requiring the state to provide funds for indigent defense but fails to provide an adequate appropriation of funds to support the provision of services. Specifically, the court granted the trial courts the authority upon motion of a defendant to terminate a prosecution if adequate funding is not available. The state is required through the Louisiana Indigent Defense Board to provide adequate appropriation for defense services, but the mechanism for funding makes it difficult to ensure adequacy. The prospect of instituting the necessary reforms of the public defender became remote with the advent of Hurricane Katrina.[66]

Adequacy of Funding

Traffic tickets and court costs provide the mechanism for funding the Orleans Parish Indigent Defender Board. Thus, funding from these sources is dependent upon revenue derived from how well the public defender is not doing his or her job. For example, every not-guilty verdict or case dismissal decreases the availability of funding, since traffic fines and court costs are not assessed in these cases. Louisiana is the only state to utilize this inconsistent and unpredictable system of funding. The disparity in resources between districts across the state is a direct result of this mechanism for funding.[67]

Post-Katrina, the funding revenue for indigent defense was totally disrupted. With the displacement of the population, fewer traffic tickets were written. With the flooding of the courthouses, fewer courtrooms were available. The state suspended funding for public defenders, prosecutors, and the prison, leaving the system even more crippled as it dealt with the additional reality of missing almost half of its private defense bar. Without lawyers to provide effective representation, the administration of the criminal justice system was and will be further hampered.[68]

The Public Defender's Office was forced to make dramatic cuts, as the funds for 2006 were reported to have dropped to less than 20 percent of the projected budget of 2.3 million dollars. Denise "Denny" LeBoeuf was sworn in as the new chair of the Orleans Parish Indigent Defender Board in April 2006. According to LeBoeuf, forty-two lawyers were employed to provide indigent representation before Katrina. Most of these lawyers worked part-time while maintaining private practices. After Katrina, the Orleans Parish Indigent Defense Program laid off thirty public defenders, more than two-thirds of its staff. Ultimately it was necessary for the members of the public and private criminal defense bar to step in and provide assistance. The Ohio and Michigan Bar Associations donated funds designated to hiring staff attorneys in compliance with American Bar Association caseload limits.[69]

As the crisis grew, attorneys from outside Louisiana poured in to help. Many efforts were met with opposition caused by prison rules, however. For example, only a member of the Louisiana bar could visit a client in jail. Even if the attorney is a member of the Louisiana bar, the jail further required verification of bar membership with the Louisiana Bar Association, which is located in New Orleans. Yet verification was not possible because the office was closed following the storm. Eventually, Mann was able to get the jail to agree that Louisiana attorneys could present their wallet bar cards for identification and that these lawyers would not be restricted to visiting only their clients. Out-of-state lawyers were still unable to visit the prisoners. The volunteer lawyers interviewed thousands of inmates, gathering and relaying information to their families and lawyers.[70]

In March 2006 law student volunteers from across the country came to the law clinics of Tulane and Loyola Universities to assist in the effort "to sort out" the prison population serving "Katrina Time."[71] The search to find these defendants left students asking whether the Constitution of the United States applied in Louisiana. The students combed through criminal court dockets to identify and secure the freedom of defendants who remained in jail after having already served their time.[72]

Like the public defender's office, the district attorney's office flooded and suffered damage as a result of the storm. It, too, lost funding with the collapse of the city and subsequent loss of the traffic fines and the court cost–driven revenue source. In fact, after failing to receive funds from the city, fifty-four employees of the district attorney's office were laid off. Temporary offices were set up at "Camp Greyhound," along with the office of the U.S. attorney. The office was relocated to a nightclub immediately after Katrina but is now in a temporary office space. It was not until the beginning of 2007 that all eighty-eight district attorneys returned to work.[73]

Almost one year after Hurricane Katrina and almost three months after the opening of the Broad and Tulane courthouses in June 2006, New Orleans district attorney Eddie Jordan "considers it a success" that his office had tried almost thirty felony cases, while clearing about three hundred others. Critics, however, disagreed with Jordan's assessment regarding the success of his office. On June 2, 2006, in the first jury trial completed since Katrina, the jury acquitted the two defendants charged with a single count of distribution of cocaine and purchase of cocaine, respectively. The first actual jury trial, which began on June 5, 2006, ended on that same day when a jury was unable to reach a verdict in the case of a stolen vehicle. Defense attorney Gary Wainwright noted, "The victims of murder and rape wait while they tied up the courtroom with this garbage."[74] Though the courthouses reopened, the New Orleans court system remains backlogged and, in many ways, ineffectual.[75]

Reorganization of Office

Although it would be easy to blame the chaos in the criminal justice system on Katrina, pre-Katrina assessments of the system were far less than sterling. Plagued by corruption, high crime, poor funding, and mismanagement, the pre-Katrina criminal justice system was problematic. According to a report from the National Legal Aid and Defender Association and the National Association of Criminal Defense Lawyers, Louisiana's system for providing legal defense to the indigent was left to public defenders, who worked part-time handling six times the caseload of a full-time attorney.[76]

Some of the pre-Katrina problems were addressed following the storm. Post-Katrina, the apparent deficiency of public defenders in the system was confronted directly with the employment of full-time attorneys. The new public defender board, appointed in April 2006, increased salaries and required lawyers to relinquish their private practices. Several lawyers refused to abandon their private practices and quit, leaving the office shorthanded. Judge Arthur Hunter noted, "The Louisiana Legislature has allowed the public defender system in New Orleans to remain a 'legal hell.'" He vowed to refuse to allow the program to represent indigent defendants in his courtroom.[77]

Other improvements of pre-Katrina problems continue. Today, public defenders have offices across from the courthouse and, for the first time, a computerized organizational system, according to LeBoeuf. In order to improve attorney-client relationships, the system has moved toward "vertical representation," meaning lawyers are assigned to clients, not courtrooms.[78] The Louisiana State Bar Association formed a new committee dedicated exclusively to indigent defense. The Right to Counsel Committee has held several meetings and continues to work to ensure the ethical and efficient use of the outpouring of resources to indigent defense programs in New Orleans.[79]

Conclusion

The aftermath of Hurricane Katrina is inextricably tied to issues of inequality, which are themselves inextricably tied to racism.[80] Racism, therefore, is inextricably tied to New Orleans and the aftermath of Hurricane Katrina. The New Orleans prison system's long history of cruelty and neglect was exemplified in the lack of planning, preparation, and leadership of the sheriff and his administration. These issues were already present, though they became more evident after the storm. While the criminal justice system appeared impervious to the continued incarceration of those held illegally in the aftermath of Hurricane Katrina, the reality revealed the contrary. Judges appeared ready to respond to, act on, and transform issues of inequality.

That the system of criminal representation for the indigent

collapsed under the pressure of underfunding and work overload is a fact that remains most prevalent in the aftermath of Hurricane Katrina. The Orleans Parish Indigent Defense system is inextricably tied to the inequality of funding and racism. The imprisoned, the poor, and the unrepresented became the most visible victims of Hurricane Katrina because of the enormity and severity of the storm and its effects. As Johnson explained, "We learned some bitter lessons from the Katrina experience that we do not want to repeat. . . . The entire criminal justice system needs to work together in a coordinated fashion to be able to maintain order within the system, should the city need to be evacuated again."[81]

Notes

1. Michael A. Fletcher and Jonathan Weisman, "Bush Says Spending Cuts Will Be Needed, Tax Increase Not Part of His Gulf Relief Plan," *Washington Post*, September 17, 2005, A-1.

2. Vesna Jaksic, "A Fresh Start: The Stories of Those Who Left," *National Law Journal*, February 13, 2007, http://www.law.com.

3. Human Rights Watch, "Shielded from Justice: Police Brutality and Accountability in the United States," http://www.hrw.org/reports98.

4. American Civil Liberties Union Report, "Abandoned and Abused: Complete Report," National Prison Project of the American Civil Liberties Union, August 9, 2006, 15. In 1969 Louis Hamilton, a prisoner, filed a class action lawsuit regarding the living conditions at his jail. In 1993 a suit was filed on behalf of juveniles for physical abuse and denial of education and for medical and mental health care. In the two years preceding the storm, at least two deaths are alleged to have occurred at OPP as a result of neglect or abuse.

5. Jeff Duncan, Bruce Eggler, and Steve Ritea, "Fielkow Looks at Seat on City Council, Holding Court," *New Orleans Times-Picayune*, December 5, 2005, B-1; "Independent Monitor Urged for N.O. Police, Brutality Complaints Revive 2002 Proposal," *New Orleans Times-Picayune*, April 28, 2006.

6. U.S. Department of Justice, Bureau of Justice Statistics Bulletin, "Prison and Jail Inmates at Midyear 2004," April 2005, 10; ACLU Report, "Abandoned and Abused," 13.

7. Paul Purpura, "Inmates Ordered Released after Months of Waiting," *New Orleans Times-Picayune*, December 23, 2005, B3; ACLU Report, "Abandoned and

Abused," 13. A reliable and precise figure of those incarcerated is unavailable. This is the city-owned juvenile facility.

8. Purpura, "Inmates Ordered Released." The name of the remaining eleven facilities are the Templeman (Buildings I–V), Central Lock-Up, the Community Correctional Center, Conchetta, Fisk Work Release, the House of Detention, and South White Street. U.S. Department of Justice, "Prison and Jail Inmates at Midyear 2004," 10.

9. Transcript of CNN coverage of Press Conference, August 28, 2005, http://transcripts.cnn.com/TRANSCRIPTS/0508/28/bn.04.html. Estimates range from as low as 6,000 to as high as 8,000.

10. Douglas Brinkley, *The Great Deluge: Hurricane Katrina, New Orleans and the Mississippi Gulf Coast* (New York: William Morrow, 2006), 2–3.

11. ACLU Report, "Abandoned and Abused," 17. It was noted that the sheriff failed to adhere to procedural and legal guidelines mandated to ensure the safety of buildings reopened after the storm.

12. Interview with Rhonda Ducre by author, March 15, 2006, notes on file with the ACLU National Prison Project. Ducre, who was four months pregnant, brought her husband, four children, and a few close friends.

13. Ducre interview.

14. Ducre interview. Finally, on the Friday after the storm, Ducre was evacuated to safety.

15. Brady Richard, e-mail interview, notes on file with the ACLU National Prison Project. Brady is no longer employed by CCC and provided information in an email to and interviews with the ACLU.

16. Richard interview.

17. Richard interview.

18. Interview with Renard Reed by author, June 22, 2006, notes on file with the ACLU National Prison Project.

19. Reed interview.

20. Reed interview.

21. Reed interview.

22. Testimonial from Inmate #144, October 27, 2005, original on file with the ACLU National Prison Project.

23. Reed interview.

24. ACLU Report, "Abandoned and Abused," 32.

25. Reed interview. The deputies called former sheriff Charles Foti, who arranged for shelter and evacuation. The Coast Guard dropped MRE and cases of water. ACLU Report, "Abandoned and Abused," 32; Ducre interview. Ducre was four months pregnant and a deputy on duty at HOD at the time of that Katrina hit.

She has been a deputy for four years. She reported to work on Sunday, August 28, after she began spotting and cramping on Monday. Her supervisor told her not to report at all if she could not return to work immediately. She returned her badge in January 2006. Interview with Marlin Gusman, sheriff of Orleans Parish, by author, New Orleans, March 13, 2006.

26. *Cook v. Gusman*, Civil District Court, Parish of Orleans, No. 2005-12477.

27. *Cook v. Gusman*.

28. Interview with anonymous employee by author, October 11, 2005, notes on file with the ACLU Prison Project.

29. Interview with Glynedale Stevenson by author, June 6, 2006, and May 24, 2006, notes on file with the ACLU Prison Project; Brandon L. Garrett and Tania Tetlow, "Criminal Justice Collapse: The Constitution after Katrina," *Duke Law Journal* 56 (2006): 127, 128.

30. Stevenson interview.

31. Stevenson interview; Peter Whoriskey, "In New Orleans, Justice on Trial: Katrina Strains Public Defender's Office," *Washington Post*, April 16, 2006, A1."

32. Whoriskey, "In New Orleans, Justice on Trial."

33. Orleans Parish Criminal Sheriff's Office, "Analysis of Daily Cost Per Inmate, 2003–2006," attached to letter from Sheriff Marlin Gusman to Members of the New Orleans City Council, November 10, 2005; Garrett and Tetlow, "Criminal Justice Collapse," 128.

34. Gwen Filosa, "Suspect Lost in Court System; Stuck for 10 Months, She Gets Out Today," *New Orleans Times-Picayune*, June 12, 2006.

35. Filosa, "Suspect Lost in Court System."

36. Filosa, "Suspect Lost in Court System"; ACLU Report, "Abandoned and Abused."

37. Matthew Crawford, "Recovery Zone: Orleans Parish Sheriff Shares His Experiences after Katrina," CorrectionalNews.Com, May/June 2006, http://correctionalnews.com/ME2/Audiences.

38. ACLU Report, "Abandoned and Abused," 87.

39. Whoriskey, "In New Orleans, Justice on Trial."

40. Whoriskey, "In New Orleans, Justice on Trial."

41. Garrett and Tetlow, "Criminal Justice Collapse," 127.

42. Associated Press, "New Orleans Holds First Trial since Katrina," June 6, 2006, <http://www.foxnews.com>; Laura Parker, "People Arrested before Katrina Still Await Trial," *USA Today*, February 27, 2006, A4.

43. Garrett and Tetlow, "Criminal Justice Collapse," 148.

44. Filosa, "Suspect Lost in Court System"; Garrett and Tetlow, "Criminal Justice Collapse," 145, 151.

45. Phyllis Mann, "Hurricane Relief Aid," *Advocate* (Louisiana Association of Criminal Defense Lawyers, Baton Rouge), Fall 2005, 3.

46. Mann, "Hurricane Relief Aid," 3.

47. Mann, "Hurricane Relief Aid," 3; Garrett and Tetlow, "Criminal Justice Collapse," 151.

48. *Hooks v. Kennedy*, 913 So. 2d 833 (La. 2005); *Porter v. City of New Iberia*, 913 So. 2d 834 (La. 2005).

49. *Ansari v. State*, 913 So. 2d 834 (La. 2005).

50. Garrett and Tetlow, "Criminal Justice Collapse," 148.

51. Susan Finch, "New Orleans Courts Carry On in Gonzales and Baton Rouge," *New Orleans Times-Picayune*, October 12, 2005, at B1; Filosa, "Suspect Lost in Court System; Garrett and Tetlow, "Criminal Justice Collapse," 138, 148; Gwen Filosa, "Judge Says He'll Release Inmate Unless the State Pays for Lawyers," *New Orleans Times-Picayune*, April 7, 2006, B1; Gwen Filosa, "Orleans Trials Resume with Familiar Themes," *New Orleans Times-Picayune*, June 8, 2006, B1. The Tulane Avenue and South Broad Streets Courthouses were opened.

52. Jeff Duncan, Bruce Eggler, and Steve Ritea, "Fielko Looks at Seat on City Council. Also: "No Comment on Baker Plan"; "Educational Optimism"; "Information Still Sparse, Holding Court"; "A Public Speaker"; all in *New Orleans Times-Picayune*, December 3, 2005.

53. Laura Maggi, "Judge Orders Many Inmates Be Released without Bail; Dozens Never Charged but Held for Months," *New Orleans Times-Picayune*, December 7, 2005, A-2; Garrett and Tetlow, "Criminal Justice Collapse," 146; ACLU Report, "Abandoned and Abused," 88.

54. Garrett and Tetlow, "Criminal Justice Collapse," 149.

55. Garrett and Tetlow, "Criminal Justice Collapse," 149; *Ansari v. State*, 69.

56. *Kimbrough v. Cooper*, 915 So. 2d 344, 345 (La. 2005).

57. *Kimbrough v. Cooper*; Robert Crowe, "Big Easy's Court System Still in State of Emergency; Judge Looking at Releasing Some Prisoners Jailed before Katrina but Still Not Charged," *Houston Chronicle*, August 27, 2006, A-19; Garrett and Tetlow, "Criminal Justice Collapse," 150.

58. Whoriskey, "In New Orleans, Justice on Trial."

59. The order specifically excluded charges against persons including, but not limited to, domestic violence, battery, and driving while intoxicated. Whoriskey, "In New Orleans, Justice on Trial."

60. Crowe, "Big Easy's Court System."

61. Susan Finch, "Criminal Courthouse Bounces Back; Wheels of Justice Expected to Speed Up," *New Orleans Times-Picayune*, October 31, 2006, B-1.

62. Finch, "Criminal Courthouse Bounces Back."

63. Crowe, "Big Easy's Court System."

64. *State (of Louisiana) v. Tomlinson*, 621 So. 2d 780 (La. 1993); Jaksic, "Fresh Start."

65. *State v. Tomlinson*, 621 So. 2d 780 (La. 1993).

66. *State (of Louisiana) v. Citizen*, 898 So. 2d 325 (La. 2005).

67. Garrett and Tetlow, "Criminal Justice Collapse," 132; Louisiana Justice Coalition, "Hurricane Brings Attention to Long Broken Public Defense System," http://www.lajusticecoalition.org/news/katrina.

68. "Hurricane Brings Attention."

69. "Hurricane Brings Attention"; Jaksic, "Fresh Start"; Henry Weinstein, "New Orleans Justice System Scrutinized," *Los Angeles Times*, February 9, 2006.

70. Garrett and Tetlow, "Criminal Justice Collapse," 149.

71. Gwen Filosa, "Katrina Leaves Inmates in Limbo; Many Still Jailed Are 'Doing Katrina Time,'" *New Orleans Times-Picayune*, March 18, 2006, B1.

72. Filosa, "Katrina Leaves Inmates in Limbo."

73. Garrett and Tetlow, "Criminal Justice Collapse," 147; Filosa, "Katrina Leaves Inmates in Limbo"; Jaksic, "Fresh Start."

74. Filosa, "Katrina Leaves Inmates in Limbo." In an editorial James Gill blasts the district attorney and his office for its ineptitude when the judge is forced to dismiss a murder case that was not retried after a mistrial within the statutory period. James Gill, "DA's Office Mired in Deep Chaos," *New Orleans Times-Picayune*, September 1, 2006, B-7. See also "DA Should Aspire to Justice, Not Just Convictions," *New Orleans Times-Picayune*, editorial, September 6, 2006, B-6.

75. Crowe, "Big Easy's Court System"; Filosa, "Katrina Leaves Inmates in Limbo."

76. Whoriskey, "In New Orleans, Justice on Trial."

77. Whoriskey, "In New Orleans, Justice on Trial," 69; Laura Maggi, "Public Defenders Board, Judges Agree to Truce; Contempt Hearing Called Off, Compromise Attempted," *New Orleans Times-Picayune*, December 8, 2006, B1.

78. Jaksic, "Fresh Start."

79. Louisiana Justice Coalition, "Hurricane Brings Attention."

80. Garrett and Tetlow, "Criminal Justice Collapse," 133.

81. Staff reports, "Orleans OK's Inmate Evacuation Plan; Court Hopes to Avoid Katrina-Type Chaos," *New Orleans Times-Picayune*, August 12, 2006, B-1.

SIX

From Worse to Where?

African Americans, Hurricane Katrina, and the Continuing Public Health Crisis

ALYSSA G. ROBILLARD

The relationship among race, socioeconomics, and health, particularly for African Americans, has a long and arduous history.[1] Racism and the history of prejudice and discrimination toward Americans of African descent contributed significantly to the health disparities experienced by African Americans centuries ago; it continues to contribute to health disparities today. Additionally, and not surprisingly, those with lower incomes do not fare nearly as well on indexes of health as do those with higher incomes. One in four African Americans lives in poverty. This complex mix of race, class, and poverty has had dire consequences on the health of African Americans, resulting in disparities in health and health care, the likes of which constitute a public health crisis.

Hurricane Katrina brought to light a great many societal ills including poverty, racism, debilitating political partisanship, and governmental neglect. These ills also included an implicit disregard for the health and well-being of a people whose health was already severely compromised. Every individual directly touched by the hurricane has, in all likelihood, experienced health consequences as a result. These consequences range from minor cuts and bruises to pervasive post-traumatic stress disorder to the greatest of all consequences, death. The notion of health, for many individuals, is a ubiquitous yet often suppressed concern, until it becomes too great to ignore. Before, during, and after the storm, residents faced unparalleled health challenges, and this is especially true for African Americans. Their health needs remain too great to ignore.

Defining Health

In the Preamble of the Constitution of the World Health Organization (WHO), "the highest possible attainment of health" is described as a fundamental right of every human being. The WHO defines health as "the state of complete physical, mental and social well-being and not merely the absence of disease or infirmity."[2] Others see health along additional dimensions that include emotional, spiritual, and environmental health as well. While these definitions may be overly holistic, especially to those who see them as too lofty a goal for individuals to achieve, such definitions represent the pursuit of total well-being that extends far beyond simply "not being sick." In fact, these definitions are highly suggestive of the intrinsic value of health. Definitions of health may vary according to individuals, but the value of one's health cannot be denied. When health is robust, communities flourish; when health is compromised, communities are weakened. Poor health reduces the ability to maximize one's contribution to society. It robs individuals, families, and communities of valued relationships, heritage, and the sense of history that serves to strengthen each.[3]

Healthy People 2010, a national prevention framework coordinated by the U.S. Department of Health and Human Services (USDHHS), has two overarching goals: to increase the years and quality of life and to eliminate health disparities. The term "health disparities" refers to the differences in the incidence, prevalence, burden of disease, deaths, and other health outcomes, as well as health care access among specific populations in the United States. African Americans constitute approximately 13 percent of the U.S. population, yet they experience a disproportionately high burden of disease, injury, death, and disability as a consequence of health conditions such as cardiovascular disease, stroke, cancer, diabetes, homicide, HIV/AIDS, and others.[4]

African American Health

The health disparities between African Americans and other racial or ethnic groups are markedly different. The three leading causes of death among all Americans are heart disease, cancer, and stroke. For these three conditions as well as others, African Americans suffer from greater mortality and morbidity than other groups.[5]

African Americans and low-income populations carry a disproportionate burden of death and disability from cardiovascular disease, including stroke. The age-adjusted death rate from cardiovascular disease in 2004 was over 23 percent higher among black adults than among the total U.S. adult population. According to the American Heart Association, African Americans have twice the risk of "first-ever stroke" compared to whites. One of the major risk factors for heart disease and stroke is hypertension, and African Americans have the highest prevalence of hypertension in the world. They also tend to develop it at younger ages, with greater severity, when compared to whites. Nearly half of adult African Americans have cardiovascular disease.[6]

Disparities also exist for most types of cancer, including colon/rectal, stomach, and prostate. African Americans have a higher age-adjusted incidence of cancer. Although African American women have a lower incidence of breast cancer compared to white women,

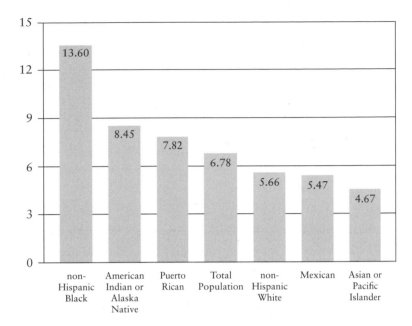

FIGURE 1. Total infant mortality by race/ethnicity, 2004.

Source: National Center for Health Statistics, "Infant Mortality Statistics from the 2004 Period Linked Birth/Infant Death Data Set," *National Vital Statistics Reports* (Hyattsville MD: National Center for Health Statistics, 2007).

they are more likely to die as a result of the disease. This difference is primarily because they see medical professionals at later stages of the disease, which severely impacts the likelihood of effective treatment. Overall, African Americans have the highest rates of death due to cancer and the shortest survival times of any racial or ethnic group.[7]

In addition to these chronic conditions, African Americans are also more prone to develop diabetes and face other health consequences. African Americans are almost twice as likely to have Type 2 diabetes when compared to whites. They have higher rates of diabetes-related complications, such as kidney disease and amputations. African Americans are also disproportionately impacted by infectious diseases like HIV and make up almost half of new HIV

TABLE 1. Life Expectancy (Years) at Birth, United States, 2004

	Black	White
Female	76.3	80.8
Male	69.5	75.7

Source: National Center for Health Statistics, "Health, United States, 2006 with Chartbook on Trends in the Health of Americans" (Hyattsville MD: National Center for Health Statistics, 2006).

infections. HIV is now the third leading cause of death for black women between the ages of 25 and 44. Homicide and death by legal intervention are also a major concern for African Americans, especially young men between the ages of 15 and 34.[8]

Infant mortality and life expectancy are additional indicators of the overall health and well-being of a population, and racial disparities exist along both criteria. Infant mortality rates indicate the number of deaths among babies younger than one year of age, within a given population during a specific period of time. In 2004 non-Hispanic black women had the highest rates of infant mortality at 13.60 deaths per 1,000 live births, while white women had a much lower rate of 5.66 deaths per 1,000 live births (see figure 1).[9]

African Americans also face different life expectancies than do people of other racial identities. Life expectancy is an estimate of the average number of years of life from birth, if current death rates were to remain the same. Although life expectancy has seen an increase over the twentieth century, black men continue to have the lowest life expectancy of 69.5 years of age, whereas white women enjoy a life expectancy of 80.8 years of age (see table 1). Researchers have suggested that this gap in mortality between blacks and whites exists as a consequence of heart disease, homicide, HIV, and infant mortality.[10]

The health of African Americans is indeed in crisis. The disproportionately high rates of chronic conditions such as heart disease, strokes, cancer, hypertension, and diabetes, as well as infectious diseases like HIV, are a consequence of a myriad of factors. Efforts to address these disparities began with the "President's Initiative to Eliminate Racial and Ethnic Disparities," established in 1998 under President Bill Clinton. Surgeon General David Satcher was responsible for leading this charge. Although efforts to address health disparities have begun and stand as a prominent goal for the decade, data indicate that great disparities in the United States, particularly for African Americans, remain.[11]

Before the Storm

In the Gulf region and especially in New Orleans, the dire picture of health for African Americans before Hurricane Katrina was certainly no better than that reflected nationally. In fact, data suggest it was much worse. Per capita health care consumption was extremely high in the region, but overall health status ranked very low. In fact, the region ranked last or second to last for the past fifteen years. Dr. Kevin Joseph, a local physician, explained: "Everyone knew that health care was bad in Louisiana. It was almost to the point where if you had a serious illness, you should live in a different state."[12] Louisiana faced numerous problems in its health care.[13]

In Louisiana citizens suffer from disproportionately high rates of infant mortality, heart disease, stroke, diabetes, overweight/obesity, and HIV/AIDS. African Americans, who represent approximately 32 percent of the state population and two-thirds of the city of New Orleans, were disproportionately impacted by these health conditions. Immediately before the hurricane, 23 percent of the city's population lived in poverty. Additionally, approximately half of the residents in Orleans Parish and one-third of those in Jefferson Parish were low income. With one of the highest rates of uninsurance in the country, more than one in every five residents lacked health

insurance. Two-thirds of those enrolled in Medicaid in the city resided in areas affected by Katrina, though adults without dependent
children were ineligible for Medicaid regardless of income.[14]

Most of these residents relied on the public hospital system, which
served the city's large poor and uninsured population. This "safety-
net system," run by Louisiana State University, included both Charity and University Hospitals—-the primary source of care before the
storm for 62 percent of evacuees in Houston shelters. Displaced citizens housed in Houston shelters were disproportionately African
American and low income, with little or no health insurance and
limited education. Forty-one percent of these displaced citizens reported chronic health conditions including heart disease, hypertension, diabetes, or asthma. Hospitals served as the main source of
care for many evacuees (41 percent), which is indicative of a lack
of health care coverage. Another indication of the limited access
to primary care and preventive services was the fact that hospital
emergency rooms in Louisiana ranked fourth highest in the nation
in 2004; many in Louisiana did not access health care until their
conditions became emergencies and could not be avoided.[15]

Before the storm, the number of uninsured was increasing as resources decreased. The health care system was truly in crisis, and
the health care and public health systems were not prepared for a
disaster of the magnitude of Hurricane Katrina and its subsequent
flooding.[16]

After the Storm

A great deal of criticism was leveled at residents of New Orleans
who did not evacuate in advance of the hurricane; criticism was
also rightly aimed at city officials who did not adequately provide
for a clear and timely evacuation. The obvious and legitimate economic barriers that prevented evacuation for the vast majority of
residents were all but ignored. There is also, however, a particular
native perspective about leaving the city that existed with respect

to evacuation. A study of evacuees found that native New Orleanians were less likely to leave. One resident explained, "People just don't like to leave. Because of previous experiences with weaker hurricanes, [they] didn't leave. [They] thought 'my house is safe.' or 'I'm elderly. If the good Lord wants me, he'll take me.'"[17] Residents of New Orleans remained in the city for a host of reasons as the storm approached.[18]

While some may have underestimated the storm or expressed fatalistic views about its outcome, a large proportion of Katrina's victims also lacked the economic means to leave the city quickly. Among evacuees housed in a Houston shelter who did not evacuate in advance of the storm, 34 percent had no transportation to get out. Another 28 percent underestimated the storm. Twelve percent were physically unable to leave or had to stay behind to care for someone physically unable to leave. Those who did not leave included 42 percent who said there would have been no way for them to leave, and the majority of these individuals reported earning less than $10,000 in the previous year.[19]

Evacuation and shelter, unfortunately, created additional problems. A large proportion of the evacuees (42 percent) spent time in either the Superdome or the New Orleans Convention Center. These locations became sites of horrific images of abandoned people who mostly were poor and mostly were black. Fourteen percent of the evacuees reported losses of a family member, neighbor, or close friend who had been killed during the storm, and another 31 percent did not know the fates of their family, neighbors, and friends at the time they were questioned. Over half went without adequate food (56 percent) or water (54 percent) during or after the storm.[20]

The experiences of Katrina survivors have been harrowing at best. Many mourned the losses of some 1,820 missing or dead relatives, neighbors, and friends. Those who escaped with their lives were soon forced to come to terms with their own losses; many lost their possessions, home, family, community, culture, and sense of familiarity. As one survivor put it, "I had the clothes on my back period and that was it."[21] Many survivors also had to come to terms with issues related to their health and health care needs, and are continuing to do so.[22]

Availability of Health Care

The biggest health issue after the hurricane was locating medical assistance. According to Joseph, who returned to his hospital outside of New Orleans within weeks of the storm to work alongside his colleagues: "Many doctors left with their families. Medical offices in the New Orleans area were destroyed and could no longer provide services. Doctors saw [ruined] offices and [a] low population, and saw [the] patient populous gone. Doctors who would return thought that they couldn't make a living. [Some] who planned on staying, had family who insisted they go. Those who came back couldn't find [a] paying patient population and found that they couldn't survive . . . Many didn't. . . . For many people, their doctors are gone."[23] With many hospitals in New Orleans closed after the hurricane, medical centers in suburban areas were left to pick up the slack even while short-staffed and with limited availability of services. Joseph agreed that the practice of medicine changed after the hurricane. During the first month following the storm, his hospital facility had to revert back from electronic charts to paper charts or whatever was available.[24]

Joseph and the hospital staff nonetheless labored to find ways to provide care despite limited supplies. Medical staff served patients from varying economic backgrounds on a first-come, first-served basis, working in, according to Joseph, "like a 'MASH unit' type of thing."[25] Patients were asked to pay on a sliding scale and were seen for as little as $5 for those who qualified. The hospital regained some semblance of normalcy once medical assistance volunteers arrived; Joseph explained that these volunteers "helped tremendously."[26] Volunteer assistance groups were able to send boats of medications, including antibiotics and hypertension medication. Concerning the issue of shortages in medical staff, Joseph also suggested, "The doctor who needs to come down here is the person who wants to work in a high volume area with people with little or no insurance . . . for long hours. [They should be] doctors who are dedicated to healing."[27]

Since a large portion of the population was poor and uninsured, the city relied heavily on the public hospital system. Charity Hospital, for many, was considered a New Orleans institution. Established in 1736 when a French seaman left his life's earnings to build and maintain "L'Hospital des Pauvres de la Charité," it stood as the second oldest public hospital in the United States. Charity Hospital began a long tradition as the primary source of care for the poor and uninsured in and around the city of New Orleans, until the damage and destruction of Hurricane Katrina permanently shut its doors. In fact, both Charity and University Hospitals, the public hospitals run by the Louisiana State University Health Care Services Division, have been declared "unsalvageable" due to a combined total of more than $445 million in damage as a result of the storm and flooding. With a patient population of approximately half a million each year before the storm, these two public hospitals served the indigent population of the city. According to Joseph, many patients held the following sentiment: "Charity's gone—there's no place to get health care."[28] The residents of New Orleans who lack insurance have even fewer health care options in the continued aftermath of Katrina.[29]

With few hospitals in the area open, emergency rooms now see an overflow of patients with significant wait times. Some wait times were reported to be as high as nine and a half hours. Tents at the Ernest N. Morial Convention Center housed an emergency room staffed by Charity Hospital doctors. These "medical tents" have since moved to a vacant department store in the New Orleans Center next door to the Superdome. Health care has diminished significantly since the storm, from approximately 53,000 hospital beds before the hurricane to only 15,000 beds eighteen months post-Katrina. The reduction in hospital beds and this limited access to health care are cause for concern.[30]

A comprehensive in-person survey of residents living in New Orleans one year after the hurricane was conducted by the Kaiser Family Foundation to "give voice" to the people of New Orleans and help document the changing needs of the population.[31] The survey found that more than one-third of those living in the Greater New Orleans area have experienced a reduction in their access to health care. About one in five reported declines in their physical health since the storm, and one in six reported a similar decline for their mental health. African Americans were more likely than whites to report challenges in their quality of life and report that life was still disrupted a year after the storm. They were also more than twice as likely to report ongoing health care access or coverage problems when compared to whites. Half of the African American residents surveyed were relying on the emergency room for care or had no place to go for health care compared to only 15 percent of whites who faced similar problems. The African American residents were also more worried that medical services will not be available to them when needed. With traditional services of health care closed, this is a legitimate concern, especially for the poor and uninsured, who cannot afford health care expenses. A key finding from interviews with Katrina survivors found the same: the loss of health care facilities and medical providers made it harder to get health care.[32]

Lapses in Care

A third of evacuees in Houston shelters, in the weeks immediately following the storm, experienced health problems or injuries as a result of the hurricane. Morbidity surveillance data for Arkansas,

Louisiana, Mississippi, and Texas from the Centers for Disease Control and Prevention immediately following the hurricane indicated chronic illnesses, such as diabetes, asthma, and heart disease, as the most commonly reported health conditions among those affected by Hurricane Katrina. About a third of evacuees had gone without prescribed medication, and a quarter went without medical care. A key finding from interviews with forty survivors revealed that many went without necessary health care and medication after the storm.[33]

Using the analogy of oxygen masks on planes, "in the event of a reduction in cabin pressure" where individuals should first place the mask on themselves before placing a mask on anyone else, Joseph described patients who were diligent with their medication before the storm but not after. "After the hurricane, other issues were at the forefront. Everyone was taking care of others [first]."[34] According to Joseph, the shock of the event pushed health care issues into the background. Only recently has he stopped hearing from patients, "I was on medication before Katrina, and this is [my] first appointment after 2 years."[35] The shock and trauma of the event interrupted health care–seeking behavior, as Joseph noted. After Katrina, there was a higher estimated prevalence of mental illness than before. With large numbers of the population suffering from post-traumatic stress disorder and other mental illnesses, the disaster may have adversely impacted the health of many in the area.[36]

Environmental Health Concerns

While early environmental threats did not turn out to be as immediately catastrophic and widespread as initially thought, environmental health concerns still threaten the rebuilding and recovery process: "Threats lie in the mountainous debris; faulty sewage treatment, toxic chemical and oil spills; contaminated water; swirling dust, pesky insects and vermin, and mold."[37] Mold, a significant problem, is responsible for the razing of homes and places of business. Many, however, have likely rebuilt (or are rebuilding) their homes and businesses with this fungus hidden within the walls. The severity of these threats remains unclear. In fact, these concerns extend beyond the affected areas. FEMA trailers, intended to serve as temporary housing for displaced residents, are still "home" for many two years after the storm. Tests conducted by the Sierra Club found that 83 percent of FEMA trailers in Mississippi, Louisiana, and Alabama had formaldehyde levels that exceeded the recommended limit. News reports of levels as high as three times the recommended limit and persistent coughs in children living in FEMA trailers indicate additional environmental health threats, particularly for those who should have escaped them. Researchers emphasize the need to follow up and track the health status of those living in areas affected by the hurricane to determine any effects from environmental exposure. This follow-up should be done with all residents affected by the hurricane.[38]

Special Concern for HIV/AIDS

HIV/AIDS was among the many health issues faced by some of the displaced residents. Approximately 21,000 people were living with HIV/AIDS in the affected areas of Louisiana, Mississippi, and Alabama; the bulk of these individuals resided in Louisiana (see figure 2). The greatest numbers of people living with HIV/AIDS were located in Orleans Parish (5,549), East Baton Rouge Parish (2,555), and Jefferson Parish (1,275).[39]

The health of those with HIV/AIDS requires special consideration, given the nature of the disease. Individuals living with HIV/AIDS are often beset with symptoms related to HIV/AIDS as well as co-morbidities, such as mental health or substance abuse issues.

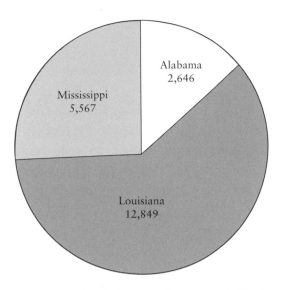

FIGURE 2. People estimated to be living with HIV/AIDS in Katrina-affected disaster areas. *Source*: Kaiser Family Foundation, "HIV/AIDS Policy Fact Sheet."

Additionally, they may also experience debilitating side effects from the medications they take to treat the infectious disease. The challenges noted in general by survivors, including barriers to medical and social support services, loss of shelter, lack of food, and physical and emotional stress, can impact individuals with a weakened immune system much more severely.[40]

Added to these challenges is the difficulty in accessing necessary antiretroviral medication. Lapses in antiretroviral medication can lead to an increased viral load, which can then cause HIV resistance to antiretroviral therapy. Those who are bothered by symptoms are those who have difficulty with or forgot to take their medication. The involuntary lapses in medication of Katrina survivors with HIV/AIDS may be associated with an increase in symptoms. When there are competing life stressors, adherence is not always perceived as a high priority.[41]

The storm did indeed impact the health care of some survivors.

Eight low-income individuals living with HIV/AIDS and having an HIV/AIDS medical provider were interviewed as part of an overall assessment of the health challenges facing Katrina survivors shortly after the storm. A key finding was that survivors with HIV/AIDS did in fact experience difficulty connecting with health care resources. They lost contact with their providers and also experienced gaps in medications. Displaced persons with HIV/AIDS had the added burden of trying to navigate their specialized care in unfamiliar settings.[42]

Even in instances where HIV/AIDS patients were finally able to identify care in new surroundings, confidentiality was likely a major concern. The social stigma associated with HIV/AIDS may have increased in a new surrounding, leading to an increased desire for confidentiality and a related decrease in medication adherence. Those who are highly concerned about revealing their HIV status are more likely to be non-adherent than those who are less concerned. Further, the treatment regimen can be very complex and difficult, so the privacy of "pill-taking" can become more challenging for those who wish to maintain confidentiality about their disease, particularly in shelters housing large numbers of people with little privacy.[43]

HIV/AIDS provides a clear example of health disparities facing African Americans. Where African Americans make up approximately 13 percent of the U.S. population, they account for almost 50 percent of new HIV/AIDS infections, as reported earlier in this chapter. This is especially a concern given that the rates of HIV and AIDS for the state of Louisiana as well as Mississippi are much higher than average, at 194.8 and 209.7 per 100,000, respectively.[44]

Disaster Preparedness

The inability of the local, state, and federal governments to respond to a major disaster was clearly displayed time and time again during and after the hurricane. From inadequate planning and resources for evacuation of poor residents before the storm to the delays in the federal response for those left behind, the combination of Hurricane Katrina, the levee breach, and the subsequent flooding revealed a city, state, and nation ill-prepared to protect its citizens. In fact, this response sorely questioned the degree to which these entities truly valued the life, health, and well-being of the overwhelmingly black and overwhelmingly poor individuals left behind.

The devastation caused as a result of Hurricane Katrina raised critical "textbook" public health issues of "sanitation and hygiene, water safety, infection control, surveillance, immunizations, environmental health, and access to care."[45] Though these issues may have been "textbook," or clearly identifiable problems for which to devise a structured response, few entities were prepared for the level of response necessary in this case. Kevin Joseph provided his own perspective as a resident of the city: "No one had a plan for what to do in case of a 'city-hitting' hurricane or anything that would cause a serious-level disaster. Charity Hospital . . . [its] all important generators were in the basement."[46] According to Joseph, none of the major hospitals had provisions for what to do if the generators were out for an extended period of time, nor did they have a serious plan for evacuating patients. He explained, "They had a serious plan for if it got 'a little bad,' but not for a major catastrophe."[47] His smaller hospital knew its limitations and planned for them, but the big hospitals did not make plans and were "caught with their pants down."[48] An analysis of the medical response in the aftermath of the hurricane found that disaster plans at all levels of government did not include a plan to keep hospitals functioning during a large-scale emergency. It is unfortunate that it took Hurricane Katrina to facilitate more attention and greater funding to address disaster preparedness. To be sure, the hurricane uncovered a health care system unable to survive the long-term effects of a major disaster.[49]

A subsequent and periodic re-evaluation of disaster preparedness and response programs is warranted post-Katrina. Mistakes
were made on multiple levels. One indication of how ill-prepared
the nation's public health entity was for a disaster on this level is
the fact that the Centers for Disease Control and Prevention (CDC)
decided not to release the Hurricane Katrina Response Report, but
instead chose to use it to improve preparedness. They further acknowledged the need to develop a coordinated approach to multi-
jurisdictional surveillance during large-scale disasters.[50]

Conclusion

Guidance for mental health professionals and others working with
people during major disasters describes several overlapping phases
of disasters: (1) the Warning or Threat phase, when people are made
aware of an impending disaster; (2) the Impact phase, when the disaster is occurring; (3) the Heroic or Rescue phase, after the disaster starts until the rescue is complete; (4) the Honeymoon or Remedy phase, occurring after the rescue when resources are readily
available; (5) the Inventory phase, when survivors realize the limitations of disaster assistance; (6) the Disillusionment phase, when
outside resources are decreasing, and one realizes the lack of personal resources to meet needs; and (7) the Reconstruction or Recovery phase, when people are able to accept and come to terms
with the changes in their lives that now reflect a "new normal" or
newly accepted way of life. In this last phase, which can take years,
survivors come to realize the need to engage in the rebuilding process and have slowly begun to do this. Hurricane Katrina survivors are charting the long and difficult course through the phases
of disaster.[51]

These phases represent a period filled with overwhelming stress,
anxiety, and uncertainty. For many, the rebuilding and recovery

phase holds the most uncertainty. It is at this point that individuals and communities alike stand on the brink of change. As with survivors of any major disaster who are able to successfully reach the recovery phase, Katrina survivors are finding themselves able to juxtapose great loss with great personal strength. As the larger community seeks to do the same, it will be very important to remember that health is a critical component of recovery for Katrina survivors and for the community as a whole.

Certainly, the hurricane exposed the problems of an "already ailing and compromised" health care system.[52] Rebuilding health care services is paramount because accessible and affordable health care are necessary for basic health and safety. A successful plan for rebuilding, however, must also include a comprehensive approach to address the goals of Healthy People 2010: increasing the years and quality of life *and* eliminating disparities. Public health must have a leadership role in recovery. In order to rebuild, health needs to be prioritized, and prevention must be meaningfully incorporated into this structure.[53]

The current model of health care for the poor and disenfranchised is one that drives people to seek care only when health is so debilitating that one can do nothing else. It is a model that relies on the emergency room for primary care and encourages people to think of their health as secondary at best. In Louisiana the term "lagniappe" is often used to describe something "extra—a bonus given as a nicety."[54] Health, particularly for the poor, disenfranchised, and mostly African American citizens of New Orleans, should not be viewed in this way. General health and well-being should be regarded as "standard—normal or the usual case," and not as "lagniappe."[55] Health is intricately intertwined with issues that are primary in the rebuilding and recovery effort.

Developing a comprehensive health care infrastructure is a key first step in recovery, but the larger elements contributing to the high rates of disease and death among African Americans should be acknowledged. Addressing these social, economic, and political barriers will lead to improved health, but prevention should also be emphasized. There is a need to treat the large numbers of people with existing conditions, but also a need to apply models of prevention that acknowledge and address, where possible, the broader barriers to eliminating health disparities. In the long term, prevention may be the best use of money in a strained economy with limited resources for health care. Preventing disease eliminates the need for costly health care services to treat individuals with disease. Prevention efforts should be incorporated into all aspects of the recovery and rebuilding process. In fact, communities should absolutely have a significant role in this process through community mobilization and community-based participatory research that allows for the valuable input from those who best understand the problem.

It is certainly true that disasters most severely affect the disenfranchised. Atkins and Moy describe Hurricane Katrina as a "teachable moment," an opportunity that clearly presents the impact of poverty and race on health.[56] The social, historical, and political milieu that has contributed to health disparities is also the one in which disasters occur. In the aftermath of Hurricane Katrina, the recommendations of Atkins and Moy to fund prevention, as opposed to rescue, and to strengthen the infrastructure of public health are critical to the goal of eliminating health disparities. In fact, it is necessary to use this teachable moment to address the "underlying vulnerabilities of poor and minority communities" if reduction and elimination of health disparities are to occur.[57] Among the many points of emphasis upon reflection of Hurricane Katrina is the importance of eliminating health disparities and the real commitment to the achievement of this goal.[58]

City, state, and federal officials, including leaders in public health, must ensure that Hurricane Katrina will not further widen the gap in disparities for African Americans, but instead will provide an opportunity to develop a strategic approach to closing and eliminating the disparities. According to the Preamble of the Constitution of the WHO, it is a nation's obligation to contribute to the health of their people. Immediately after the storm, New Orleans did seem to be the "city that care forgot." In the rebuilding and recovery ahead, the health and well-being of all its citizens must not be forgotten.[59]

Notes

1. The author wishes to thank Dr. Kevin Joseph for sharing his professional experiences post-Katrina. Sincere thanks are also extended to Sarah and Ruffin Robillard and Elizabeth Russ for their assistance in collecting health-related local media reports.

2. World Health Organization, Constitution, Geneva, 1948.

3. Rebecca J. Donatelle, *Health: The Basics*, 4th ed. (Boston: Allyn and Bacon, 2000).

4. U.S. Department of Health and Human Services, *Healthy People 2010: Understanding and Improving Health*, 2nd ed. (Washington DC: Government Printing Office, 2000); National Institutes of Health, "Addressing Health Disparities: The NIH Program of Action; What Are Health Disparities?" n.d., accessed May 20, 2007, http://healthdisparities.nih.gov/whatare.html; U.S. Department of Health and Human Services, "Health Disparities Experienced by Blacks or African Americans—United States," *Morbidity and Mortality Weekly Report* 54 (January 14, 2005): 1–3.

5. A. M. Minino, M. P. Heron, and B. L. Smith, "Deaths: Preliminary Data for 2004," *National Vital Statistics Reports* 54 (2006): 1–50.

6. American Heart Association, "Heart Facts 2007: All Americans/African Americans; Cardiovascular Diseases Still No. 1," December 2006, accessed May 22, 2007, http://www.americanheart.org/downloadable/heart/11769 27558476AllAmAfAm%20HeartFacts07_lores.pdf; American Stroke Association, "What about African Americans and High Blood Pressure?" 2005, accessed May 22, 2007, http://www.americanheart.org/downloadable/heart/11208317263815%20 ABH%20WhatAboutAfcnAmHBP.pdf.

7. U.S. Department of Health and Human Services, "Health Disparities Experienced"; American Cancer Society, "Cancer Facts and Figures for African Americans, 2007–2008" (Atlanta: American Cancer Society, 2007).

8. Office of Minority Health, "Diabetes Fact Sheet: Eliminate Disparities in Diabetes," May 11, 2007, accessed May 22, 2007, http://www.cdc.gov/omh/AMH/factsheets/diabetes.htm; Centers for Disease Control and Prevention, "Cases of HIV Infection and AIDS in the United States and Dependent Areas, 2005," *HIV/AIDS Surveillance Report, 2005* 17 (2006): 1–54; M. P. Heron and B. L. Smith, "Deaths: Final Data for 2003," *National Vital Statistics Reports* 55 (2007): 1–96.

9. Office of Minority Health, "Infant Mortality Fact Sheet: Eliminate Disparities in Infant Mortality," May 11, 2007, accessed May 22, 2007, http://www.cdc.gov/omh/AMH/factsheets/infant.htm.

10. National Center for Health Statistics, "Infant Mortality Statistics from the 2004 Period Linked Birth/Infant Death Data Set," *National Vital Statistics Reports* (Hyattsville MD: National Center for Health Statistics, 2007)"; S. Harper et al., "Trends in the Black-White Life Expectancy Gap in the United States, 1983–2003," *Journal of the American Medical Association* 297 (2007): 1224–32.

11. D. Satcher, "Our Commitment to Eliminate Racial and Ethnic Health Disparities," *Yale Journal of Health Policy, Law and Ethics* 1 (2001): 1–14.

12. Kevin Joseph, personal communication, May 23, 2007.

13. H. Larkin, "Louisiana's Second Chance," *Hospitals and Health Networks* 81 (February 2007): 54–56, 58, 60; United Health Foundation, *America's Health Rankings: A Call to Action for People and Their Communities* (Minnetonka MN: United Health Foundation, 2006).

14. Kaiser Family Foundation, "Number of Infant Deaths, 2002," accessed May 22, 2007, http://www.statehealthfacts.org/cgi-bin/healthfacts.cgi?action=comparecategory=Health+Status&subcategory=Infants&topic=Number+of+Infant+Deaths; Centers for Disease Control and Prevention, "Cases of HIV Infection"; Kaiser Family Foundation, "A Pre-Katrina Look at the Health Care Delivery System for Low-Income People in New Orleans," (2006), accessed April 20, 2007, <http://www.kff.org/uninsured/upload/7442.pdf>.

15. M. Brodie, E. Weltzien, A. Drew, R. J. Blendon, and M. A. Benson, "Experiences of Hurricane Katrina Evacuees in Houston Shelters: Implications for Future Planning," *American Journal of Public Health* 96 (2006): 1402–8; Kaiser Family Foundation, "Number of Infant Deaths, 2002."

16. Kaiser Family Foundation, "Pre-Katrina Look."

17. Joseph, personal communication.

18. Brodie et al., "Experiences of Hurricane Katrina."

19. Brodie et al., "Experiences of Hurricane Katrina."

20. Brodie et al., "Experiences of Hurricane Katrina."

21. Kaiser Family Foundation, "Pre-Katrina Look," p. 24

22. Earth Institute at Columbia University, "Hurricane Katrina Deceased-

Victims List," n.d., accessed May 18, 2007, http://www.katrinalist.columbiz.edu/stats.php.

23. Joseph, personal communication.

24. B. Hamilton, "E. R. Trauma," *New Orleans Times Picayune*, February 5, 2006: A-1, A-12; Joseph, personal communication.

25. Joseph, personal communication.

26. Joseph, personal communication.

27. Joseph, personal communication.

28. Joseph, personal communication.

29. J. Salvaggio, *New Orleans' Charity Hospital: A Story of Physicians, Politics, and Poverty* (Baton Rouge: Louisiana State University Press, 1992); J. Harper, "Big Easy Hospitals Deemed Unsafe," *Washington Times*, October 6, 2005, A-12.

30. Hamilton, "E. R. Trauma."

31. Kaiser Family Foundation, "Giving Voice to the People of New Orleans: The Kaiser Post-Katrina Baseline Survey," Executive Summary, May 2007, accessed May 14, 2007, http://www.allhealth.org/briefingmaterials/GivingVoicetothePeopleofNewOrleans-KaiserPost-KatrinaBaselineSurvey-718.pdf.

32. Kaiser Family Foundation, "Pre-Katrina Look."

33. Brodie et al., "Experiences of Hurricane Katrina"; Centers for Disease Control, "Cases of HIV Infection 2005"; U.S. Department of Health and Human Services, "Morbidity Surveillance after Hurricane Katrina—Arkansas, Louisiana, Mississippi, and Texas, September 2005," *Morbidity and Mortality Weekly Report* 55 (July 7, 2006): 727–31; Kaiser Family Foundation, "Pre-Katrina Look."

34. Joseph, personal communication.

35. Joseph, personal communication.

36. Joseph, personal communication; R. C. Kessler, S. Galea, R. T. Jones, and H. A. Parker, "Mental Illness and Suicidality after Hurricane Katrina," *Bulletin of the World Health Organization* 84 (2006): 930–38.

37. J. Wilson, "Health and the Environment after Hurricane Katrina," *Annals of Internal Medicine* 144 (2006): 153.

38. Sierra Club, "Toxic Trailers? Tests Reveal High Formaldehyde Levels in FEMA Trailers," n.d., accessed May 22, 2007, http://www.sierraclub.org/gulfcoast/downloads/formaldehyde_test.pdf; K. Nelson, "High Levels of Formaldehyde Found in Some FEMA Trailers," (May 22, 2007), accessed May 23, 2007, http://www.wafb.com/Global/story.asp?s=6527613; J. Wilson, "Health and the Environment."

39. Kaiser Family Foundation, "Assessing the Number of People with HIV/AIDS in Areas Affected by Hurricane Katrina," accessed September 1, 2005, http://www.kff.org/katrina/upload/7407.pdf.

40. J. C. Walsh, R. Horne, M. Dalton, A. P. Burgess, and B. G. Gazzard, "Reasons

for Non-adherence to Antiretroviral Therapy: Patients' Perspectives Provide Evidence of Multiple Causes," *AIDS Care* 13 (2001): 709–20; Kaiser Family Foundation, "Assessing the Number of People with HIV/AIDS."

41. I. B. Corless, et al., "Symptom Status and Medication Adherence in HIV Disease," *International Conference on AIDS Abstracts* 14 (2002); R. H. Remien, A. E. Hirky, M. O. Jonson, D. W. Weinhardt, and G. M. Le, "Adherence to Medication Treatment: A Qualitative Study of Facilitators and Barriers among a Diverse Sample of HIV+ Men and Women in Four U.S. Cities," *AIDS and Behavior* 7 (2003): 61–72.

42. Kaiser Family Foundation, "Pre-Katrina Look."

43. L. S. Rintamaki, T. C. Davis, S. Skripkauskas, C. L. Bennett, and M. S. Wolf, "Social Stigma Concerns and HIV Medication Adherence," *AIDS Patient Care and STDs* 20 (2006): 359–68; G. Davies et al., "Overview and Implementation of an Intervention to Prevent Adherence Failure among HIV-Infected Adults Initiating Antiretroviral Therapy: Lessons Learned from Project HEART," *AIDS Care* 18 (2006): 895–903.

44. Centers for Disease Control and Prevention, "Cases of HIV Infection"; Centers for Disease Control and Prevention, "HIV/AIDS among African Americans," accessed February 1, 2007, http://www.cdc.gov/HIV/topics/aa/resources/factsheets/pdf/aa.pdf.

45. P. G. Greenough and T. D. Kirsch, "Public Health Response—Assessing Needs," *New England Journal of Medicine* 353 (2005): 1544.

46. Joseph, personal communication.

47. Joseph, personal communication.

48. Joseph, personal communication.

49. C. Franco et al., "Systemic Collapse: Medical Care in the Aftermath of Hurricane Katrina," *Biosecurity and Bioterrorism* 4 (2006): 135–46; S. Rosenbaum, "U.S. Health Policy in the Aftermath of Hurricane Katrina," *Journal of the American Medical Association* 295 (2006): 437–40.

50. J. N. Logue, "The Public Health Response to Disasters in the 21st Century: Reflections on Hurricane Katrina," *Journal of Environmental Health* 69 (2006): 9–13; Kaiser Family Foundation, "CDC Will Not Release Hurricane Katrina Response Report, Will Use Analysis to Improve Preparedness, Officials Say," accessed November 1, 2006, http://www.kaisernetwork.org/daily_reports/print_report.cfm?DR_ID=40919&dr_cat=3; U.S. Department of Health and Human Services, "Morbidity Surveillance."

51. D. J. DeWolfe, "Training Manual for Mental Health and Human Service Workers in Major Disasters" (Washington DC: Substance Abuse and Mental Health Services Administration Center for Mental Health Services, 2000);

R. T. Boland, "Can It Get Any Worse?" *Frontiers of Health Services Management* 23 (2006): 31–34.

52. H. Rodriguez and B. E. Aguirre, "Hurricane Katrina and the Healthcare Infrastructure: A Focus on Disaster Preparedness, Response, and Resiliency," *Frontiers of Health Services Management* 23 (2006): 13–23; R. Rudowitz, D. Rowland, and A. Shartzer, "Health Care in New Orleans before and after Hurricane Katrina," *Health Affairs* 25 (2006): 393–406.

53. Rosenbaum, "U.S. Health Policy"; S. C. Quinn, "Hurricane Katrina: A Social and Public Health Disaster," *American Journal of Public Health* 96 (2006): 204.

54. Quinn, "Hurricane Katrina," 204.

55. Quinn, "Hurricane Katrina," 204.

56. D. Atkins and E. M. Moy, "Left Behind: The Legacy of Hurricane Katrina," *British Medical Journal* 331 (2005): 916–18.

57. Quinn, "Hurricane Katrina," 204.

58. Greenough and Kirsch, "Public Health Response"; Quinn, "Hurricane Katrina"; Atkins and Moy, "Left Behind"; Logue, "Public Health Response."

59. WHO Constitution; F. P. Grad, "The Preamble of the Constitution of the World Health Organization," *Bulletin of the World* 80 (2002): 981–84.

SEVEN

Failed Plans and Planned Failures

The Lower Ninth Ward, Hurricane Katrina, and the Continuing Story of Environmental Injustice

CARLTON WATERHOUSE

An independent investigation of the New Orleans flood protection system revealed that the catastrophic destruction and devastation that followed Hurricane Katrina resulted from local, state, and federal governments' failure to plan and implement a sufficient system of protection for citizens of the Lower Ninth Ward from the infrequent but known risks caused by major hurricanes. This phenomenon typifies the experience of African Americans, Latinos, Asians, Native Americans, and poor whites in facing environmental and ecological hazards nationwide. Federal, state, and local governments routinely provide lower protection standards, fewer resources, and slower responses to the risk faced by people of color and poor whites.[1]

This chapter explores the New Orleans levee system failures as an example of environmental injustices experienced by people of color and poor whites. It also examines the results of levee failure investigations in light of existing complaints and studies regarding the inferior quality of environmental protection provided to minority and poor white communities, ranging from the design and implementation of Superfund cleanups to the issuance and enforcement of permits under the Clean Air and Clean Water Acts. Based on the similarity between the planning failures and failed plans concerning the New Orleans levee system, and the planning failures and failed plans of federal and state agencies to provide the proper environmental protection for people of color and the poor, the chapter argues that the environmental injustices of Hurricane Katrina mirror the environmental injustices devastating other communities around the country and the globe.[2]

Environmental justice is the desire and the demand that poor and oppressed people in the United States and around the world be provided with the protection, consideration, and decision-making authority provided to their wealthier or whiter counterparts locally and globally. The environmental justice movement began as an offshoot of the civil rights movement, focusing on racism in the environmental arena. Its watershed moment, in Warren County, North Carolina, under the leadership of Congressman Walter Fauntleroy, mirrored the "campaigns" of the civil rights movement. Organizers fighting against the placement of a hazardous waste landfill in the area protested and used civil disobedience to challenge what they understood to be "environmental racism." After a truck driver traversed the state from the northern to the southern border and back again, discharging waste oils along the shoulders of Interstate Highway 85, state officials decided to place a toxic waste landfill in Warren County to hold the contaminated soils gathered from across the state. Protestors challenged the action as racism because of the heightened concentration of black residents in the area chosen for the site. Congressman Fauntleroy was arrested along with 500 others during the protest. Upon his return to Washington DC, he requested a General Accounting Office (GAO) study examining the demographics of communities with hazardous waste sites in the Southeast.[3]

The 1985 GAO study found that three out of five hazardous waste landfills in the southeast region were located in predominantly black or Latino areas. It was soon followed by a 1987 report, entitled "Toxic Waste and Race" by the Commission for Racial Justice of the United Church of Christ. That report was more extensive than the GAO study. It looked at the list of uncontrolled toxic waste sites contained in the Environmental Protection Agency's (EPA) Comprehensive Environmental Response Compensation and Liability Information System (CERCLIS) database and mapped them onto zip codes across the country. Using census data, the study then correlated the zip codes with waste sites and the demographic data for nearby residents. Beyond analyzing the racial makeup of residents, the study also examined residential income to assess its relative significance in the location of waste sites. The report's authors, who included Charles Lee, found that regardless of their income, African Americans disproportionately lived in zip codes with uncontrolled toxic waste sites.[4]

Studies of environmental racism continued. Within a year, a book by sociologist Robert D. Bullard entitled *Dumping in Dixie* provided an academic examination of a historic and continuing phenomenon that relegated many undesirable waste disposal and polluting facilities to predominantly black areas. With the GAO study, the Commission for Racial Justice report, and Bullard's book bolstering their claims, local activists and more prominent civil rights leaders began to draw attention to racial disparities in the siting of pollution-related facilities. In response to growing awareness and pressure, in 1990 EPA administrator William Reilly commissioned an agency task force to determine what relationship existed between race and pollution. Rejecting the activists' claims that EPA and others participated in environmental racism, the administrator adopted the name "Environmental Equity" to describe the concerns raised by activists.[5]

EPA created an Office of Environmental Justice in the agency administrator's office. It was tasked with investigating the issue and educating agency personnel on how to approach citizens' concerns. Clarice Gaylord, the first director, had a PhD in atmospheric science and brought a scientific perspective and background to the issue. She was assisted in the task with corresponding regional directors. In Region Four, where a substantial number of "environmental justice" hot spots existed, Vivian Malone Jones was hired to direct the office. A love-hate relationship between EPA and Environmental Justice activists soon developed as William Jefferson Clinton was elected president of the United States and the EPA announced that "environmental justice" was one of its top five priorities. Serving as a clearinghouse for activists to voice their concerns, the EPA modified many of its policies and practices of community relations and took substantial strides to give voice to the concerns raised by "EJ communities." The agency provided numerous grants, sponsored several conferences, and created a National Environmental Justice Advisory Committee (NEJAC) to inform the agency on ways to achieve its environmental justice goals.[6]

One of the greatest benefits of these developments was the raised awareness gained by Native American, African American, Latino, and other community members near Superfund sites and other pollution-related facilities. During this time period, communities began to share stories, ideas, and knowledge to assist each other in learning about the risks they faced and the tools available to decrease or eliminate these risks. In 1994 President Clinton supported these developments across the federal government by issuing Executive Order (EO) 12898, directing federal agencies to identify and address disproportionately high and adverse human health effects impacting minority and low-income populations.[7]

Under this regime, environmental justice became an exercise in community relations for the EPA, state agencies, and corporations.

In the absence of either legislation or case law supporting reform in the legal and regulatory regime that governs the vast majority of environmental decisions, EO 12898 provided enough authority to raise public expectations but not to raise the level of environmental protection for minority communities. In fact, to date the EPA has never implemented the primary directive of the executive order to "identify and address the disproportionately high and adverse human health effects of its programs and procedures on low income and minority populations."[8] A 2004 EPA Inspector General (IG) report concludes that the EPA "has not developed a clear vision or a comprehensive strategic plan, and has not established values, goals, expectations, and performance measurements" to meet the directive.[9] Rather than develop an environmental policy that attended to the alleged disparity in pollution exposure, the environmental justice movement raised the awareness of community members concerning their role in environmental decision making. The movement also challenged agency officials to develop a more effective means of responding to the concerns of "minority" and "low income" populations.[10]

The EPA is not alone in this regard. Executive Order 12898 directs each federal agency to "make achieving environmental justice part of its mission by identifying and addressing, as appropriate, disproportionately high and adverse human health or environmental effects of its programs, policies, and activities on minority populations and low-income populations in the United States."[11] Despite this directive, when called on the carpet, agencies have rarely integrated this order into their substantive decision making. Most agencies covered by the executive order limited their implementation to enhanced community outreach efforts and small grant programs to low-income and minority communities.[12]

The 1997 decision of the Nuclear Regulatory Commission's (NRC) Atomic Safety and Licensing Board regarding the license application for a privately owned uranium enrichment plant provides an instructive example. Louisiana Energy Services (LES) applied for a permit to construct the plant in the mostly poor and African American communities of Forest Grove and Center Springs in Claiborne Parish, Louisiana. The Atomic Safety Board denied the license request, pending an analysis of the site selection process pursuant to EO 12898. Prior to granting the permit, the NRC purported to consider environmental justice through a one-page section of an otherwise lengthy environmental impact statement; it concluded that the facility would have no adverse effects because its operations would meet the state and federal environmental standards. An analysis of the site selection process indicated that areas with larger white populations were consistently removed from consideration, however, in favor of sites with larger black populations. In reviewing the matter, the licensing board heard testimony that the list of potential sites was narrowed from 78 sites with an average black population of 28 percent within a one-mile radius at the beginning of the process to 37 sites with an average black population of 37 percent after initial cuts.[13]

LES further narrowed its choices during a fine screening process to 6 possible sites with an average black population of 65 percent within a one-mile radius of the site, before ultimately selecting the Forest Grove and Center Springs communities, which have a 97 percent black population within a one-mile radius. Based on this and other testimony, the Atomic Safety Board decided that the NRC had failed to meet the requirements of EO 12898 before issuing its license. Following this decision, the Atomic Safety Board has never again used the executive order as a standard in evaluating license requests. Just as the IG found regarding the EPA, agencies have done little to integrate Executive Order obligations into their substantive decisions. The Army Corps of Engineers is no exception. Although the Army Corps stated an intention to develop implementation directives or "guidance" for EO 12898, it never did so. After considering how environmental injustices flow out of environmental decisions below, this chapter assesses how an analysis under EO 12898 could have guided the Army Corps to address the New Orleans levee problems in a way that would have prevented much of the damage to the Lower Ninth Ward and New Orleans East.[14]

Rather than an anomaly, the destruction that Hurricane Katrina wrought on the poor and the minority residents of the New Orleans Ninth Ward exemplifies the experience of environmental injustice faced by millions of people in America and worldwide. Environmental justice efforts seek to counteract the neglect, apathy, and disregard shown for African American, Latino, Asian American, Native American, and poor and working-class white communities in environmental decision making, planning, and practices. At the national level, these injustices range from the issuance of new pollution permits in Latino and African American communities already overburdened with multiple pollution sources and pathways to the targeting of tribal lands in the Midwest for the receipt of radioactive and other hazardous waste. Globally, environmental injustices range from the massive ecological devastation of the Niger Delta region of Nigeria in pursuit of oil revenues to the destruction of forests on tribal lands in Latin America. In each of these cases, the formula for environmental injustice remains the same. Environmental decision makers in both the public and private sectors discount the well-being of racial or ethnic minority groups who otherwise lack the power to control the environmental protection they receive. When this happens, community members suffer from increased disease and death and their quality of life decreases.[15]

Although private business forces often contribute to environmental injustices, responsibility for protecting the public from pollution rests with federal, state, and local governments. Individually and collectively, these entities bear the burden of reducing and mitigating the threats posed by pollution and other practices that compromise environmental quality.

The "environmental justice discount" represents the assortment of ways that environmental injustices flow out of and result from socially prevailing views about the value of communities based on the race and the class of the residents. Property values represent a proxy for those views as they reflect the value associated with living in certain communities as much as the value of any particular home. In turn, the "value" placed on communities drives business and governmental decision making about the goods, services, and level of protection afforded to these communities.

In the environmental arena, environmental justice discounts reflect the lower value associated with certain communities in the plans and pronouncements of local, state, and federal environmental decision makers. These discounts result in

1. less extensive cleanup of toxic waste sites in African American and Latino neighborhoods;
2. less enforcement for permit violations for facilities in or near African American and Latino areas and communities;
3. disregard for substantially higher rates of asthma and lead poisoning in African American and Hispanic children in setting conditions for pollution permits;
4. disregard for the subsistence fish diets of Native Americans and other minority groups in establishing mercury levels in pollution permits;
5. neglect of cumulative effects caused by exposure to multiple pollution sources and pathways in permitting decisions;
6. exclusion from decision making, or the neglect of community views and wishes;
7. valuing of profits or savings over community long-term well-being; and comfort with the compromised well-being of minority and low-income communities.

In each of the forgoing cases, decision makers knowingly set policies and carried out practices that failed to provide or promote the highest level of protection for communities made up of racial minorities or low-income whites. EPA and other environmental policy agencies explain some of these practices through the concept of "risk management." In the ideal case, risk management allows decision makers to balance the costs of providing certain levels of environmental protection with the likely health consequences of the decision. In the Superfund context, the EPA has established a range to guide it in decisions about when and how to clean up a site. When the risk posed suggests that more than one in ten thousand people will derive cancer from the pollution, then the EPA will presumptively act to eliminate the risk. In contrast, when the risk posed suggests that fewer than one in one million people will derive cancer from the pollution, the EPA will presumptively refrain from eliminating the risk. This type of formula, used by the EPA and other organizations, aids them in deciding how to manage a limited number of resources. When a risk does not warrant elimination or reduction, the situation is deemed "acceptable."[16]

Environmental injustices worldwide result from decisions in which the risks and hardships are avoided by the decision makers themselves and born instead by ethnic, religious, and low-income communities. In Nigeria, the Muslim majority in the North avoids the ecological devastation visited upon the Ogoni and other people of the Niger Delta. In Argentina, the Mataco and other Indian groups who live in the Gran Chaco forest suffer the immediate consequences of deforestation that deprives them of the plant, animal, and water resources they need for survival. In India, Dalits relegated to sewerage work suffer the risks of death and disease caused by routine bare-skinned immersion in the country's industrial and domestic waste. While these decisions may lack a conscious desire to harm any of the groups mentioned, decision makers' failure to recognize and reject the risks imposed upon these groups reflects a valuation that the well-being of these group's members is substantially lower than what they would accept for themselves and their loved ones. Essentially, these persons decide that the increased risk of death and disease faced by these groups is "acceptable" even though the same level of risk would not be found acceptable if imposed on the class of persons represented by the decision makers themselves. This phenomenon rests at the heart of environmental injustices across the United States, the world, and, ultimately, New Orleans.[17]

Planned Failure

Even if fully implemented, the Army Corps of Engineers levee plan would have only prepared the New Orleans levees to withstand a Category 3 storm. This meant that residents would benefit from protection against low- and medium-level storms but not against the high-level storms that weather experts had repeatedly predicted for the area. By only planning for a low-level storm, the Army Corps acquiesced to the catastrophic risk of harm posed to certain parts of the city by a higher-level storm. Unfortunately, the Army Corps failed to fully and satisfactorily implement even that inadequate plan. As a result, many New Orleans residents were knowingly placed at an even greater risk of harm.[18]

Despite the recognized risk caused by the failure to complete the New Orleans levee system over several years, neither the Army Corps nor the U.S. Congress nor the past three presidents prioritized the federal project. At the executive level, President George W. Bush cut the proposed budget of the Army Corps by two-thirds, from $6 billion to $4 billion. The director of the Army Corps ultimately resigned the position after making public comments that the president's budget cuts harmed the national interest. More specifically, the Army Corps received only $5.7 million of the $27 million dollars it requested for levee projects at Louisiana's Lake Pontchartrain. As a result, funding problems forced the Army Corps to delay multiple levee improvement contracts. These delays affected some of the specific levee failures during Hurricane Katrina.[19]

The New Orleans Flood System Report provides a comprehensive examination of the flood protection system's performance during Hurricane Katrina. This independent engineering analysis made the following conclusions regarding the flooding in the Lower Ninth Ward and New Orleans East caused by Hurricane Katrina:

> the catastrophic flooding of the St. Bernard and Lower Ninth Ward protected basin was primarily due to: catastrophic erosion of the Mississippi River Gulf Outlet (MRGO) frontage levees, and a pair of large failures (and breaches) on the east bank of the IHNC [Inner Habor Navigational Canal] at the west end of the Lower Ninth Ward. The catastrophic erosion of large portions of the nearly 11-mile long MRGO frontage levees was the result in large part of the use of unsuitable sand and shell sand fills, with low resistance to erosion, for major portions of these embankments. Large portions of these fill materials came from spoils dredged from the excavation of the adjacent MRGO channel. The short-term savings achieved by the use of these soils now pale in comparison to the massive damages and loss of life that resulted.[20]

Beyond this, investigations revealed that the MRGO channel served as the chief cause of the flooding in New Orleans. Like a funnel, the MRGO directed the water surging from Lake Borgne to St. Bernard Parish and the Lower Ninth Ward. Rather than such action being a surprise, the storm fulfilled scientific predictions that, with even Category 3 conditions, the MRGO would act like "a shot gun pointed straight at New Orleans."[21]

Executive Order 12898

An environmental justice analysis using Executive Order 12898 could have prevented much of the damage to New Orleans, and especially to New Orleans East and the Lower Ninth Ward. To date, the Army Corps has not developed any implementation guidance regarding the 1994 executive order. Yet, a serious effort to carry out the dictates of EO 12898 required that the Army Corps identify and address the disparately high and adverse human health and environmental effects of its policies and activities regarding the New Orleans flood protection system. As a planning tool, the executive order could have alerted the Army Corps to the significant crisis facing some residents under its plan. This potential flows from the executive order's fundamental directive that each federal agency examine its policies to make sure that the policies did not cause disproportionate adverse effects upon minority or low-income populations. Although adequate guidance exists to enable federal agencies to fully comply with EO 12898, few have complied with the executive mandate to "identify and address" the adverse effects of their activities on low-income and minority populations as required by the order. According to the Army Corps' July 30, 1999, General Policy Statement, the Corps was developing environmental justice implementation guidance. The Army Corps' failure to follow through with this before Hurricane Katrina certainly hampered the organization's compliance with the order.[22]

As mentioned above, EO 12898 was never fully integrated into federal agency operations, even though it has improved community relations efforts by some agencies. This can be seen in agency directives requiring the translation of public information into the languages used within particular communities and the use of public service announcements on local radio stations and in newspapers geared toward ethnic or racial minorities. In other situations, however, the order has been interpreted as *not* to affect the way agencies operate. In these cases agencies carry out their statutory and regulatory mandates with little regard for the requirements of the executive order. The failure of federal agencies to robustly implement the executive order certainly contributes to environmental injustices around the country. It is important to clarify what I mean by environmental injustice, however, and how this concept relates to the action of federal agencies.[23]

From early on, some have challenged the legitimacy of domestic environmental justice claims based on race. Challenges to claims of race-based bias rest upon three different arguments: (1) environmental siting decisions are made based on economics and not race; (2) minority populations move to areas with pollution because of lower housing prices; and (3) working-class whites, rather than African Americans, Latinos, or other minority groups, are disproportionately burdened by toxic waste and other pollution sources in their census tracts. In response to these challenges, new national studies were conducted, and old national studies were reexamined, that continued to link toxic waste disproportionately to racial minorities.[24]

While efforts to accurately understand the relationship between race, income, and pollution all contribute to a better understanding of where pollution sources are located and can ultimately help us improve environmental protection, efforts to "disprove" environmental injustices based on race miss the point. Pollution exists in American society. Many neighborhoods in urban and rural settings have pollution sources located in them or nearby. In some cases African American, Latino, Native American, or other minority groups at diverse income levels have pollution concentrated in or around the places they live. In other cases low-income and working-class whites find themselves in close proximity to pollution sources. Neither of these phenomena disproves the other; each reflects different forms of environmental injustice addressed by EO 12898. Yet, to effectively promote environmental justice and the implementation of the executive order by federal agencies, a better understanding of environmental justice as both a goal and a process is needed.

Federal, state, and private actors, like some commentators, may view environmental justice claims by racial minorities as baseless cries of racism where no bad faith exists. In turn, decision makers often adopt a defensive posture that seeks to disprove racial bias claims rather than to consider how to pursue environmental justice as a goal and a process. In one of the earliest accounts of justice, Aristotle discusses the concept in his book entitled *Nichomachean Ethics*. In that discussion, he describes justice as both a process of deciding disputes and a way of distributing things in a society. Today, we distinguish these as procedural and distributive justice, respectively. In the environmental context, justice can be viewed as a process and a means of distribution as well. As a process, environmental justice relates to the procedures used to decide how and when the risks of environmental harms will be distributed. This aspect of environmental justice focuses on who makes the decisions, the criteria used for decision making, and the fairness of the decision-making process. Aristotle maintained that objective decision makers, judging between parties, had to treat people as equals and without bias in order to make fair decisions. Environmental justice advocates seek to establish environmental decision-making procedures that provide equal treatment for racial minorities and low-income whites. As a concern about distribution, environmental justice relates to the distribution of environmental harms and risks across communities and the larger society.[25]

Aristotle claimed that the just distribution of goods, positions, and rewards in a society should be determined based on what the members of that society deserved. A good example of this today is the process we go through at the checkout counter of a grocery store. The items in the store that we pay for are the items that we feel we "deserve." A shopper who leaves a store without some items that were paid for, however, feels that she did not get what she "deserved." The opposite is also true. The individual who leaves a checkout counter with items that he did not pay for then received something that he did not "deserve." In this example money allows a purchase of something desired or needed at an advertised price. Because the purchase was made at the price that was advertised, shoppers feel that they "deserve" to leave the store with the item. If they are then told that they cannot leave the store with the item they paid for, then they will probably feel that they have been wronged because they have been denied something that they "deserved."

There is another way that people commonly deserve things, however. If a fire starts in the place where people live, then they will likely feel that they "deserve" to have available firefighters come to help them in the same way that they help others. When people feel that they deserve available firefighters' help, it is not because they have paid the firefighters for help or that the help has been earned, but because as residents of that particular city or town, they "deserve" the same help that any other resident would get. Unlike a grocery store, where the people who pay more money at the checkout "deserve" to leave with either more items or items that are more expensive, residents who face fires "deserve" help regardless of how much money they have or how much money they have spent to live where they do.[26]

Environmental injustices take place when the environmental protection that people deserve to receive as fellow citizens, residents, or human beings is based on their race, their religion, their ethnicity, or the amount of money they have. These injustices take place because decision makers do not employ protective procedures designed to ensure that everyone receives treatment as equals. Due to well-documented historic and contemporary racial discrimination, racial minorities at varying income levels lack the same opportunities to minimize their risk of environmental harm that middle-class and wealthy whites receive by their housing choices. This results in the inequitable distribution of environmental harms and risks across race and class lines, so that racial minorities and low-income whites suffer more than their fair share of environmental problems.

Federal, state, and local government agencies charged with the responsibility to protect public health and safety, which includes environmental protection, can increase existing injustices, maintain existing injustices, decrease existing injustices, or ignore them while fulfilling their public duties. The historical mistreatment of racial minorities and the contemporary indifference to the needs of all poor and working-class people necessitate that thoughtful planning consider the impact of decisions on these groups; this must become a central part of government decision making to decrease existing injustices and prevent new ones. Governments' continued use of "business as usual" approaches to environmentally related decisions will only increase existing disparities in the health and safety risks faced by the public.

The standard approach follows a pattern across local, state, and federal agencies. At present, a developer or some other commercial entity might spot a business opportunity and approach political officials for their support of the project; they likewise might recognize that an existing business venture that they enjoy is threatened because of the environmental risks that it poses, and they might enlist the support of political leaders to help them maintain the benefit that they enjoy. At the local level, the important initial decisions to protect the public are often made by zoning and planning boards. These groups meet with little public input and in many cases decide how the public health and safety risks will be distributed across a county or a municipality. In New Orleans, critical decisions before Katrina were also made by the Orleans Levee Board and the Water and Sewerage Board. Each of these boards, along with the Army Corps, made decisions that contributed to the devastation of the Lower Ninth Ward, New Orleans East, and other parts of the city. Although hindsight allows us to see the missteps of these groups that may not have been apparent at the time, it also shows how the failure to require public entities to consider the impact of their efforts on the society's most vulnerable groups increases existing injustices.[27]

The Orleans Levee Board shared responsibility with the Army Corps of Engineers for the maintenance of the New Orleans Flood Protection System. This was carried out under two protection projects: the West Bank, Louisiana, and Vicinity Hurricane Project and the Lake Pontchartrain and Vicinity Hurricane Project. The levee systems associated with the massive flooding from Hurricane Katrina were part of the Lake Pontchartrain and Vicinity project. While the Army Corps was tasked with the technical design and construction of these levees, the Levee Board held responsibility for covering 30 percent of the costs as well as inspection, maintenance, and operation of the project. In the years leading up to Katrina, the Levee Board spent most of its time undertaking and managing development projects. These board projects included local parks, marinas, a "cash strapped" airport, and a dock.[28]

One former board member stated that the one thing they never discussed was the levees themselves. Although the Orleans Levee Board did not have the "lead" on design and construction of the system, as local sponsors and financial partners they clearly had an active role to play in its maintenance and in the creation of a viable flood protection system for New Orleans. The development and investment projects of the board presumably provided the financial resources needed to cover their 30 percent share of levee projects. Yet for more than a decade, the board was enmeshed in high-profile real estate management and financial scandal that distracted it from its primary mission and deprived it of its ability to fund the improvements needed for the levee system. This aspect of the board's history provides a prime example of the way that public officials, who narrowly focused on the "financial promise" of development deals, neglected public safety and environmental protection responsibilities that leave vulnerable populations exposed to elevated risks.[29]

These concerns also relate to the work of the Army Corps in the area. Overall, congressional budget restrictions affected the speed and the quality of the Army Corps' levee plan. However, the agency also contributed to the levee system's failure in significant ways. One substantial agency failure was the position it adopted regarding the MRGO. The MRGO was intended to provide large cargo ships with a seventy-plus-mile shortcut to the Port of Orleans from the Gulf of Mexico. Prior to Katrina, the MRGO suffered from decreasing usage for over a decade. Attracting fewer and fewer vessels each year, the MRGO accounted for less than 3 percent of the port's total cargo. Although the port's freight total had increased since 1994, the freight carried down the MRGO had decreased by 50 percent. Not even one ship per day used the MRGO at a cost that critics estimate exceeded $12,000 per vessel per day. Moreover, the Army Corps expended $13 million dollars of its limited budget the year before Katrina to dredge the MRGO to enhance the quality of the channel as a commercial shipping way.[30]

Amid recurring calls to close the waterway because of the threat it posed to local residents, Army Corps personnel continued to defend its operation because of its importance to the local economy. Sixteen months before Katrina struck, a local official summed up one community's concerns about the MRGO and the risks it posed: "This is not working for St. Bernard. This is about lives and the people who live here. It's not about the dollars. It's killing us and it's going to devastate our area."[31] Just as predicted, when Katrina struck, water from Lake Borgne funneled down the MRGO to the Inner Harbor Navigational Canal (Industrial Canal). The effects of this journey wrought the massive devastation of the Lower Ninth Ward and New Orleans East. Statistics show that the majority of deaths caused by Katrina were of African Americans, at roughly 42 percent. Likewise, the death tolls were highest in predominantly black areas like the Lower Ninth Ward.[32]

An Ounce of Prevention

Everyone agrees that better planning would have spared New Orleans a great deal of the devastation and death caused by Hurricane Katrina. Beyond the common need for disaster preparedness, however, a particular investigation into the risks posed to low-income and minority populations was necessary to avoid one of America's most acute experiences of environmental injustice.

The Army Corps should have identified these and other impacts as risks associated with the use of the soils from the MRGO in the levee system. Likewise, the Corps should have recognized and made clear the elevated risks faced by the most vulnerable citizens of New Orleans because of the outdated science used in selecting the heights of the levees as well as the continued operation of the MRGO. In fact, the 1994 Executive Order on Environmental Justice directed that federal agencies including the Army Corps "identify and address disproportionately high and adverse human health or environmental effects of its programs, policies, and activities on minority populations."[33] From the issuance of the executive order to Hurricane Katrina, the Army Corps had a decade to undertake such an analysis. The benefits of the investigation would have become immediately clear. New Orleans residents in the Ninth Ward,

New Orleans East, and elsewhere who were predominantly African American or poor faced a greater likelihood of catastrophic loss of life and property during a Category 3 or higher-level hurricane. Based on such an investigation, the executive order then directs agencies to address the disproportionately high and adverse effects. Using that information, the Army Corps could have worked with the Orleans Levee Board to mitigate the identified effects. Another local levee board in Jefferson Parish took exceptional steps to provide additional protection for its levee system in the absence of Army Corps funding. To make sure that the residents were protected, the board spent $200,000 enhancing its levee system with additional structures that held up under Katrina's 145-mile-per-hour winds. Such mitigation efforts could have decreased the most significant threats identified in the heavily populated Orleans district even though financial difficulties delayed completion of all the changes needed to protect the entire city.[34]

Mitigation efforts by the Army Corps or the Orleans Levee Board could have gone a long way in lessening the impact of the environmental injustices resulting from Katrina. Rather than some radical approach, however, this type of advance planning represents the standard operating procedure called for in the Department of Transportation (DOT) Order on Environmental Justice. The order, published a decade ago as a way to implement EO 12898, presents a process for the integration of environmental justice into the agency's operations. Three valuable commitments from the DOT guidelines provide an important example for the Army Corps as well as other federal agencies. In integrating environmental justice with existing operations, DOT prescribed observing the following principles:

1. Planning and programming activities that have the potential to have a disproportionately high and adverse effect on human health or the environment shall include explicit consideration of

175

the effects on minority populations and low-income populations. Procedures shall be established or expanded, as necessary, to provide meaningful opportunities for public involvement by members of minority populations and low-income populations during the planning and development of programs, policies, and activities (including the identification of potential effects, alternatives, and mitigation measures).

2. Steps shall be taken to provide the public, including members of minority populations and low-income populations, access to public information concerning the human health or environmental impacts of programs, policies, and activities, including information that will address the concerns of minority and low-income populations regarding the health and environmental impacts of the proposed action.

To prevent "disproportionately high and adverse effects," the Order on Environmental Justice stated:

> It is DOT policy to actively administer and monitor its operations and decision making to assure that nondiscrimination is an integral part of its programs, policies, and activities. DOT currently administers policies, programs, and activities which are subject to the requirements of NEPA, Title VI, URA, ISTEA and other statutes that involve human health or environmental matters, or interrelated social and economic impacts. These requirements will be administered so as to identify, early in the development of the program, policy or activity, the risk of discrimination so that positive corrective action can be taken. In implementing these requirements, the following information should be obtained where relevant, appropriate and practical: Population served and/or affected by race, color or national origin, and income level; Proposed steps to guard against disproportionately high and adverse effects on persons on the basis of race, color, or

national origin; present and proposed membership by race, color, or national origin, in any planning or advisory body which is part of the program.[35]

These directives provide guidance for the Army Corps, as well as other agencies covered by Executive Order 12898 on the steps that they can take to counteract the "environmental justice discount" experienced by minority and low-income populations when environmental decisions are made.

As an initial matter, the effects of proposed projects and activities on minority and low-income populations should be "explicitly" considered, instead of examined only as an afterthought of public officials who are otherwise focused on promoting business interests. Second, procedures should be put in place to allow meaningful participation by minority and low-income communities in the planning and development of agency policies and activities. These procedures should include community involvement in identifying potential effects, alternative options, and measures to mitigate adverse impacts. As a necessary part of this process, community members should be provided with information about the effects of the proposed agency program or activity. This initial engagement of the residents of these often overlooked communities will starkly contrast with the typical exclusion and neglect that low-income and minority communities receive in the planning process. Finally, agencies should identify the risk of discrimination in carrying out Army Corps requirements under NEPA and other statutes early in the development of the program or activity by gathering the following information: race and income demographics of the affected and served populations; the steps proposed to prevent disproportionately high and adverse effects; and the race of present and proposed members of local or other bodies participating in the program or activity. These steps would ensure that the Army Corps gathered the background information needed to help prevent discriminatory effects from taking place. Although the entire DOT guidance document can help Army Corps employees to understand how to carry out EO 12898, the sections above show vital steps the Army Corps should take in its actions in New Orleans and elsewhere to avoid future environmental injustices heaped against the people who are least able to survive them.

Hurricane Katrina's devastation of the Lower Ninth Ward and New Orleans East represent another sad example of the environmental injustice caused by decision making that fails to take seriously the need to decrease the risks born by low-income and minority communities. Like other environmental protection mechanisms that "discount" the increased risk and precarious position of low-income and minority communities, the New Orleans levee system and those responsible for its development and maintenance neglected the protection of these communities and others in order to support what seemed to be more promising financial priorities. To prevent the continued replay of the environmental injustice experienced in New Orleans and elsewhere, the Army Corps of Engineers and other federal agencies need to meet the central requirement of EO 12898 by identifying and addressing the disproportionately high and adverse effects of their programs and activities on minority and low-income populations. By following the example provided by the Department of Transportation's Environmental Justice Order, the Army Corps of Engineers and other agencies can plan to succeed, and succeed in planning, for the protection of America's most at-risk environmental communities.

Notes

1. "Investigation of Performance of the New Orleans Flood Protection Systems in Hurricane Katrina on August 29, 2005," Independent Levee Investigation Team Final System Report, July 31, 2006, accessed April 21, 2007, http://www

.ce.berkeley.edu/~new_orleans/; Luke Cole and Sheila Foster, *From the Ground Up: Environmental Racism and the Rise of the Environmental Justice Movement* (New York: New York University Press, 2001).

2. "Investigation of Performance."

3. Cole and Foster, *From the Ground Up*. Walter Fauntleroy, the nonvoting delegate to the U.S. House of Representatives for the District of Columbia, was a former civil rights organizer and lieutenant of Dr. Martin Luther King Jr. Robert D. Bullard, *Dumping in Dixie: Race, Class, and Environmental Quality* (Boulder CO: Westview Press, 2000), 30–31. Over 30,000 gallons of PCB-laced oil was dumped and left on the side of over 210 miles of road in North Carolina for four years before the state and the EPA began cleanup efforts. Warren County was more than 84 percent black at the time. U.S. General Accounting Office (GAO), "Siting of Hazardous Waste Landfills and Their Correlation with Racial and Economic Status of Surrounding Communities," June 1, 1983, accessed March 19, 2007, http://archive.gao.gov/d48t13/121648.pdf.

4. U.S. GAO, "Siting of Hazardous Waste Landfills"; Charles Lee, "Toxic Wastes and Race in the United States: A National Report on Racial and Socio-Economic Characteristics of Communities with Hazardous Waste Sites," Commission for Racial Justice, United Church of Christ (1987). Charles Lee currently serves as the deputy director of the Office of Environmental Justice, Environmental Protection Agency (EPA), and chair of the EPA's National Environmental Justice Advisory Council.

5. Lee, "Toxic Wastes and Race"; Environmental Protection Agency EPA, "Environmental Equity: Reducing Risks for All Communities," accessed March 20, 2007, http://www.epa.gov/compliance/resources/publications/ej/reducing_risk_com_vol1.pdf.

6. Unlike Clarice Gaylord, Vivian Malone Jones's background was in civil rights. Best known for integrating the University of Alabama despite George Wallace's personal refusal to deny her entrance to the university, Jones provided the agency with a level of credibility in dealing with a new breed of environmental activists. Now deceased, Jones served as director from 1992 to 1996. During this time, the author served as the primary contact and support for the Regional Office of Environmental Justice and the lead attorney addressing "environmental justice" issues for the region. Carol M. Browner, Administrator of the EPA, "Before the Committee on Finance," U.S. Senate, accessed January 28, 2006, http://www.epa.gov/history/topics/justice/01.htm; Clifford Rechtschaffen and Eileen P. Gauna, *Environmental Justice: Law, Policy, and Regulation* (Durham NC: Carolina Academic Press, 2002) (describing the history of the National Environmental Justice Advisory Committee).

7. Meredith J. Bowers, "The Executive's Response to Environmental Injustice: Executive Order 12898," *Environmental Law* 1 (1995): 645.

8. Executive Order No. 12898, 59 Fed. Reg. 7629 (February 16, 1994).

9. EPA, Office of Inspector General, "Evaluation Report: EPA Needs to Consistently Implement the Intent of the Executive Order on Environmental Justice," Report No. 2004-P-00007, accessed March 1, 2004, http://www.epa.gov/oig/reports/2004/ 20040301-2004-P-00007.pdf.

10. EPA, Office of Inspector General, "Evaluation Report: EPA Needs to Consistently Implement." A 2006 report finds that the agency has also failed to conduct Environmental Justice reviews of its programs as required by the executive order. EPA, Office of Inspector General, "Evaluation Report: EPA Needs to Conduct Environmental Justice Reviews of Its Programs, Policies, and Activities," Report No. 2006-P-00034, accessed September 18, 2006, http://www.epa.gov/oig/reports/2006/20060918-2006-P-00034.pdf.

11. Executive Order No. 12898.

12. Denis Binder, Colin Crawford, Eileen P. Gauna, et al., "A Survey of Federal Agency Response to President Clinton's Executive Order No. 12898 on Environmental Justice," *Environmental Law Reporter* 31 (2001): 11133.

13. *In the Matter of Louisiana Energy Service*, L.P., 69 Fed. Reg. 25 (February 6, 2004).

14. *In the Matter of Louisiana Energy Service*. In 2006 the NRC licensed LES to construct the facility in Eunice, New Mexico. "NRC Issues License to Louisiana Energy Services for Gas Centrifuge Uranium Enrichment Plant in New Mexico," *NRC News*, Press Release No. 06-084, accessed June 23, 2006, http://www.nrc.gov/reading-rm/doc-collections/news/2006/06-084.html.

15. Cole and Foster, *From the Ground Up*; Robert D. Bullard, *Unequal Protection: Environmental Justice and Communities of Color* (San Francisco: Sierra Club Books, 1997).

16. EPA, National Center for Environmental Assessment, "Human Health Guidelines," accessed November 12, 2007, http://cfpub.epa.gov/ncea/cfm/nceaguid_human.cfm; EPA, "Superfund Risk Assessment: Human Health Risk Characterization, Waste and Clean Up Risk Assessment," accessed November 12, 2007, http://www.epa.gov/oswer/riskassessment/superfund_hh_characterization.htm; Joseph V. Rodricks, "Some Attributes of Risk Influencing Decision Making by Public Health and Regulatory Officials," *American Journal of Epidemiology* 154, no. 12 (2001): November 12, 2007, http://aje.oxfordjournals.org/cgi/reprint/154/12/S7.pdf.

17. Ibibia Lucky Worika, "Deprivation, Despoilation and Destitution: Whither Environment and Human Rights in Nigeria's Niger Delta?" *ILSA Journal of International and Comparative Law* 8 (Fall 2001): 1.

18. "Investigation of Performance," 2–8.

19. Bob Marshall, "300 Years of Decisions Contributed to Disaster," *New Orleans Times Picayune*, August 25, 2006, A1. However, the levee problems cannot all be placed at the feet of the Army Corps. As discussed below, local decisions also hampered the levee implementation process.

20. "Investigation of Performance."

21. Robert R. M. Verchick, statement to U.S. Senate, Committee on Environment and Public Works hearing, accessed November 17, 2005, http://epw.senate .gov/hearing_statements.cfm?id=248927.

22. Executive Order No. 12898; U.S. Army Corps of Engineers, "General Policies," accessed July 30, 1999, http://www.usace.army.mil/publications/eng-pam phlets/ep1165-2-1/c-3.pdf (maintaining that the general policy of the Army Corps of Engineers is to develop, control, maintain, and conserve the nation's water resources in accordance with the laws and policies enacted by the U.S. Congress and administration).

23. Binder, Crawford, Gauna, et al., "Survey of Federal Agency Response," 11133.

24. See Thomas Lambert and Christopher Boerner, "Environmental Inequality: Economic Causes, Economic Solutions," *Yale Journal on Regulation* 14 (Winter 1997): 195; Vicki Been, "Market Dynamics and the Siting of Lulus: Questions to Raise in the Classroom about Existing Research," *West Virginia Law Review* 96 (1994): 1069; "Toxic Waste and Race in the United States: A National Report on the Racial and Socioeconomic Characteristics of Communities with Hazardous Waste Sites," United Church of Christ Commission for Racial Justice (1987); "Toxic Wastes and Race Revisited: An Update on the 1987 Report on the Racial and Socioeconomic Characteristics of Communities with Hazardous Waste Sites," Center for Policy Alternatives, National Association for the Advancement of Coloured People, and United Church of Christ Commission for Racial Justice (1994); "Toxic Wastes and Race at Twenty, 1987–2007, A Report Prepared for the United Church of Christ Justice and Witness Ministries," accessed November 12, 2007 http://www.ucc.org/justice/pdfs/toxic20.pdf.

25. Rechtschaffen and Gauna, *Environmental Justice*; Aristotle, *The Nicomachmean Ethics*, trans. W. D. Ross (350 BC; New York: Oxford University Press, 1998).

26. Some may connect the feeling of desert with their payment of taxes. However, few persons would suggest that an exemption from taxes or even a delinquent tax bill would justify an available firefighter's abandonment of persons and property threatened by a fire.

27. Marshall, "300 Years," A1.

28. Marshall, "300 Years," A1; James Huey, congressional testimony before the Senate Committee on Homeland Security and Governmental Affairs, 5–7,

accessed December 15, 2005, http://hsgac.senate.gov/_files/121505Huey.pdf; Ann Carns, "Long before Flood, New Orleans Was Prime for Leaks," *Wall Street Journal*, November 25, 2005.

29. Carns, "Long before Flood." "The board has a well-established reputation as a free-spending and often wasteful agency that has never hesitated to stray from its primary mission of providing flood protection." Frank Doze, "Levee Board Tax a Hard Sale Bad Image, Timing Create Obstacles," *New Orleans Times-Picayune*, November 18, 1999.

30. Marshall, "300 Years," A1; Michael Grunwald, "Canal May Have Worsened City's Flooding: Disputed Project Was a 'Funnel' for Surge, Some Say," *Washington Post*, September 14, 2005, A21.

31. Karen Turni Bazile, "Defense of Gulf Outlet Doubted: St. Bernard Officials Say Army Corps Is Wrong," *New Orleans Times-Picayune*, April 7, 2004, A1.

32. See State of Louisiana, News, "Task Force Pelican Updates, Fatalities," accessed October 25, 2005, http://www.gov.state.la.us/index.cfm?md=newsroom& tmp=detail&articleID=1074; Ceci Connolly and Manuel Roig-Franzia, "Grim Map Details Toll in 9th Ward and Beyond: Katrina Proved Deadly in Every Section of New Orleans," *Washington Post*, October 23, 2005, A14.

33. Executive Order No. 12898.

34. Carns, "Long before Flood."

35. U.S. Department of Transportation, Order on Environmental Justice, 62 Fed. Reg. 72 (April 15, 1997).

EIGHT

"Still Up on the Roof"

Race, Victimology, and the Response to Hurricane Katrina

KENNETH B. NUNN

One of the most important functions of law in a civilized society is to deter harmful behavior. In tort law, this is accomplished by ensuring that wrongdoers bear the financial costs of their harmful acts. In criminal law, the threat of fine or imprisonment is used to prevent wrongdoers from harming others. Yet things do not always work out as planned. This aphorism of life also applies to the law. This is particularly the case when matters are complicated by race. As Charles Hamilton Houston once famously said, "Nobody needs to explain to the Negro the difference between the law in books and the law in action."[1] On the books people are punished or assessed damages for intentional, reckless, and negligent acts that bring avoidable harm to others. Although the loss of life and property that came as a result of Hurricane Katrina could have been prevented, no one has been held legally responsible for this tragedy. Is it because of race?

Hurricane Katrina was the worse hurricane in recent American history. It resulted in over 1,417 deaths and over 75 billion dollars in damage. Yet Hurricane Katrina was not an unexpected occurrence.

The vulnerability of the Gulf Coast, particularly New Orleans, to this kind of destruction was well understood. Furthermore, as the hurricane approached the Gulf Coast, multiple warnings were issued about the approaching catastrophe. The loss of lives and property in New Orleans and the Gulf Coast was not the result of inadequate warnings, but, as I argue, the result of a failure to act on the part of local, state, and national authorities.

In this chapter, I examine whether the failure of authorities to prepare, warn, and rescue could be characterized as a crime. I look at the appropriate legal standards for criminal liability and examine the events leading up to and occurring in the aftermath of Katrina in light of these standards. Secondly, I examine the Katrina catastrophe with an eye on the characteristics of the victims. I argue that the government's failure to assist Katrina victims—U.S. citizens—was colored by race and class. Finally, having determined the centrality of race and class in the Katrina response, I consider the meaning Katrina holds for the African American community. I conclude that the African American community must develop community-controlled, grassroots methods to respond to catastrophes.

Was New Orleans the Scene of a Crime?

New Orleans has always played a central role in the development of America and Africans in America. As such, New Orleans was stage for some of the greatest achievements in African American life and some of the greatest degradations. The city was a huge slave market, and through its doors poured thousands of enslaved Africans, torn away from their motherland. Yet the culture that these enslaved Africans created in New Orleans was a thing of beauty. Its music, food, religion, and art were widely influential and shaped not only Louisiana but the nation and the world. One legacy of slavery, and the vicious brand of Jim Crow that followed it in New

Orleans, was a large population of wretchedly poor African American residents. Concentrated mainly in the Ninth Ward, these residents struggled to survive but nonetheless defined the urban life of New Orleans and made it one of the most vibrant and entertaining cities in the country.[2]

Prior to Hurricane Katrina, New Orleans was a site of concentrated poverty. Among the nation's fifty largest cities, New Orleans ranked second among those with poor families clustered in extremely poor neighborhoods; 38 percent of its poor residents lived in high-poverty census tracts. Before Katrina, 28 percent of New Orleanians lived below the poverty line, and most of these—over 53 percent—lived in deep poverty at less than one-half the official poverty line. In the city's deeply impoverished areas, "the average household barely earned $20,000 annually, only one in twelve adults held a college degree, four in five children were raised in single-parent families, and four in ten working-age adults—many of them disabled—were not connected to the labor force."[3] This level of impoverishment left New Orleans' poor residents with few resources to call upon in the event of an emergency. The Washington DC-based Center on Budget and Policy Priorities found that "more than half of the poor households in New Orleans—54 percent— did not have a car, truck, or van in 2000."[4]

Pre-Katrina New Orleans was also highly segregated. Based on the 2000 census, it was one of the most segregated cities in the United States, so much so that a 2005 Brookings Institution report claimed, "Blacks and whites were living in quite literally different worlds before the storm hit."[5] African Americans accounted for 68 percent of the New Orleans population, and 34 percent of the African American population lived in poverty. In total, 85 percent of New Orleans poor were African American.[6]

The poor, black residents of New Orleans lived in the most vulnerable parts of the city. The core city areas they inhabited were, geographically, the lowest and were afforded the least protection from New Orleans' aging levee system. Consequently African Americans were disproportionately affected by the storm's fury. African Americans were 45.8 percent of the population in areas damaged by Katrina, and yet were only 20.9 percent of the population in undamaged areas.

Arguably the vulnerability of the New Orleans black and poor, standing alone, is unfortunate, but not legally significant. What turns New Orleans into a potential crime scene is the fact that the vulnerability of the black urban poor was well known to local, state, and federal officials. Public officials and disaster preparation experts knew for decades that New Orleans was a disaster waiting to happen. Multiple investigations had predicted that if a major hurricane ever hit New Orleans, the levee system would be quickly overwhelmed and most of the population would be unable to escape. Joel Bourne, a writer for *National Geographic Magazine*, wrote the following about the effects of a hurricane on the New Orleans area:

> The storm gathered steam and drew a bead on the city. As the whirling maelstrom approached the coast, more than a million people evacuated to higher ground. Some 200,000 remained, however—the car-less, the homeless, the aged and infirm, and those die-hard New Orleanians who look for any excuse to throw a party.
>
> The storm hit Breton Sound with the fury of a nuclear warhead, pushing a deadly storm surge into Lake Pontchartrain. The water crept to the top of the massive berm that holds back the lake and then spilled over. Nearly 80 percent of New Orleans lies below sea level—more than eight feet below in places—so the water poured in. A liquid brown wall washed over the brick ranch homes of Gentilly, over the clapboard houses of the Ninth Ward, over the white-columned porches of the Garden District, until it

raced through the bars and strip joints on Bourbon Street like the
pale rider of the Apocalypse. As it reached 25 feet (eight meters)
over parts of the city, people climbed onto roofs to escape it.[7]

Bourne's comments are a dead-on description of Katrina's impact.
Yet this article was written in October 2004, almost a year *before*
Katrina hit. Either Bourne was a prophet, or he had access to data
and experts who clearly demonstrated these expected outcomes.[8]

If you lived in New Orleans or were responsible for its safety,
would you have read this article? Yes, you would have read it, if
only out of curiosity. And if you had read it, you could not have
helped but learn the following: "The killer for Louisiana is a Category Three storm at 72 hours before landfall that becomes a Category Four at 48 hours and a Category Five at 24 hours—coming
from the worst direction."[9] More importantly, not only would you
have read the article, but you would have, or at least *should* have,
had access to the same if not better information than that offered
by *National Geographic*. Thus, you would have known that due
to dredging and diverting the natural flow of the Mississippi River,
Louisiana loses 25 square miles of coastal wetland a year. This wetland provides a critical buffer against incoming storms. You would
have also known that the Army Corps of Engineers was aware of
these risks, and that they had developed a thirty-year, $14 billion
plan to deal with the situation. And you would have known that although the plan was accepted by a variety of environmental groups,
it was opposed by President George W. Bush and his administration
and stalled in Congress over concern that it was too costly.

If you were a New Orleans government official, odds are you
would be familiar with the five-part series the *New Orleans Times-
Picayune* published in 2002, three years prior to Hurricane Katrina. Had you read that series, you would have known that the
nightmare scenario that unfolded in the days after Katrina struck

was not unexpected. The first article in the series outlined the extent of the danger:

> If enough water from Lake Pontchartrain topped the levee system along its south shore, the result would be apocalyptic. Vast areas would be submerged for days or weeks until engineers dynamited the levees to let the water escape. Some places on the east bank of Orleans and Jefferson parishes are as low as 10 feet below sea level. Adding a 20-foot storm surge from a Category 4 or 5 storm would mean 30 feet of standing water.
>
> Whoever remained in the city would be at grave risk. According to the American Red Cross, a likely death toll would be between 25,000 and 100,000 people, dwarfing estimated death tolls for other natural disasters and all but the most nightmarish potential terrorist attacks. Tens of thousands more would be stranded on rooftops and high ground, awaiting rescue that could take days or longer. They would face thirst, hunger and exposure to toxic chemicals.[10]

Later articles in the *Times-Picayune* series also presaged what happened after Katrina with startling precision:

> Ninety percent of the structures in the city are likely to be destroyed by the combination of water and wind accompanying a Category 5 storm, said Robert Eichorn, former director of the New Orleans Office of Emergency Preparedness. The LSU Hurricane Center surveyed numerous large public buildings in Jefferson Parish in hopes of identifying those that might withstand such catastrophic winds. They found none.
>
> Amid this maelstrom, the estimated 200,000 or more people left behind in an evacuation will be struggling to survive. Some will be housed at the Superdome, the designated shelter in New Orleans for people too sick or infirm to leave the city. Others will

end up in last-minute emergency refuges that will offer minimal
safety. But many will simply be on their own, in homes or looking for high ground.[11]

The New Orleans local paper provided detailed and startling information about the risks to the city's residents.

Other sources also graphically detailed the destruction that a major hurricane could bring to the New Orleans area, including well-
known articles published in 2001 in *Popular Mechanics*, *Scientific
American*, and the *Houston Chronicle*. As the final report of the
House Select Bipartisan Committee to Investigate the Preparation
for and Response to Hurricane Katrina concluded, Hurricane Katrina "had been predicted in theory for many years, and forecast
with startling accuracy for five days."[12] Public officials had every
reason to prepare for this disaster.[13]

As the Select Committee indicated, public officials were told precisely what to expect as Hurricane Katrina bore down on the Gulf
Coast. Three days before the hurricane struck, Max Mayfield, the
director of the National Hurricane Center in Miami, called New Orleans mayor Ray Nagin to express concern over the apparent lack
of urgency in the city's preparations. The following day, Mayfield
participated in a video conference call with President Bush, Homeland Security Chief Michael Chertoff, and Federal Emergency and
Management Agency Director Michael Brown. During the tele-
conference, Mayfield specifically warned that the New Orleans levees could be topped by floodwaters. That same day, the New Orleans field office of the National Weather Service issued a bulletin
predicting catastrophic damage to the New Orleans area from the
approaching storm.[14] The bulletin warned that "most of the area
would be uninhabitable for weeks," that all gabled roofs in the city
would fail, that most industrial buildings would suffer severe damage, and that all "wood framed low rising apartment buildings will

be destroyed."[15] The bulletin predicted that blown debris, power outages, and water shortages "will make human suffering incredible by modern standards."[16] The impending storm was no surprise to any authority who had access to information.

Notwithstanding their knowledge of New Orleans' vulnerability in the event of a hurricane and the specific warnings they received from meteorologists and other scientists, public officials at the state, local, and national levels grossly failed in their duty to protect the lives and property of the citizens of New Orleans. At the outset the city was inadequately prepared for a hurricane of any sort, let alone a major hurricane like Katrina. The levee system designed to protect the city from Lake Pontchartrain and the Mississippi River could not hold back the storm surge of a major hurricane. In the event of flooding, there was insufficient pumping capacity to keep up with the rising waters. There were no safe places in the city to shelter civilians from floodwaters and hurricane-force winds. And in light of all of the above, the most critical failure is that there was no plan to evacuate the city that accounted for the tens of thousands of residents who lacked private transportation.

These failures alone were inexcusable. What was damning was that once Katrina struck, and public officials either knew or certainly should have known what threats the public faced, days passed before any organized and coordinated efforts were made to rescue New Orleans residents. Residents were left stranded on roofs until private citizens organized private flotillas to attempt to rescue them. Food was not provided. Water was not made available. Medical facilities were nonexistent. Dead bodies were left to lie in the street. Transportation out of New Orleans was not organized. On at least one key occasion, residents trying to leave New Orleans were turned back at gunpoint. To make matters worse, not only did public officials fail to ameliorate the situation, but it appears they did everything they could to stop private relief efforts from assisting New Orleans residents as well.

In well-publicized comments on NBC's *Meet the Press*, Aaron Broussard, president of Jefferson Parish near New Orleans, described how federal officials hampered relief efforts:

> The aftermath of Hurricane Katrina will go down as one of the worst abandonments of Americans on American soil ever in U.S. history. . . . It's not just Katrina that caused all these deaths in New Orleans here. Bureaucracy has committed murder here in the greater New Orleans area. . . . Three quick examples. We had Wal-Mart deliver three trucks of water. FEMA turned them back. They said we didn't need them. This was a week ago. FEMA, we had 1,000 gallons of diesel fuel on a Coast Guard vessel docked in my parish. When we got there with our trucks, FEMA says don't give you the fuel. Yesterday—yesterday—FEMAA comes in and cuts all of our emergency communication lines. They cut them without notice.[17]

Crime and Katrina

A crime is a violation of law so disturbing that the perpetrator deserves to be punished. Criminal liability for the governmental failures that exacerbated the effects of Hurricane Katrina could be based on two potential theories. First, various actors could be liable for the failure to mitigate conditions that led to harm. Second, individuals could be held criminally responsible for failing to rescue the victims of Katrina.

Criminal liability for failing to mitigate harm is a well-established rule in American courts. *Commonwealth v. Welansky* is the most important case explaining this rule. In *Welansky*, a Boston nightclub owner was prosecuted for failing to ameliorate conditions that led to a fire in his establishment. The fire took place on a weekend following an important Boston College football game, and the nightclub, the Cocoanut Grove, was filled with football fans. Over a thousand people packed the club, pushing the building to more than double its capacity. The fire started when a busboy climbed up a ladder to change a light bulb and lit a match to illuminate the darkened area. Flammable paper decorations near the ceiling accidentally caught on fire from the match. The fire spread quickly, and patrons stampeded the exits. Many doors to the club, however, were locked shut to prevent patrons from leaving without paying their bills. Other doors opened inward and were useless against the press of the panicked crowd. Over 492 people died, mostly as a result of the lack of operable exits.[18]

According to the Massachusetts Supreme Court, Welansky could be held responsible for manslaughter even though he was not present at the time of the fire and did not directly cause the flames. The prosecution proceeded on a theory of involuntary manslaughter based on recklessness, or what the court called "wanton or reckless conduct." According to the court, Welansky had a duty to care for the patrons of his establishment; consequently "wanton or reckless conduct may consist of intentional failure to take such care in disregard of the probable harmful consequences to them or of their right to care."[19] In other words, the court held that since Welansky was aware of the flammable material in the club and the restricted exits from the club, *and did nothing to correct them*, he was criminally responsible for the death of the patrons in his club.[20]

This same argument could be made in respect to the public officials who were charged with protecting New Orleans from a natural disaster. They were aware that the city was vulnerable to a major hurricane, and that such hurricanes were foreseeable occurrences in the Gulf region. Yet someone made the decision not to upgrade the levees to provide the required level of protection. Compounding matters further—knowing that there was inadequate protection for New Orleans residents in the city bowl—public officials failed to make a plan for their orderly evacuation prior to the hurricane's landfall, failed to evacuate them after the storm, and failed to provide food, clothing, water, shelter, medicine, security, and other life-sustaining necessities. That is to say, in much the same way that the fire in the Cocoanut Grove was predictable, Hurricane Katrina was an entirely foreseeable and avoidable tragedy.

Welansky involved the prosecution of a private citizen. Could state, federal, and local bureaucrats be held criminally liable, as government officials, for failing to do their jobs? The underlying incident in *Welansky* provides some guidance on this score as well. Three public officials had criminal charges lodged against them as a result of the Cocoanut Grove fire. A fire lieutenant, who inspected the nightclub eight days before the fire, a building commissioner, and a police captain were all charged with criminal negligence for failing to correct the hazardous conditions found at the club. None of the officials were convicted; the fire lieutenant was acquitted at trial, and charges were dropped against the other two. Yet their status as public officials did not immunize them from prosecution for any acts of criminal negligence.

In a more recent case, three government engineers were convicted of several criminal violations of the Resource Conservation and Recovery Act. The three engineers were civilian employees of the U.S. Army engaged in the development of chemical warfare systems at the Aberdeen Proving Ground in Maryland. They were alleged to have stored toxic chemicals in violation of the act. The 4th U.S. Circuit Court of Appeal quickly dispensed with the defendants' argument that, as employees of the federal government, they were entitled to immunity from prosecution. Noting that the defendants were prosecuted as individuals, the court held "sovereign immunity does not attach to individual government employees so as to immunize them from prosecution for their criminal acts."[21] The

193

court did observe, however, "In certain circumstances, federal officers may avoid criminal prosecution by a state when the alleged crime arose from performance of federal duties."[22] Governmental employees may be held responsible, then, for certain crimes caused by the ways that they fulfill their duties for the government.[23]

A federal agent is shielded from state prosecution when his or her acts are (1) authorized by federal law and (2) necessary to the performance of federal duties. This type of federally protective immunity arose at the time of Reconstruction and is designed to prevent state governments from thwarting the enforcement of federal laws, such as civil rights provisions, with which they disagree. Yet the rule-granting immunity to federal officers does not allow them to violate any and all state criminal laws with impunity. This limited immunity is only intended to prevent state interference with federal purposes. Thus, for example, federal agents could be prosecuted in California courts for driving under the influence.

The prosecution of federal agents for failing to mitigate the harm of Katrina would not give rise to any immunity if the prosecutions took place in federal court. To the extent federal agents are prosecuted in Louisiana courts, there would not appear to be any bar to prosecution, either. A claim of criminal negligence or recklessness, as made in the *Welansky* case, would not appear to involve acts necessary to the performance of federal duties. Rather, the claim in such a case would be that federal officials did *not* perform their federally required obligations when they failed to mitigate the conditions that existed prior to and immediately following the impact of the hurricane. It would be this failure to perform federal duties that would give rise to state prosecution.

Another well-established ground for criminal prosecution is failure to rescue. Say a person fell into a public swimming pool and started to drown. In most states a passer-by would have no obligation to rescue the drowning person. The failure to rescue would be called an omission and would not give rise to criminal responsibility, except in limited circumstances. On the other hand, a lifeguard *would* be obliged to rescue the drowning person and could be convicted of a crime if he or she failed to attempt the rescue. A lifeguard would be viewed as having a duty to rescue under either a contract or a statute setting forth the lifeguard's duties. Thus, the general rule that an omission to act does not give rise to criminal liability will not apply in the lifeguard's situation.

In the 1936 case of *State v. Benton*, a Delaware court found a railroad crossing watchman guilty of involuntary manslaughter for failing to signal the approach of a train to an oncoming car. Since the watchman had a contractual duty to look out for the pubic safety, an omission to act defense would not have provided him any protection. Under similar reasoning firefighters, emergency medical technicians, police officers, and other emergency responders could be held responsible for negligent performance of their duties. The same would be true of emergency planners and governmental officials who negligently directed emergency responders during and after Hurricane Katrina, thereby hampering relief efforts. Each of these actors has an affirmative duty to provide for the public safety and to rescue members of the public in the event of an emergency.[24]

So long as the acts of emergency planners and responders in failing to rescue rise to the level of criminal negligence, then they cannot claim governmental immunity for their acts. Immunity *is* available for public officials engaged in governmental functions like disaster planning and emergency rescue in a *civil* lawsuit. In such cases, courts point out that the only way to punish delinquent government officials accused of negligence is through criminal prosecution.

Louisiana Revised Statutes Section 14.12 describes criminal negligence in the state of Louisiana: "Criminal negligence exists when . . . there is such disregard of the interest of others that the offender's conduct amounts a gross deviation below the standard of care expected to be maintained by a reasonably careful man under like circumstances." Under this statute, unless a reasonably careful man would fail to evacuate the citizens of New Orleans as a Category 5 hurricane approached, fail to rescue them from their rooftops for several days after the storm, and leave them stranded in New Orleans without adequate food, shelter, clothing, and so forth for weeks, then criminal negligence was committed by the government officials who failed to rescue the citizens of New Orleans in the aftermath of Hurricane Katrina.[25]

Yet, as of the time that this chapter is being written, there are no criminal prosecutions of any public officials in Louisiana for their abandonment of their public responsibilities during the time of Katrina. There have been a number of investigations and special reports by various political bodies, and there has been at least one criminal prosecution of private citizens for failing to evacuate a nursing home. I In another case murder charges were leveled at medical personnel for euthanizing patients at the height of the storm. Yet there has not been any movement toward filing criminal charges against officials at any level—federal, state, or local—for their dereliction of duty in the face of one of the country's greatest catastrophes. To paraphrase Jefferson Parish president Aaron Broussard, bureaucracy has gotten away with murder in the greater New Orleans area.[26]

When Victims Are Black

The images of residents clinging to their roofs and waving makeshift "help" signs at passing camera crews have been seared into the nation's memory. Also unforgettable are the scenes of families wading through chest-high water, corpses left to rot in the streets, and thousands lined up outside the Superdome with nothing but the tattered clothes on their backs. These images led viewers around the world to ask, "Is this America, or is this an impoverished Third World country?" Days of this kind of coverage finally embarrassed the federal government into action, especially after Kanye West and others began to publicly question the government's racial motives. During an NBC telethon for Hurricane Katrina victims on September 2, 2005, West blurted out, "George Bush doesn't care about black people!"[27] West only articulated what everyone else was thinking. It was clear to anyone who could see that all of these stranded, struggling people were of African descent. Was it just a coincidence that all of these people were black, and that they were trapped in New Orleans with no hope and no place to go?

Similar questions could be asked about the lack of prosecution for this entirely avoidable tragedy. Maybe the intrusion of the race issue was enough to get the evacuation buses rolling and the rescue helicopters flying, but not enough for the powers that be to contemplate putting someone behind bars for shirking their responsibilities when the waters started rising. Is it really possible that the decision whether to charge anyone could be influenced by race this late into our nation's history? Or, is this just wild and irresponsible speculation?

Victimology is the study of victims and their treatment by the legal system. Victimologists often study the lifestyle, background, and physical characteristics of victims to determine why they became targets of crimes and other social wrongs. Often victimologists also advocate for victims and their rights in their dealings with the justice system. What victimologists have learned about race in the criminal justice system and its impact on crime victims could help us sort out the remaining questions over race and Katrina.

Victimologists have focused on race in a number of contexts. Scholars of tort damage awards have demonstrated that the race of the tort victim, or the race of the plaintiff, matters in determining how much money the tort victim receives for restitution. The calculation of damages in personal injury and wrongful death actions is often racially biased because courts rely on race-based actuarial tables to determine loss of future earning capacity. Since African Americans generally earn less than whites due to several factors—including historic and present discrimination, shorter life spans, and a greater likelihood of illness—the use of these tables replicates existing racial disparities in income. Jurors can harbor conscious or unconscious racial biases that lead to reduced awards for minority plaintiffs. Finally, African American plaintiffs may be disadvantaged in seeking damage awards due to the general lack of credibility afforded to black experts and witnesses by jurors and judges.

African American victims also fair less well in the criminal justice system. A number of studies have found that prosecutors are less likely to file criminal charges when the victims are black. When charges are filed, they tend to be for lesser crimes than those prosecuted when the victims are white. Black male defendants fare especially poorly when their victims are white females. In a 1985 study Michael Radelet and Glenn Pierce found that charging decisions were affected by the race of the victim. Crimes involving white victims and black defendants resulted in more serious charges than crimes involving black victims and white defendants. An earlier study of charging practices in Indianapolis also found that prosecutors treated cases more seriously when the victim was white.[28]

Not only do the racial attributes of victims affect the seriousness of charges that are brought in court, but they also affect the severity of the defendant's sentence. Researchers have consistently found racial disparities in sentencing since these studies were first undertaken in the 1930s. This racial impact is particularly evident in death penalty cases. A number of studies have found that death sentences are more likely to be imposed when the victim is white. The most important of these is the Baldus study of capital sentencing in Georgia reviewed in the Supreme Court case of *Mc-Cleskey v. Kemp*. After controlling for over 230 nonracial factors, the Baldus study found that race of the victim was the determining factor in whether a defendant received a death sentence in Georgia. They found that defendants who killed white victims were four times more likely to receive the death penalty. Black defendants who killed white victims were eleven times more likely to receive the death penalty than white defendants who killed African American victims. In addition, a number of mock jury experiments by social science researchers have also suggested jurors are influenced by the race of the victim and may be more likely to find the defendant guilty when the victim is white.[29]

Fear of potential race discrimination has led some judges and many legal scholars to oppose the use of victim impact statements in criminal sentencing. As one law professor explains, the use of such statements "increases the likelihood of racial distortion."[30] In light of the evidence I have detailed here, a conclusion that prosecutors have failed to investigate or charge any government officials with crimes related to the Katrina response is patently reasonable. The race of the victim has a well-documented impact on who is charged, who is sentenced, and how severe a sentence is imposed upon the defendant. Plainly, the fact that the televised victims of Katrina were dark-skinned affected the degree of sympathy that they were accorded, not only by prosecutors but also by the American public. The way that Katrina victims were labeled as "refugees" and depicted as law-breakers by the early press coverage coming out of New Orleans clearly shows they were perceived as different and deviant. They were not granted the privilege of being viewed as victims of a potential crime. Instead, they were the ones who were constructed as criminals.[31]

In a law review article, now almost twenty years old, Yale law professor Stephen Carter pointed out that "victimhood" is a socially constructed concept that makes little sense outside of the context in which it is used. When crime provides the context, blacks are viewed as threats, not victims. Therefore, according to Carter: "There are two varieties of people who are involved in criminal activity, black people and victims. So perhaps when victims happen to be black, the culture rationalizes the seeming contradiction by denying that there has been a crime."[32]

So it was in New Orleans. At the time Katrina hit, no one saw the black crowds who were left behind as victims. And while the nation was shamed into belatedly providing assistance, it would not be so shamed as to call what happened in New Orleans a crime. This failure to identify what happened in New Orleans as a crime is in itself criminal. Identifying conduct as a crime and prosecuting it as such do more than manage the behavior of wayward individuals. Naming conduct as criminal makes a statement about what kind of behavior is accepted and legitimate in the society, and what kind of behavior is not. By failing to treat the literal abandonment of blacks by their government as criminal behavior, the state sends the message that the African American community is not important, and that blacks are not full citizens. Thus, the victims of Katrina are forced to suffer a double mugging: one by the officials who abandoned them and one by the criminal justice system that refused to do anything about it.

"A Bus and a Boat": A Plan for Looking Out for Our Own

Our exploration of the reasons for the lack of prosecution of potential criminal conduct during Hurricane Katrina leaves us with two key observations. First, America's first response upon seeing black citizens in need was not to rush to their aid. Some aid did come in the initial hours after the storm, and a lot of that assistance could not have been provided without the heroic assistance of many white people. Yet the institutional response left the black community vulnerable; this institutional response was to stand by and act as if nothing out of the ordinary had happened at all. The second observation was that Americans can be shamed into doing right. Yet in between the standing by and the shame is a critical period in which many hundreds needlessly died.

Those of us with any sense know that America is a racist society, no matter what some blowhard talk show hosts and even the mainstream corporate media may say. We do our communities and ourselves a disservice when we fail to account for this sad reality. Katrina teaches African Americans that it is foolish, indeed dangerous, to assume that the government is going to take care of us in the event of a catastrophe. Rather than rely solely on the government, we must take steps to care for ourselves in the event that the cavalry does not come. The failure of government agencies to prepare for the occurrence of a major hurricane in the New Orleans area was grossly negligent. It was also negligent for African Americans as a community not to prepare for such an event as well, however.

African Americans in New Orleans knew that in the event of an evacuation, large numbers of black people would be without means of transportation. As tax-paying citizens, it was appropriate for them to expect that their government would make reasonable efforts to supply buses or other means of needed transportation. Yet as conscious and aware community members, they should have known that the government cannot be trusted to care for the black community. They should have had a Plan B.

African Americans do not have the resources to provide needed social services to the African American community when so many of our community members live in concentrated poverty. Thus, part of any strategy must be to do exactly what Kanye West and others did when they embarrassed, cajoled, and shamed the government into doing something about our people who were stranded in New

Orleans. That is why the community needs leaders like Jesse Jackson and Al Sharpton. These men are often maligned, but in a crisis the community needs leaders who can appropriately and effectively "play the race card" to get critical resources. Condoleezza Rice and Colin Powell were no help when Katrina struck. Even Mayor Ray Nagin was no help so long as he was "Ray-Nagin-the-corporate-executive-mayor." It was not until Mayor Nagin had a meltdown on the radio and began to sound like Al Sharpton that he started to be effective.

While African American communities do not have extensive resources, we do have some. It would not be too difficult for communities to organize ride-sharing lists on a neighborhood basis. Block captains could be assigned to determine who had rides and who needed rides. These lists could be shared with organizations within the African American community, like sororities and fraternities with members who may have available space in their cars.

An effective makeshift solution would be for community-based relief efforts to be organized around African American churches. Following Katrina, all African American churches in the Gulf Coast region should invest in a bus and a boat. Most churches should be able to raise enough money to purchase at least a van and a small skiff. Those that do not have the financial backing to do so should be able to seek foundation and corporate support. In the event of an evacuation order, buses could be used to take citizens out of the area. Following the storm, buses and boats from undamaged areas can enter the area of concern to support rescue efforts, if needed.

Certainly buses, boats, and ride sharing are not enough to address a tragedy as significant as Katrina. By necessity, the greatest obligation is on the federal government during and following catastrophes of this magnitude. Nonetheless, African Americans can and should organize to develop an alternative plan should local, state, or federal governments again shirk their responsibilities in the event of future disasters.

Notes

1. Charles Hamilton Houston, "Don't Shout Too Soon," *Crisis* 43 (1936): 14.

2. See Frederick Bancroft, *Slave Trading in the Old South* (Columbia: University of South Carolina Press, 1959), 312. For an exhaustive treatment of the New Orleans slave markets during the late enslavement period, see Walter Johnson, *Soul by Soul: Life in the Antebellum Slave Market* (Cambridge MA: Harvard University Press, 1999).

3. Alan Berube and Bruce Katz, "Katrina's Window: Confronting Concentrated Poverty across America" (Washington DC: Brookings Institution, October 2005), 1.

4. Arloc Sherman and Isaac Shapiro, "Essential Facts about the Victims of Hurricane Katrina," Center on Budget and Policy Priorities, September 19, 2005, http://www.cbpp.org/9-19-05pov.htm, 2.

5. Brookings Institution, "New Orleans after the Storm: Lessons from the Past, a Plan for the Future" (Washington DC: Brookings Institution, 2005), 6.

6. Sherman and Shapiro, "Essential Facts," 3.

7. Joe Suhayda, a retired Louisiana State University coastal engineer, quoted in Joel K. Bourne Jr., "Gone with the Water," *National Geographic Magazine*, October 2004, 1.

8. Suhayda, in Bourne, "Gone with the Water," 1.

9. Suhayda, in Bourne, "Gone with the Water," 1.

10. Mark Schleifstein and John McQuaid, "The Big One," *New Orleans Times-Picayune*, June 23, 2002, 9.

11. Schleifstein and McQuaid, "Big One," 9.

12. U.S. House of Representatives, Select Bipartisan Committee to Investigate the Preparation for and Response to Hurricane Katrina, "A Failure of Initiative: Final Report of the Select Bipartisan Committee to Investigate the Preparation for and Response to Hurricane Katrina" (Washington DC: Government Printing Office, February 19, 2006).

13. Jim Wilson, "New Orleans Is Sinking," *Popular Mechanics*, September 11, 2001, 5; Mark Fischetti, "Drowning New Orleans," *Scientific American*, October 2001, 6; Eric Berger, "Keeping Its Head above Water: New Orleans Faces Doomsday Scenario," *Houston Chronicle*, December 1, 2001, 3.

14. Spencer S. Hsu and Linton Weeks, "Officials Detailed a Dire Threat to New Orleans," *Washington Post*, March 2, 2006, A1; "Urgent Weather Message,"

National Weather Service/New Orleans, Louisiana, August 28, 2005, at 10:11 a.m.

15. "Urgent Weather Message."

16. "Urgent Weather Message."

17. *Meet the Press*, NBC News, National Broadcasting Company, transcript from September 4, 2005, http://www.msnbc.msn.com/id/9179790/.

18. Wayne R. LaFave and Austin W. Scott Jr., *Criminal Law* § 3.7(a), 2nd ed. (Toronto, Canada: Thompson, 1986); *Commonwealth v. (Barnett) Welansky*, 316 Mass. 383, 55 N.E.2nd 902 (1944).

19. *Commonwealth v. Welansky*, 909.

20. *Commonwealth v. Welansky*, 909.

21. *U.S. v. Dee*, 912 F.2d 741, 744 (4th Cir. 1990).

22. *U.S. v. Dee*.

23. *U.S. v. Dee*.

24. *State (of Delaware) v. Benton*, 187 A. 609 (Del. 1936).

25. *State v. Benton*.

26. *Meet the Press*, transcript.

27. Lisa de Moraes, "Kanye West's Torrent of Criticism, Live on NBC," *Washington Post*, September 3, 2005, C01.

28. Michael L. Radelet and Glenn L. Pierce, "Race and Prosecutorial Discretion in Homicide Cases," *Law and Society Review* 19 (1985): 587, 615–19; Martha A. Myers and John Hagan, "Private and Public Trouble: Prosecutors and the Allocation of Court Resources," *Social Problems* 26 (1979): 439, 441–47.

29. Samuel Walker et al., *The Color of Justice: Race, Ethnicity and Crime in America* (New York: Wadsworth, 2000), 186; David C. Baldus et al., "Racial Discrimination and the Death Penalty in the Post-Furman Era: An Empirical and Legal Overview, with Recent Findings from Philadelphia," *Cornell Law Review* 83 (1998): 1638, 1661 (finding evidence of race-of-victim disparities in 90 percent of states studied); David C. Baldus et al., "Comparative Review of Death Sentences: An Empirical Study of the Georgia Experience," *Journal of Criminal Law and Criminology* 74 (1983): 661; Cynthia K. Y. Lee, "Race and the Victim: An Examination of Capital Sentencing and Guilt Attribution Studies," *Chicago-Kent Law Review* 73 (1998): 533.

30. Anthony V. Alfieri, "Race Trials," *Texas Law Review* 76 (1998): 1293, 1321.

31. In an aspect of his televised criticism of President Bush that is often overlooked, Kanye West showed a remarkable insight into how media images are used to construct African Americans as criminals. He made the following impromptu comments on the award show: "I hate the way they portray us in the media. You see a black family, it says, 'They're looting.' You see a white family, it says, 'They're

looking for food.' And, you know, it's been five days [waiting for federal help] because most of the people are black. And even for me to complain about it, I would
be a hypocrite because I've tried to turn away from the TV because it's too hard to
watch. I've even been shopping before even giving a donation, so now I'm calling
my business manager right now to see what is the biggest amount I can give, and
just to imagine if I was down there, and those are my people down there. So anybody out there that wants to do anything that we can help—with the way America
is set up to help the poor, the black people, the less well-off, as slow as possible. I
mean, the Red Cross is doing everything they can. We already realize a lot of people that could help are at war right now, fighting another way—and they've given
them permission to go down and shoot us!" Lisa de Moraes, "Kanye West's Torrent of Criticism, Live on NBC," *Washington Post*, September 3, 2005, C01.

32. Stephen L. Carter, "When Victims Happen to Be Black," *Yale Law Journal* 97 (1988): 420.

NINE

Governmental Liability for the Katrina Failure

LINDA S. GREENE

Katrina's initial imagery was that of a natural disaster without a timely or comprehensive governmental response. People on rooftops awaited rescue. Ten people clung to an overturned car as the water rose. People stood on overpasses and bridges. Private citizens rescued people with battered motorboats. People waded through water and searched for food and drinking water in small boats. They waited to enter the Superdome and carried the few belongings they were able to save before the water rose over their rooftops. Hurricane Katrina survivors walked down railroad tracks. These images are the visible reminders of a disaster that left as many as 2,000 dead, 727 dead in New Orleans alone, and over one-half million people displaced. The initial impression was that an unforeseeable natural disaster had occurred, which caught local, state, and federal governments off guard. Yet just two years after this cataclysmic event, there is now substantial evidence that the havoc wreaked by Hurricane Katrina resulted from the failure of government to protect its citizens.[1]

In the aftermath of Hurricane Katrina, citizens, primarily of

New Orleans, have brought lawsuits to hold local, state, and federal governments accountable for actions before, during, and after the hurricane. In this chapter, I explore whether local, state, or federal governments may be liable for decisions that left the Louisiana coastline, and especially New Orleans, vulnerable to Hurricane Katrina. May the governments be held responsible for exacerbating Hurricane Katrina's effects? Initially I explore the mounting evidence that local, state, and federal governments acted to create the risk that tragic losses would occur in the event of a Katrina-like storm. When the storm occurred, these governments failed to act promptly to mitigate that catastrophic risk.

Next I examine the litigation mounted against state, local, and federal governments by Hurricane Katrina survivors. The governmental defendants have responded uniformly to this litigation with the defense of "governmental immunity," or "sovereign immunity," based on longstanding legal doctrines that limit the circumstances in which courts may review governmental actions. Though I write while the Katrina Litigation is at an early stage, it is clear that prospects for victim recovery will depend on whether courts accept or reject the defense of governmental immunity. Ultimately, immunity doctrines may limit the effectiveness of litigation to redress the human and economic losses due to Hurricane Katrina. Nonetheless, I conclude that this litigation is important because it provides an opportunity to reflect on the inadequacy of existing law to redress these catastrophic failures of government.

It is necessary to look beyond litigation and existing law to set standards for full redress to Hurricane Katrina victims and for governmental responsibility to protection against future catastrophic disasters. Full redress for Hurricane Katrina must include both reparation-scale measures and a reconception of the duty of government to its citizens. Thus, full redress would include compensation for tangible economic and intangible psychological injuries, resources sufficient to resurrect and reconstruct social and governmental institutions with the full participation of citizens, and protective measures that ensure that a Katrina-like governmental failure will never occur again.

The Katrina Failure

The failures of government in the context of Hurricane Katrina have been well documented. The U.S. Senate committee that investigated the Katrina Failure characterized the government performance as a "long term failure."[2] The Committee on Homeland Security observed that government officials failed to heed disaster warnings, made poor decisions before and after the hurricane hit, failed to provide effective leadership, and failed to develop the capacity to respond to catastrophic events. The result was the "tragic loss of life and human suffering on a massive scale, and an undermining of confidence in our government's ability to plan, prepare for, and respond to national catastrophes."[3] This committee noted that government officials failed the victims of Katrina.

A number of factors and errors led to the devastation of New Orleans. One of the important levee breaches that caused flooding of New Orleans at the 17th Street Canal floodwall failed due to design flaws. Three days passed before the city, state, and federal governments resolved their conflicts over authority and responsibility to repair it. A six-mile portion of the Mississippi River Gulf Outlet (MRGO), the construction of which was authorized by Congress, was constructed in a manner that increased the flow of water in the direction of New Orleans. Manmade changes in dams, the construction design of the MRGO, and natural changes in the coastland left New Orleans without the natural shelter it had from hurricanes from the eighteenth century. Drilling for oil and gas, as well as the extraction of oil, caused the land to sink and exposed the city to greater flood risk. These changes caused salt water to flood the freshwater wetlands on the coast, where vegetation normally provides protection to the coastlands from floods by absorbing water before it reaches flood stage.[4]

Moreover, two detailed reports by the U.S. Army Corps of Engineers document decades of decisions in connection with the so-called New Orleans and Southeast Louisiana Protection System. These decisions led to incomplete as well as inadequate protection for the region, over fifty breaches, and the consequent catastrophic loss of lives and property. The New Orleans Levee District, the local partner with the federal government in the Lake Pontchartrain Project to protect New Orleans against floods, knew that levees were below the height necessary to protect the city against flooding, yet used its bonding and taxing authority to pursue business rather than flood-control projects.[5]

The failure of the U.S. government to prepare for a Katrina-like storm is also well documented. Despite warnings that a Katrina-like hurricane would require meticulous and comprehensive protection and relief effort, the Federal Emergency Management Agency (FEMA) anticipated the challenge but did not prepare to meet its demands. State government delayed its response and discouraged agencies including the Red Cross from involvement. There is also ample documentation that confusion and competition among state, local, and federal governments cost lives and property.[6]

There are at least three grounds on which claim may be made that Hurricane Katrina was less a natural disaster, but rather a massive failure of government. Voluminous reports show that government did not prepare for predictable consequences of hurricane activity, including mass starvation. Moreover, the U.S. government made and authorized changes in the Mississippi Delta region to promote commerce and development that altered the environment to make the Louisiana coastline more vulnerable. As the hurricane approached this vulnerable coastline, the U.S. government, the only government with sufficient resources to respond to the hurricane's threat, failed to act in time to save lives and property after the enormity of the potential Hurricane Katrina–related disaster was evident. When the government did act, it herded hurricane survivors into confined conditions, including overpasses and convention centers, and left them without food, water, or medical attention.

Although the U.S. government has already expended more than $6 billion in aid, the aid to individuals has been limited in amount. One program provided $2,000 to Hurricane Katrina victims for their immediate emergency needs, temporary housing expenses, and real property repair and replacement, with a cap of $26,000 per person. Not surprisingly, many Hurricane Katrina survivors have concluded that these payments, as well as the government's acknowledgments of responsibility, are inadequate. They have sought redress in state and federal courts against the federal government.

The Katrina Litigation

Litigation is one predictable response to the Katrina Failure. At the time of this writing, Hurricane Katrina victims have filed thousands of lawsuits. Although some of this litigation is insurance litigation in which policyholders have sued to require insurance companies to cover Hurricane Katrina–related damages, a great deal of it concerns the responsibility of local, state, and federal governments for the human and property losses that flowed from the storm.

Some of the cases pending are wrongful death lawsuits filed against the U.S. government. In three of those lawsuits, collectively titled *Freeman v. United States Department of Homeland Security*, plaintiffs alleged that their relatives died when the federal government assumed disaster relief responsibility and then left their relatives to die. One family said that the government was negligent when it left hurricane evacuees in the Convention Center without medical care, food, or water. In another lawsuit relatives claimed that the government was negligent when it moved a man out of an assisted living home to a causeway, where he died without any medical attention. In the third case relatives also claimed the government was negligent when it rescued their relatives, transported them to the Convention Center, and then left them to die without proper emergency services. With regret, the judge dismissed the claims against the governmental defendants on the ground that rules of governmental immunity to suit protected the government defendants from lawsuits based on their Hurricane Katrina decisions.

In a lengthy decision, the court explained that the doctrines of sovereign immunity shields the U.S. government from lawsuits for damages, except where the Congress has enacted statutes that permit lawsuits against the United States, thereby waiving immunity from suit. Although the court agreed that one lawsuit was based on a federal statute that permitted a lawsuit against U.S. government officials, the Federal Tort Claims Act, the court concluded that the lawsuit could only succeed if the government failed to perform duties specifically set forth in the statute. Thus, if federal legislation imposed a vague duty on governmental officials but did not require specific actions to be undertaken, the officials may not be held *judicially* responsible for the consequences of actions or failure to act, even where the consequences of governmental action or failure to act are human fatalities.[7]

In another case Hurricane Katrina survivors have sought to hold FEMA responsible for its botched disaster relief. Here too, governmental immunity doctrines did not foreclose relief. In *McWaters v. Federal Emergency Mgmt. Agency*, the plaintiffs asserted that FEMA violated federal statutes as well as the Constitution by failing to provide the emergency housing relief authorized in federal statutes. Predictably FEMA argued that it was immune to suit under the doctrine of sovereign immunity and that its decision whether to provide aid was a discretionary activity that could not be reviewed by a court. The court disagreed, however, concluding that FEMA is "not immune from all judicial review and could be held accountable for failing to provide specific relief mandated in federal statutes." In *McWaters*, as to those duties that were unambiguously set forth in relevant statutes, such as the provision of temporary housing assistance, the court ordered that FEMA comply with those statutory provisions. The distinction between discretionary and mandatory duties did limit the relief ordered by the court, and because the federal disaster statutes did not specifically require that FEMA notify victims that disaster relief was available, the court could not hold that FEMA's decision to withhold relief information from victims violated federal law. Yet the judge seized the opportunity to chastise the federal government for its indifference to its citizens during the Katrina emergency. Even if there was no legal duty mandated by statute, argued the judge, there was a moral duty to tell Hurricane Katrina victims about their rights. The "foundations of . . . our government and FEMA itself, are individual people—human beings who must also be cared for equally, equitably, and fairly."[8]

Other Hurricane Katrina survivors sued city, state, and the federal governments for failure to warn and provide a timely evacuation. The court dismissed *Armstead v. Nagin* on governmental immunity grounds as well. The Armsteads had sued for monetary compensation from the mayor of New Orleans, the governor of Louisiana, and the president of the United States, among others. Relying on *McWaters*, the court concluded that federal sovereign immunity doctrines precluded any recovery against the federal government where the Congress allows government officials to exercise discretion in the performance of their duties. Moreover, the court concluded that under longstanding doctrine the president is immune from monetary judgments. As to the governor of the state of Louisiana, the court relied on long-standing Supreme Court decisions holding that the Eleventh Amendment to the U.S. Constitution precludes lawsuits for monetary or injunctive relief against state officials in their official capacity—at least in the absence of a specific congressional authorization for such a suit. The allegation that Governor Blanco violated the Constitution when the governor failed to provide rescue from Katrina also failed on the basis of immunity doctrine. An official may be held personally responsible for misconduct if he or she breaches a duty clearly established by law. Yet the court concluded that there is no duty to rescue that is clearly established in the rulings of federal courts, nor is there any federal law that establishes liability for the negligent performance of an official's duties. In addition, the court relied on several immunity doctrines as a basis for its dismissal of claims against the city and its officials.[9]

With one exception to date, the cases in which Katrina victims have sought relief against the government have run afoul of various governmental immunity doctrines. In one case, however, the federal court refused to accept the government's immunity claims, at least at the outset of the litigation. This lawsuit was one brought by property owners against the U.S. Army Corps of Engineers. The property owners argued that the design of the MRGO intensified the Katrina storm surge and that these design flaws—not Katrina itself—caused the loss of their property. Here, the court concluded that the Army Corps of Engineers, which constructed the MRGO, was not immune from lawsuits for its design decisions. Although federal statutes do explicitly extend the shield of immunity to the federal government for flood control projects, the court concluded that statutory governmental immunity did not extend to projects designed to ease navigation. The MRGO was a navigation project that Congress did not shield with a specific grant of governmental immunity. In order to ensure that its decision would not be misread, the court warned that its decision was a preliminary one that did not hold that the federal government must pay damages for the intensification of the storm surge attributable to the MRGO design. In addition, the court also warned that there might be other immunity doctrines that might protect the federal government from damage liability even if its MRGO decisions caused harm.[10]

The question of U.S. governmental responsibility for Hurricane Katrina has also arisen in other cases in which Hurricane Katrina survivors sued insurance companies that refused to pay claims for Hurricane Katrina–related property losses. In these cases the insurance companies have argued that their policies excluded payment for losses due to flooding. Those who have suffered losses have argued that their losses are not due to flooding, but rather are due to the negligence of the Army Corps of Engineers and its poor maintenance of levees and canals. Trial courts have thus far refused to dismiss the cases in their early stages, thereby allowing the claimants an opportunity to prove their cases. Although these lawsuits will not result in federal government liability for Hurricane Katrina–related losses, they will involve litigation identifying federal governmental responsibility for damage from Hurricane Katrina.[11]

As these cases show, there are many obstacles to holding government and its officials responsible for Hurricane Katrina–related damage. Doctrines of immunity protect governmental defendants from litigation over the exercise of their responsibilities. Only responsibilities defined in mandatory terms may provide a basis for recovery, and courts have been unwilling to interpret the Constitution to require an affirmative duty of protection to its citizens. There is faint hope that litigation against local, state, or federal government will provide redress for the human and economic losses. No matter what the outcome of these myriad lawsuits, Hurricane Katrina litigation has revealed the limitations of judicial relief for government failures with catastrophic consequences. There is a renewed debate about the legitimacy of immunity doctrines that shield the government from damage suits, as well as the extent of any constitutional protection when the government fails to act to prevent or redress harm to its citizens.[12]

The judicial response to cases in which citizens seek to hold the government liable for Hurricane Katrina–related losses is understandable, as lower courts are bound by longstanding preexisting doctrine. These doctrines developed to preserve the division of authority between the courts and the legislature by limiting the circumstances in which the judiciary can commit the financial resources of the local, state, or federal governments. Immunity doctrines are also based on concerns that court supervision of the executive branch would intrude on that branch. These doctrines transfer the authority to carry out the laws to the courts. Both of these bases for governmental immunity doctrines are long-standing. Although these preliminary cases show that the courts have been willing to enforce those federal statutory obligations that are stated in very specific terms, such as an entitlement to temporary housing assistance, a range of immunity doctrines will prevent courts from becoming a forum in which Hurricane Katrina grievances are aired and redressed.

Our democracy rests on the assumption that citizens authorize the government to act in a manner that will produce results that advance the common good. Yet the governmental actions before, during, and after Hurricane Katrina suggest that concern for the common good did not include concern about the potential loss of life along the Gulf Coast, and in New Orleans specifically. In particular, the elimination of governmental immunity doctrines, or the curtailment of them in the context of the Katrina Failure, would encourage government to invest in safety measures and vigorously protect citizens in the event of catastrophic disasters.

Immunity doctrines aside, there are legitimate questions regarding whether courts, rather than legislatures, are the right institutions to address the consequences of the Katrina Failure. Government decisions that contributed to the vulnerability of the Gulf Coast span decades and involve many thousands of actors at all levels of government: local, state, and federal. In addition, court processes involve an adversarial system in which plaintiffs are pitted against defendants in a contest over both facts and the appropriate relief. Such litigation is costly and lengthy; in effect the government defendants pass the costs of such litigation on to their citizens, while the citizen plaintiffs, some of whom are the plaintiffs in the lawsuits, must bear their own costs. The courts' conclusions in an individual lawsuit would not address all the Hurricane Katrina facts, nor all the consequences of Hurricane Katrina, but rather the limited facts and issues presented to the court in that particular lawsuit. Even if courts do provide relief for specific claims, the results in those lawsuits will not represent full redress for the Katrina Failure given the far-reaching, long-enduring consequences.

The results of the government's Katrina Failure far exceed loss of more than two thousand lives and hundreds of billions of dollars' worth of property. Over one million people are displaced from the Gulf Coast region to every state of the Union. That so many have lost all hope is manifest in the tripling of the New Orleans suicide rate, post–Hurricane Katrina. Virtually all of the social structure of New Orleans, as well as that of other communities, including churches, shops, places of employment, schools, music venues, parks, barbershops, was destroyed. Government, and citizen participation in government, all but ended. Moreover, the actions of the government before, during, and after Katrina destroyed the bond of trust that existed between citizens and their government. Even if courts are able to address specific questions of governmental responsibility that are not foreclosed by immunity doctrines, courts cannot provide full redress for these consequences.

The Katrina lawsuits do address the human and economic losses to which government action contributed, but their scope is inadequate to restore all that has been lost. In addition, the governmental response to litigation that challenges the legitimacy of the judicial action threatens to leave unanswered fundamental questions about governmental responsibility to citizens. Does the government owe an obligation to protect its citizens from harm due to foreseeable dangers that citizens are unable to address? Should the government have a duty to act to lessen the consequences of catastrophic disasters such as Hurricane Katrina? Does the government owe an obligation to compensate individuals and communities whose losses are directly attributable to governmental action or neglect? Is government obligated to undertake the reconstruction of communities—along with their social institutions—as a result of governmental failures? In order to fully address the question of government responsibility to its citizens, it is necessary to look beyond current law and litigation for ideas broad enough to redress the Katrina Failure.

Transitional Justice after Katrina?

In the aftermath of the moral and legal failures that allow a mass killing, called genocide, to occur, more than the assignment of blame or the conviction of war criminals is necessary to address the wrongs that have occurred. The prosecution of war criminals is an important symbolic act in a transition from conflict to peace, because it sends a clear signal about right and wrong. The prosecution of individuals may also send the message that the assignment of blame to an individual is a sufficient response to crimes against humanity. The idea of *transitional justice* addresses a range of activities that are necessary to reconstruct society in the transition from the past. The assignment of blame to individuals, and their punishment, is an important part of that transitional process.

Yet holding an individual responsible may not address the societal context that made the genocide possible, such as governmental indifference to life or disrespect for a particular ethnic group. For example, after the 1994 Rwanda Hutu massacre of over one million Tutsi tribe members, over one hundred thousand Hutu individuals were charged with war crimes. These criminal trials are ongoing. It is understood by those involved in Rwanda peacemaking, however, that these criminal trials may hold individuals accountable without addressing the historical circumstances, the long-standing distrust between the two tribes, the breakdown in government authority, or the indifference of the international community that made such a shocking and brutal genocide possible. In that context, full redress for the Rwandan genocide and the prevention of future atrocity require more than the prosecution of individuals, although individual prosecution may be important to punish and deter future genocide. It will require greater economic and political participation, restoration of property to those who fled the genocide, initiative to promote peaceful coexistence of Hutus with Tutsis, public education to eliminate misunderstanding and to communicate the changes underway, and enhanced regional and international relief and peacekeeping efforts, among a few possibilities.[13]

This comprehensive approach is known in international law as transitional justice.[14] Transitional justice encompasses the action a government takes to pave the way for a new understanding about human rights, justice, and equality. A new understanding is necessary because tolerance of widespread suffering and violence are the result of a community's values, not simply the result of the individual's action or inaction. Likewise, the individuals and the community are harmed. Transitional justice refers to the processes, or steps, that are necessary in order to heal the community and establish a new system of values. In order to establish this new system of values, it is necessary to take on the past head on: "to master the past." In this process we learn the truth about the past, determine who is responsible for the injuries that occurred, and offer some form of redress.[15] In this view "mastering the past" requires more than the assignment of blame and civil or criminal processes of accountability. The aim is to "contribute to the creation of a community based on freedom, equality, human dignity, and respect for the right to diversity."[16] Transitional justice demands restoration through multiple institutions and aspects of society.

Similarly, in the post–Hurricane Katrina context, "mastering the past" requires more than an examination and elimination of the technical engineering flaws that led to the human disaster. A full response to the Hurricane Katrina disaster would involve a close examination in public of those institutions, conditions, and forces that contributed to the catastrophe. For example, how were the needs and interests of the people who died in the Hurricane Katrina disaster represented in local, state, and federal government decision-making processes? What were the interests that may have contributed to the systematic neglect of the flood protection system infrastructure? What role did wealth, race, and politics play in the decisions that contributed to the disaster before, during, and after Hurricane Katrina? What were the values and principles relied on by government?

The haunting images of people left to fend for themselves without food, water, or medical care suggest that principles of respect for human dignity were abandoned. Though many thousands of pages have been written about the factors that led to such catastrophic lost of life and property, the people most affected, many of whom are displaced across the United States, have not been involved in the examination processes. In this respect the indifference that is represented in the government decision making that led to the disaster is replicated in the examination of the disaster. In this process of examination, it may be possible to identify the moral environment that made the governmental indifference possible. Going forward to address the construction of the future, with an affirmative commitment to human dignity and equality, would be the standard against which redress efforts are judged.

The examination of root causes of the disaster would form a basis for the reconstruction of the physical, social, and political institutions. As noted earlier, those institutions include religious, fraternal, recreational, cultural, social, political, and governmental institutions. This reconstruction requires not only economic resources necessary to restore the places in which people gather, but the human resources necessary to support and sustain these institutions until they are self-sustaining. As to the political institutions that failed the Hurricane Katrina victims, redress will not be complete until there is a quality of active citizen political participation that ensures the alignment of government decisions with human needs. Redress must include satisfaction of not only basic human needs of shelter, food, education, health care, and transportation, but also the economic and educational resources to enable vigorous political participation. As to those who have been displaced, effective measures would include economic and psychological support to ensure their return and their reintegration into the political and social community. The complete reconstruction of civic society requires the establishment of citizenship capacity, so that citizens can form their own views about the responsibilities of their governments, participate in government, and hold government officials accountable.

After Hurricane Katrina: A Responsibility to Protect?

An important part of the process of redress is the repair and reconstruction of the physical flood protection system and the design of more effective governmental rescue and relief measures for future catastrophes. This process is already underway. Yet before the government can conceptualize the scope of its responsibility to repair the past and prepare for the future, it must embrace a principle that establishes the scope of its duty. If the government acknowledged a *responsibility to protect* its citizens, we would have a basis to measure the scope of the Katrina Failure and the adequacy of the governments' response to Katrina. The idea of a responsibility to protect is sourced in the international law of humanitarian intervention. The law of humanitarian intervention involves the circumstances under which a government or international organization may enter a country to protect the people of that country from harm, usually due to violent conflict.[17]

The scope of a responsibility to protect doctrine has been debated in many contexts that are familiar: Liberia, Rwanda, Bosnia, and, more recently, Darfur. Although the international circumstances of these conflicts differ from the circumstances of Hurricane Katrina, the principles that undergird the idea of a responsibility to protect in international law may be relevant as a measure of the government's duty to its citizens in the context of Hurricane Katrina. Those principles include the basic responsibility of governments to protect the safety and lives of citizens and to promote their welfare, as well as the idea that governments are responsible and accountable for their actions as well as their failure to act. Put another way, governments have the responsibility to "respect the dignity and basic rights of all the people within the state."[18] Reframing the post–Hurricane Katrina debate in terms of the government's responsibility to protect its citizens provides a basis for the evaluation of the Katrina Failure as well as a measure to judge the adequacy of governmental effort to prepare for future catastrophic events.[19]

It is not clear what standard will be used by the state, local, and federal governments to measure the effectiveness of future disaster protection and relief efforts. The reports of the Army Corps of Engineers on the decades of decision making that led to an incomplete flood protection system provided a chronology of that decision making but did not set a standard to be met by future systems. The past demonstrated that governments were willing to accept the risk that lives would be lost in the event of serious hurricanes. The decision by government to undertake the improvement of the flood warning, protection, and relief system that failed deserves praise: the consequences of past failures require an immediate response. Yet unless the planned improvements are designed and tested against a standard that ensures protection for respect of human existence, the government has not acknowledged its "responsibility to protect."[20]

Rethinking Citizenship

Whatever the outcome of Hurricane Katrina litigation against the government, one result of the Katrina Failure will be a closer examination of laws and legal doctrines that immunize government from responsibility for its deliberate disregard of legal duties or its failure to exercise due care when performing its governmental functions. That reexamination is underway, as Hurricane Katrina survivors as well as scholars raise questions about the legitimacy of governmental immunity doctrines that limit accountability of government actors for harms to their citizens. In addition, local, state, and federal government agencies will continue to evaluate their inadequate preparation and response to the Katrina Failure, identifying "lessons learned," making disaster response system improvements, and rebuilding the physical and institutional infrastructure of protection against hurricane threats. These are necessary but insufficient developments.

These developments are insufficient because the Katrina Failure cost more than lives or property. This failure was also a failure of government. Government did not fulfill its fundamental responsibility to protect its citizens, and its failure to protect was systemic, pervasive, and long-standing. The Katrina Failure exposed the government's indifference to human life and dignity, thereby disrupting the trust and confidence in government that is the foundation of strong democratic institutions. Therefore, the Katrina Failure raises a fundamental question: what measures must be undertaken to restore the legitimacy of government as well as the capacity of citizens to hold government accountable for the fulfillment of its basic responsibility to those citizens? Rhetoric about the importance of restoring faith in democratic institutions may often ring hollow, but in the context of the Katrina Failure, the ring must be true. The litigation over that responsibility will continue, and there is still the prospect that some redress will come from the courts, but the judiciary cannot provide full redress in view of the limited conception of governmental duty encompassed in current law as well as the limited capacity of courts to redress the consequences.

The incorporation of ideas from international law would ensure a solid foundation for Hurricane Katrina redress. The transitional justice framework would require a thorough examination of the physical and moral circumstances that created the tragedy. In addition, the framework would focus on economic and other means of support to restore and empower individuals and community institutions, as well as the establishment of increased citizen participation in government. This framework would hold governmental bodies more responsive to the basic human needs of citizens. In addition, governments at all levels should explicitly embrace "a responsibility to protect," measuring the adequacy of future preparation and relief efforts against a standard fiercely protective of human life and dignity. Efforts that fall short of these standards will leave in place the circumstances that produced the Katrina Failure.

Notes

1. See KatrinaDestruction.com http://www.katrinadestruction.com/images/v/ survivors/; photo, "Rooftop, New Orleans," www.ehponline.org/.../2006/114-10/ katrina_AP.jpg; photo, "Trapped by Floodwaters, New Orleans, AP/Wide World Photo," www.boingboing.net/images/taleoftwocities_2.jpg; photo, "People standing

on the overpasses and bridges to get out of the New Orleans floodwaters, New Orleans, Louisiana, August 31, 2005," http://www.katrinadestruction.com/images/v/survivors/people+on+overpasses.html; photo, "People who did not evacuate walk through the New Orleans floodwaters to get to higher ground, New Orleans, Louisiana, August 30, 2005," http://www.katrinadestruction.com/images/v/hurricane/SIP0515508-surreall-scene.html. Also see photo, "Survivors Search for Food and Water, New Orleans, Louisiana," http://www.katrinadestruction.com/images/v/billingscr/Survivors+search+for+food+and+water.jpg.html; photo, "Residents are bringing their belongings and lining up to get into the Superdome, New Orleans, Louisiana, August 28, 2005," http://www.katrinadestruction.com/images/v/survivors/14371-afterw.jpg.html; photo, "Evacuees, carrying what few possessions they were able to save from the floodwaters of Katrina, exit a rescue helicopter," http://www.katrinadestruction.com/images/v/survivors/14533w.jpg.html; photo, "Hurricane Katrina survivor image of folks walking down railroad tracks, New Orleans, Louisiana, August 31, 2005," http://www.katrinadestruction.com/images/v/survivors/17kd271-katrina-images.html; U.S. Army Corps of Engineers, Interagency Performance Evaluation Task Force, "Performance Evaluation of the New Orleans Southeast Louisiana Hurricane Protection System," Executive Summary and Overview, American Society of Civil Engineers, vol. 1, March 26, 2007, 55; (1,600–2,000 fatalities); "The New Orleans Hurricane Protection System: What Went Wrong and Why," Report by the American Society of Civil Engineers Hurricane Katrina External Review Panel (Reston VA: American Society of Civil Engineers, 2007) (estimated 1,330 dead); U.S. Senate, Committee on Homeland Security and Governmental Affairs, "Hurricane Katrina: A Nation Still Unprepared," S. Rpt. 109-322, 2006, 2 (more than 1,500 dead); U.S. White House, "The Federal Response to Hurricane Katrina: Lessons Learned," 2006, 1 (over 1,330 dead).

2. Army Corps of Engineers, "Performance Evaluation"; "New Orleans Hurricane Protection System"; U.S. Senate, Committee on Homeland Security, "Hurricane Katrina"; U.S. White House, "Federal Response"; Douglas Kysar and Thomas McGarity, "Did NEPA Drown New Orleans? The Levees, the Blame Game, and the Hazards of Hindsight," *Duke Law Journal* 56 (2006): 179.

3. U.S. Senate, Committee on Homeland Security, ""Hurricane Katrina."

4. U.S. Senate, Committee on Homeland Security, ""Hurricane Katrina."

5. U.S. Army Corps of Engineers, "Decision Making Chronology for the Lake Pontchartrain and Vicinity Hurricane Protection—Draft Final Report," 2007; see also U.S. Army Corps of Engineers, Interagency Performance Evaluation Task Force, "Performance Evaluation," 2007.

6. Douglas Brinkley, *The Great Deluge: Hurricane Katrina, New Orleans, and the Mississippi Gulf Coast* (New York: William Morrow, 2006), 618; see also Christopher Cooper and Robert Block, *Disaster: Hurricane Katrina and the Failure of*

Homeland Security (New York: Times Books, 2006); Nathan Smith, "Water, Water Everywhere, and Not a Bite to Eat: Sovereign Immunity, Federal Disaster Relief, and Hurricane Katrina," *San Diego Law Review* 43 (2006): 699.

7. *Freeman v. United States Department of Homeland Security*, C.A. No: 06-4846 C/W 06-5689 & 06-5696 SECTION: "A" (5), D.C. E.D. La, 2007 U.S. Dist. LEXIS 31827, April 30, 2007.

8. *McWaters v. Federal Emergency Mgmt. Agency*, 436 F. Supp. 2d 802 (E.D. La. 2006).

9. *McWaters v. Federal Emergency Mgmt. Agency*, 101.

10. *In re Katrina Canal Breaches Consolidated Litigation*, 471 F. Supp. 2d 684, (E.D. La. 2007). Unless Congress otherwise states, the federal government may not be held responsible for decisions that involve the exercise of discretion or the making of policy. On the other hand, the government may be held responsible for failure to perform a mandatory duty set forth in a statute or a regulation. One question will be whether there were specific duties that the Army Corps of Engineers failed to perform that caused the MRGO to flood New Orleans.

11. *Axis Reinsurance Company v. Lanza*, No 05-6318 Section: J(3), 2007 U.S. Dist. LEXIS 22976, March 29, 2007).

12. See Nathan Smith, "Water, Water Everywhere," 699 (citing the duty to provide food to Katrina victims was not discretionary, but mandatory).

13. John Prendergast and David Smock, "Post-Genocidal Reconstruction: Building Peace in Rwanda and Burundi," Special Report no. 53, United States Institute of Peace, September 15, 1999, http://www.usip.org/pubs/specialreports/sr990915.html.

14. Ruti G. Teitel, *Transitional Justice* (New York: Oxford University Press, 2000).

15. Nenad Dimitrjevic, "Moral Responsibility for Collective Crime: Transitional Justice in the Former Yugoslavia," *Eurozine*, May 7, 2006, http://www.euro zine.com/articles/2006-07-05-dimitrijevic-en.html.

16. Dimitrjevic, "Moral Responsibility for Collective Crime."

17. Gareth Evans, "The Responsibility to Protect and the Duty to Protect," *American Society of International Law* 98 (2004): 77.

18. Jeremy Levitt, "The Responsibility to Protect: A Beaver without a Dam? Review of *The Responsibility to Protect*, by the International Commission on Intervention and State Sovereignty, and *The Responsibility to Protect: Research, Bibliography, Background*, by Thomas G. Weiss and Don Hubert (supp. vol. to *The Responsibility to Protect*), *Michigan Journal of International Law* 25 (2003): 153.

19. Gareth Evans and Mahomed Sahnoun, "The Responsibility to Protect: Rethinking Humanitarian Intervention," *Foreign Affairs* 81 (2002): 99.

20. John Schwartz, "One Billion Dollars Later, A City Still at Risk," *New York Times*, August 17, 2007, A1.

TEN

Katrina, Race, Refugees, and Images of the Third World

RUTH GORDON

Katrina, a Category 3 hurricane, hit land for the second time near the Louisiana-Mississippi border with sustained winds of 120 miles per hour on August 25, 2005. In its aftermath there was catastrophe, for the next day the levees that were to protect New Orleans from the waters of Lake Pontchartrain failed, and the waters rushed in. An old, historic, unique, and simply remarkable city was literally under water. Pictures of the flooded city were startling, indeed astonishing, for great cities are rarely so completely felled in one swift stroke. Yet the images that were to follow proved to be just as shocking, perhaps more so because in the aftermath of this dreadful disaster, another tragedy with even more far-reaching consequences was about to unfold. To our collective shock and amazement, television screens showed thousands of people in quite desperate straits, stranded in a now submerged city. People were marooned in their homes, on rooftops, and in a filthy, uninhabitable sports stadium. The streets were strewn with decomposed bodies, and residents were seen wading through waters that were polluted, disease-ridden, and riddled with oil from nearby refineries.

Thousands were in need of the most fundamental of basic necessities, including food, shelter, water, and rudimentary sanitation; they were also overwhelmingly black and obviously poor. Even more outrageously, the U.S. government seemed overwhelmed, hapless, helpless, and completely ineffectual.[1]

As these images splashed across American and international television screens, the public recoiled and then seethed with anger and startled disbelief. The bungling incompetence demonstrated by the Federal Emergency Management Agency (FEMA) was simply beyond the pale. It bespoke an ineptitude and lack of skill that most thought did not exist in the "can do" nation of the United States; yet there it was in the starkest terms for all to witness. Despite the so-called movement for small government, it seemed that Americans of almost all political stripes still expected presence and proficiency from the federal government during natural disasters. The public felt collective outrage, embarrassment, and perhaps shame.[2]

Still, this scenario seemed vaguely familiar, even if a bit out of kilter. Masses of impoverished, distressed, and distraught people of color, especially black people, were left to plead for assistance during other disasters; such spectacles have often graced American and international television screens. What was askew was that these were Americans. It was simply unacceptable, indeed shocking, for American nationals and even the most despised of America's citizens to be treated like this populace. Commentators and reporters quickly discerned such parallels and began to refer to Katrina's wounded as refugees, and New Orleans as a Third World country. These terms were viewed as unquestionably pejorative, and an uproar ensued, with the loudest objections emanating from those designated as leaders of the African American community. They charged racism. Surely their response was, at least in part, an expression of the anger and indignation regarding the unfolding inhumane treatment of American citizens by the American government, and racism was undoubtedly at the heart of this lack of response. Nevertheless, these charges also struck this author as an unambiguous declaration of how negatively we view the Third World and its peoples. While it is predictable that the U.S. media and American analysts would share this unfavorable viewpoint, it seemed that few of us, even progressive people of color, realized or thought about our position in this particularly objectionable discourse regarding those we used to call our brothers and sisters. It seemed our solidarity with the peoples of the Third World had fractured or at least was transformed in some way, even as some of those nations offered sympathy as well as financial and other assistance.[3]

This chapter explores this disconnect, or perhaps one should say connect, for as this author has opined elsewhere, "Third World" is a derogatory term in the twenty-first century. It seems that the term "refugee" has also now attained this unenviable status, at least in the United States. This terminology along with "underdeveloped," "undeveloped," and, more recently, "developing" quite often substitutes for black, colored, impoverished, downtrodden, and, indisputably and incontestably, inferior. These terms often signify gloomy, shadowy, and quite terrible places that not even the darkest and most cast-off Americans inhabit. The discourse that emerged in the aftermath of the particularly American tragedy of Katrina can help us explore how race plays out in images of the Third World, the underdeveloped, and the impoverished, and allow us to think about how African Americans are situated within this particular cauldron.[4]

Before we begin probing these issues, however, a caveat is in order. In discussing my thoughts for this chapter, colleagues and friends often had the impression, at least initially, that I was critical of Katrina victims. Nothing could be further from the truth. Indeed, this sojourn is more about the utter disregard and disrespect for impoverished peoples the world over, and for people who are, more often than not, colored people. It is my hope that we can reclaim our solidarity with those I believe are the definitively dispossessed and realize our commonalities rather than our differences.

Part I: Katrina and Its Aftermath

Natural and Unnatural Disaster

Katrina initially hit the United States twice, first striking Florida as a category 1 storm that packed winds of 80 miles per hour, and then moving into the Gulf of Mexico. The storm, all the while gathering in strength over the warm waters of the Gulf, headed back toward the U.S. coast. This time it traveled toward Louisiana and Mississippi; local and federal officials began taking various steps, such as declaring impending disaster areas, ordering FEMA and Homeland Security to prepare, and dispatching National Guard troops. The mayor of New Orleans ordered a voluntary evacuation, and residents of low-lying areas were encouraged to leave. As the authorities well knew, however, many of these residents lacked the resources to comply. The day before Katrina struck the United States its second time, it strengthened to a Category 5 storm with winds up to 160 miles per hour. Federal officials were briefed on the possibility that the levees protecting New Orleans might be breached. Issues including the possibility of catastrophic harm and the potential for a major disaster were raised. The mayor of New Orleans ordered a mandatory evacuation and announced that Regional Transit Authority buses would pick up people in twelve locations around New Orleans to take them to places of refuge and to the New Orleans Superdome.[5]

Katrina made landfall on Monday, August 29, as a Category 3 hurricane measuring 400 miles wide, with an eye 30 miles wide and maximum sustained winds of 121 miles per hour. At first, the city and nation breathed a sign of relief, believing the levees had weathered the storm. The New Orleans' levees were designed by the Army Corps of Engineers to withstand a Category 3 hurricane storm surge. When Katrina made landfall as a Category 3 storm, many mistakenly thought the worst was over. Flooding began in the Ninth Ward, a predominantly black area, as the levees were penetrated; floodwaters soon reached 6 to 8 feet. By Monday, 80 percent of the city was underwater, and some places were under as much as 20 feet of water.[6]

Katrina was a natural disaster, a hurricane whose strength and path could not be controlled by human forces. Indeed, Katrina is the largest natural disaster in U.S. history, surpassing even the 1906 San Francisco earthquake and ensuing firestorm. Like San Francisco, New Orleans experienced two distinct disasters: first, wind and water damage caused by the hurricane and second, flooding caused by several levee breaks. Unlike the San Francisco earthquake of 1906, however, New Orleans' vulnerabilities were well known, and it is here that the manmade part of the disaster exacerbated an already difficult situation. The flooding of New Orleans was very much a manmade catastrophe that led to many deaths and the destruction of many lives.[7]

Prelude to Calamity

As Isabel Medina, one of the thousands who fled New Orleans, has opined, "Natural disasters do not discriminate on the basis of race, color, gender or wealth and in this regard, Katrina was no different from other natural disasters."[8] Yet what transpired before and in the aftermath of the storm had plenty to do with human intervention, and much to do with race, color, and affluence. The abject poverty that characterized pre-Katrina New Orleans was created by an utter disregard for "basic human rights such as education, food, a healthy and secure environment, access to health care, housing and decent employment."[9] These conditions were entirely human choices that presaged the devastating impact of the hurricane's disaster on the underserved residents of New Orleans, as well as other areas of Louisiana and Mississippi. Nearly one-fifth of the population most affected by the hurricane lived in poverty before Katrina, and one in three living in the hardest-hit areas was African American.[10]

The failures and callous disregard for the welfare of the impoverished, largely black, residents of New Orleans in the wake of the hurricane was and continues to be so massive and so overwhelming that it is difficult to know where to begin; I begin with the levees. The low-lying areas of the city were the "most dependent on the network of concrete walls and levees that failed to hold back floodwaters. Yet, despite the dangerous vulnerability poor areas of the city faced, the levees were inadequately maintained and local authorities had no warning system in place in case of their breach."[11] These vulnerabilities developed over decades, with numerous missed opportunities to address such issues, due to inadequate maintenance of the levees, or to regulate development along the coast to mitigate wind damage and surges from major storms.[12]

Moreover, the specific consequences of a levee breach were known and described in numerous governmental reports, media accounts, and academic studies. Indeed, federal, state, and local emergency management authorities concluded a training exercise one year prior to Katrina to study the potential aftermath of such a disaster and concluded that the aftermath would likely lead to a catastrophic event. The scale of the disaster that would result from a powerful hurricane was hardly a surprise. Nonetheless, pre-storm planning was unusually weak, with the biggest gap made manifest in inadequate preparations to evacuate the poorest members of the New Orleans community, despite governmental awareness of the potential for devastating floods and the inability of poor residents to evacuate. Given the extraordinarily bad pre-storm planning, it

231

is not surprising that the actual response to the disaster was overwhelmingly deplorable.[13]

The Response and Its Aftermath

When Katrina struck and the city flooded, government institutions at all levels independently and collectively failed the citizens of New Orleans. Local authorities made poor decisions regarding mass evacuations and mass shelter. Local emergency management and response agencies were soon overwhelmed and often relegated to saving themselves or releasing personnel to save their own families; in many cases local governmental institutions were simply shattered. At the state level, officials were slow to realize the scale of the disaster, and state resources were not deployed quickly. State and local emergency management programs were not up to the task of evacuating residents, sheltering and feeding those who remained, conducting search and rescue operations, or initiating the recovery effort. Federal authorities were slow to respond to state requests for aid and were justifiably criticized for their reactive posture as they waited for aid requests. Moreover, once the need was realized, federal agencies were painfully slow to deliver: "Poor implementation of emergency plans, poor communication and poor decision processes were evident in the lack of congruence between conditions on the ground in the disaster areas and local, state and national decision making."[14] As a result of monumental bungling at all levels, thousands of victims were not rescued. They also received no aid for more than a week after Katrina hit.[15]

Surely the residents of New Orleans believed help would materialize with water, food, tents, and other necessities soon after the storm passed. When this did not happen, FEMA director Michael Brown became the symbol of the botched response as the federal breakdown was surely the most egregious, given the scale of the disaster and presumed federal capabilities. Yet there were severe deficiencies at all steps along the way, from city hall to the White House. At a minimum, the citizens of New Orleans who could not evacuate by their own means needed the government to provide transportation out of the vicinity of peril and sufficient lodging until they could return to their homes. Instead, transportation was nonexistent, and citizens were herded to three locations throughout the city, termed shelters of last resort, including the New Orleans Superdome and the New Orleans Convention Center. It is an understatement to note that conditions in these facilities were horrendous. The heat was overbearing, sanitation was nonexistent, and there was no power or adequate food. Meanwhile, corpses floated in the streets, and people waded through neighborhoods inundated with dreadfully polluted waters as they foraged for the bare necessities of life.[16]

The appalling response in the wake of Katrina and the debacles of the Superdome and Convention Center violated the fundamental human rights of our fellow citizens. The Katrina catastrophe was to some degree shaped by economic disparities, even as the storm destroyed multiple areas of the city. The more affluent, who could marshal resources, managed to escape, while those without means were unable to flee and consequently were caught in the cauldron that was to follow. The poor and dispossessed were left to the vagaries of an incompetent government and thus were the chief victims. The face of poverty in New Orleans, as in much of the United States, divides along racial lines. Even as poor whites, Vietnamese, and Latino residents endured this hell, the desperate faces that much of America and the world witnessed were African American. There were relentless pictures of African Americans on rooftops surrounded by flooded streets, which were often strewn with decomposed bodies, pollution, and oil from nearby refineries, and were presumed to be disease-ridden because sewer and all other systems were inundated. The desperation largely had a very black face; we saw black mothers with babies begging for food and help, and the covered corpses of black grandmothers.[17]

Then again, perhaps we should not be shocked by the disparities witnessed in the aftermath of Katrina, for disparate treatment in these circumstances has been rather routine in America. While natural disasters are inevitable and beyond the force of human beings, their aftermath is very much human created and human directed, and in America, that aftermath is often driven by racism. In chronicling the regularity of discrimination and disparate treatment of minority communities in the wake of natural and unnatural disasters, Katrina revealed that disaster response is no different from the remainder of the American landscape. Thus, perhaps we should not have been so surprised at the fates of Katrina's victims. Indeed, if not for the enormity of the crisis and twenty-four-hour news coverage, perhaps it too would have been lost to history. Nevertheless, we did observe it, and it was larger and worse than any such disaster we had witnessed in our lifetimes. We were stunned and we were bewildered.[18]

Public Reaction

Katrina challenged the nation to examine aspects of society that we prefer to hide. As one commentator noted, "Hurricane Katrina cast stark and embarrassing attention on a side of the U.S. that most Americans do not care to confront."[19] This outright poverty and stark inequality are the underbelly of American society, and the spotlight illuminating them after the storm was glaring and continuous. The "Other America" was plastered across American and international television screens, becoming the only news story in America and containing perhaps the most dramatic, disturbing, and quite shocking images of African American poverty and disenfranchisement in several generations. Outrage at what unfolded on television screens built to a crescendo. Indeed, even members of the media began to step outside of their purported neutrality to call on the government, especially the federal government, to do something, anything, to help these people.

Certainly part of the exceedingly negative reaction developed because we assumed that a nation as wealthy and resourceful as the United States would be ready, willing, and able to respond, and respond effectively, to the needs of its citizens in the face of a natural disaster of any size, including one on the scale of the flooding of New Orleans. Thus, many recoiled at the sheer incompetence of the U.S. government and were especially troubled and alarmed at its ineptitude, given that the attacks on U.S. soil on September 11, 2001, purportedly fostered greater preparation for disasters. African Americans, however, quickly concluded that the shocking level of ineffectiveness was due to the race of those in need. Although white Americans generally disagreed, many African Americans attributed the grossly inadequate response to racism, pure and simple. They believed that if white people were in such desperate straits, the government's response would be drastically different and much better executed; indeed, it did seem the response was different when it came to white communities.[20]

Nonetheless, for all the shock and outrage, the images, in fact, were vaguely familiar, if somehow askew. They appeared to be images from a Third World country, where misery and disorder seem to be almost commonplace and expected. Though disturbing events take place regularly, they usually do not occur in the United States. Members of the press share and in fact perpetuate such perceptions of the Third World. They soon began to refer to the scenes emanating from New Orleans as something from a Third World country. They also began to refer to Katrina's victims as refugees. The term suddenly took on a life, albeit a new life, of its own.[21]

The response to the term "refugee" was swift and decisive. To put it mildly, another hell broke loose, and a new debate exploded.

The Reverend Jesse Jackson declared, "It is racist to call American citizens refugees."[22] The National Association of Black Journalists called on news organizations to ban the use of the term. President George W. Bush took offense as well, maintaining that those impacted are Americans, not refugees. Others argued that the term "refugee" applies only to those who have crossed an international border, and that "internally displaced persons" would be more appropriate. A debate erupted in the media over whether it was appropriate to refer to Katrina victims as "refugees." As one journalist put it, "A few days after Katrina struck, refugees woke up to find that the term had become a slur."[23] Many news outlets decided to discontinue employing the word and replaced it with "victim" or "evacuee." MSNBC, for example, explained, "There was a sense in the word 'refugee' that it somehow made these United States citizens, people who live in Louisiana and Mississippi, into aliens or foreigners or something less than they are."[24] Evidently refugees were something less than Americans, and even fleeing, poor, black, desperate Americans could not occupy that particular space. Other media outlets, however, continued to use the term "refugee." A representative of the Associated Press noted, "Several hundred thousand people have been uprooted from their homes and communities and forced to seek refuge in more than 30 different states across America. Until such time as they are able to take up new lives in their new communities or return to their former homes, they will be refugees."[25] This more benign view of the term may have been technically correct, if we take the word out of its international legal context. Yet one wonders why the term was not applied to those on the Mississippi coast or to white refugees. Is it that refugees must be people of color: poor, miserable and abandoned by their government?[26]

The term "refugee" was also intertwined with the Third World, for it seemed that is where one finds refugees. One man, who was interviewed outside the Baton Rouge Convention Center as it housed 5,000 displaced residents, objected to being called a refugee, stating, "The image I have in my mind is people in a Third World country, the babies in Africa that have all the flies and are starving to death. . . . That's not me. I'm a law-abiding citizen who's working every day and paying taxes."[27] He was not alone; it seemed many saw refugees as Third World people, poor people, the ultimate abject "other." Similarities between the storm's victims and refugees from the Third World hint at an America that cannot take care of its citizens. Suddenly America appeared to be too much like the incompetent, ill-advised, and always colored governments of the Third World that are unable to provide for their own.[28]

Frustration regarding these similarities came from blacks and whites, rich and poor, from all points along the political and social spectrum, though these comments were articulated primarily by Americans. It seemed to this writer, however, that the underlying subtext of this outrage was that America is distinct and special, and somehow above that dark, inferior space called the Third World. This author has long contended that "Third World" has become a pejorative expression; it is regarded as a place below all of us, even black leaders, even people of color, even progressives. Even our view of our black selves appears to be intimately tied up in being American. At its heart, these concerns belie a belief in American exceptionalism, which is stridently believed along all rungs of the American economic, political, and social hierarchy and which non-Americans often find so offensive. Americans are somehow superior to all others, and even black Americans, at their lowest point, are still not the desperate, despised "other" that is too poor, too backward, and too much of the Third World. Surely, Third World solidarity was never monolithic, and our connection to it has always been complex. Katrina proved, however, that this connection was now most definitely a thing of the past, or at least on hiatus.[29]

Part II: Defining the Third World, Defining Refugees

The ideas of a Third World and a refugee have complex meanings and long and rich histories beyond the manner in which they were debated during the Katrina debacle. Some of their significance is legal, as in the case with refugees. Other aspects of the terms are part of the political and social fabric of the search for inclusion and justice. African Americans, as part of the African diaspora, have been integral elements in this struggle. Part II attempts to document some of this history and the history of the terms' evolution from expressions of liberation to language of disdain.[30]

Constructing the Third World

In its purest form, the term "Third World" designated those countries that were aligned with neither the West, as personified by the United States and its allies, nor the Soviet Union and its satellites. The term signified an important part of the "Non-Aligned Movement."[31] It has long had much broader subtexts and implications, however. The ideas at the core of the notion of a Third World ultimately emerged from the demands of colonial peoples for liberation, equality, and political, social, and economic justice.

The belief that racial discrimination and colonialism should cease, and the notion of unity among peoples of color, have been the subjects of international movements and conferences since the first Pan-African conference was held in 1900. In the aftermath of the Second World War, the momentum for decolonization built to a crescendo. The Non-Aligned Movement was born when the Asia-Africa Conference, more famously known as the Bandung Conference, convened in 1955 and birthed the conception of a Third World. While the conference itself could not be termed radical, the idea of a Third World was groundbreaking. The two-thirds of humanity who did not live in the First and Second Worlds were already classified as the underdeveloped. Those from the First and Second Worlds believe that people in the Third World would desperately need their former colonizers if they were to survive and prosper. The Bandung Conference is still viewed as a launching pad for Third World demands, as the countries of the Southern Hemisphere resolved at that time to set a distance between themselves and the big powers seeking to rule them. Hence, the term "Third World" began as a celebration of solidarity and independence from the colluding capitalist (always First) and the Communist (former Second) worlds. The term was a declaration of independence by people of color the world over who sought to end oppression emanating from whatever source.[32]

At some point, however, this expression of hope and solidarity became a surrogate for something dark and dispossessed. Legal scholar Keith Aoiki explained that the Third World has been defined "in terms of a certain set of images, including poverty, squalor, corruption, violence, calamities and disasters, irrational local fundamentalisms, bad smell, garbage, filth, technological backwardness or simply lack of modernity."[33] Moreover, the term "Fourth World" now commonly designates the most marginalized peoples or those sometimes identified as the "least developed." The distinguished law professor Anne Orford noted, "Intervention narratives regularly produce images of the people who live in nations targeted for humanitarian intervention as starving, powerless, suffering, abused and helpless victims, often women and children in need of rescue or salvation."[34] The American media's response to Katrina and commentary regarding the "Third World" designation made it obvious that this is the American view of the Third World. What is more surprising is that black Americans would so readily adopt this view, and especially that those black Americans who identify as *African* Americans would do so.[35]

Defining Refugees

For a definition of "refugee," one needs to look no further than a dictionary. The word is defined as "one that flees, especially a person who flees to a foreign country or power to escape danger or persecution."[36] Pursuant to this definition, the victims of Katrina could be termed refugees in that they were "one who flees," as they fled the ravages of their destroyed homes and city. Yet the remainder of this definition demonstrates that "one who flees" only begins the discussion.

The word also has a particularly international connotation, which rose from the lowest depths of man's inhumanity to other men, women, and children: the Nazi holocaust against the Jewish people. From these ashes came the perceived need for the nations of the world to provide refuge. In the wake of the Holocaust, and the widespread refusal of the nations of the world to receive its victims, the international community created distinct rights for refugees, which are enshrined in the 1951 Convention relating to the Status of Refugees. The Refugee Convention defines a refugee as "Any person who . . . owing to a well-founded fear of being persecuted for reasons of race, religion, nationality, membership in a particular social group or political opinion, is outside the country of his nationality and is unable, or owing to such fear, is unwilling to avail himself of the protection of that country.[37]

According to this much broader definition, it seems the victims of Hurricane Katrina were not refugees. They were not outside of the country of their nationality. Further, it did not seem that they were unable to avail themselves of the protection of their country of nationality, the United States. While African Americans overwhelmingly believed that the slow pace of assistance was due to the color of the victims, it does not seem that anyone believed that they had lost their nationality or were actually persecuted on the basis of race. The Refugee Convention was created to assist people, such as the Jewish people of Germany during the Second World War, who fled from their home of origin and sought asylum in foreign lands. While analogous genocides and other human rights trage-dies have been repeated numerous times in the ensuing fifty-five years, such was not the case in New Orleans, Louisiana, in Sep-tember 2005.[38]

Moreover, given that refugees' roots denote international disper-sion, perhaps there was a measure of legitimacy to objections re-garding the media's designations of Katrina's victims as refugees. There surely were internally displaced persons following Katrina, and victims of past U.S. natural disasters have also been labeled as refugees. Even if the term was technically erroneous, however, does that somehow make "refugee" a derogatory term? The United Na-tions Office of the High Commissioner of Refugees expressed dismay that the term "refugee" could be viewed as pejorative. War, politi-cal strife, and genocide, as well as natural disasters, have generated refugees, and it is indeed troubling that peoples already burdened with horrific circumstances would now be laden with yet another encumbrance and somehow rendered even more undesirable.[39]

If persons displaced by past American natural disasters were termed refugees, then what was so different this time? Could it be that "refugee" has taken on the same undercurrents as Third World? The word's definition has changed from peoples fleeing the worst forms of hate and oppression to, instead, the colored of the world fleeing their plight as the colored of the world. That is, Third World and refugee are part and parcel of the same paradigm; both are something to be disdained. The terms now connote that the vic-tims of this disaster were distraught, hapless, and very black.[40]

African Americans did not always subscribe to dominant views of the Third World, however. They once realized that the struggle against white supremacy was an international struggle even before there was a Third World. Indeed, when W. E. B. Du Bois made his famous observation that the problem of the twentieth century was the problem of the color line, he framed it in an international context. He explained, "The dilemma of color included the relation of the darker races to the lighter races of men in Asia, Africa, in America and the islands of the sea."[41] Still, black America's connection with the Third World has been broad, multifaceted, and complex, possibly accounting for our reactions in the aftermath of Hurricane Katrina.

Part III: Toward Rediscovering Solidarity

On some level, the destinies of black Americans and the larger Third World have always been intertwined. This connection has ranged from early nineteenth-century repatriation movements led by, among others, Martin Delaney and Alexander Cromwell to Marcus Garvey's Universal Negro Improvement Association in the 1920s, which placed black migration back to Africa and a powerful Africa at its core. Links can also be found in the work of Du Bois, who was one of the leaders of an international Pan African Movement, in which people of color the world over struggled against the forces of imperialism and racism. As African nations emerged from the throes of colonialism, black Americans emerged from the darkness of legal segregation. These movements found sources of strength and solidarity in each other. Black Americans and the future leaders of newly emerging African nations were both present at the Bandung Conference, where the concept of a Third World congealed. This bond deepened and took on a cultural component in the United States in, for example, the use of the term "African American," the now yearly celebration of Kwanzaa, which is inspired by African traditions, and African-inspired hairstyles and fashions. The connections among African Americans and the Third World can be found in the successful fight to end Apartheid, which in the U.S. was led by African Americans, and in black American lobbying on behalf of African interests including the African Growth and Opportunity Act. In addition, some African nations have recently taken up the cause of reparations for colonialism, borrowing from the black American reparations movement.[42]

Given this distinctive history, one might wonder how we arrived at a place where *African* Americans would abjure any connection to the Third World or to refugees and would seek instead to couple our demand for just treatment with efforts to distinguish ourselves from the larger colored world. Part of the seeming contradiction lies in the other side of our engagement with the South, and especially that part of the South that is Africa, and with our identities as Americans and relationships with the Anglo-Saxon culture in which we subsist. This is the other, ignoble side of an otherwise quite magnificent story. There is also an often forgotten history in which black Americans believed that Africans were uncivilized while they, because they were American, were civilized and could aid in the white man's burden to civilize the uncivilized. Black Americans possessed a sense of American superiority, even in the face of American racism and notwithstanding an awareness of some semblance of unity with our African brethren. Indeed, American Negro duality was articulated on the international stage, as was the idea of a talented tenth: a small group of blacks capable of moving the race forward. The concept of a talented tenth implied that talent was the civilized American Negro, and the rest was manifestly African.

In many respects, black Americans have constructed and yearned for some form of international racial unity. Yet they have been unable to escape their profound Americanism, which by definition sets them apart and, given American exceptionalism, above all others even when the others are the rest of the Colored of the world. Perhaps we should not be too surprised at the contemporary distance between black Americans and the Third World. "Third World" has become a pejorative term, and in our current state of disengagement from the international sphere, perhaps we have not sufficiently questioned or studied this development. African states are generally powerless on the international stage and are portrayed as being in a collective, endless, and constant crisis that is characterized by war, famine, debt, corruption, and abject poverty. Devoid of any historical, economic, social, or political context, this endless crisis appears to be due solely to their incompetence, an assumption compounded by racism and long-held core beliefs about the incompetence and inferiority of black people. Of course, while most African countries are quite impoverished and unfortunately in bottomless debt, the other markers are more limited and circumscribed. Moreover, when placed in a broader historical context, these problems are surely not caused by mere incompetence, and surely not due to racial inferiority. Nonetheless, perhaps black Americans would prefer to avoid being associated with what appears to be a hopeless morass; it is simply too close to home.[43]

We must stay connected, and not as "saviors" or through a desire to "patronize" to the "other." While there are profound cultural differences and distances between black Americans and Africans generally (with perhaps the exception of South Africans), the forces at the root of our oppressions are related and share race at their core. Just as the "international community," which is led by the United States, fails to take any meaningful steps to end genocide in Darfur, it is also somehow easier to leave the victims of Katrina stranded for days on end; black people are just not important. This is why those who were simply trying to stay alive in the aftermath of Katrina were characterized as looters if they were black and helping their families if they were white. It is why so many poor New Orleanians are black in the first place and why economic, social, and civil distances were so broad from the outset.[44]

These same assumptions are on display internationally in the fates of the peoples who have been exploited in the most horrendous manner from their initial encounters with Europeans, and yet were perceived as inferior and the white man's burden. They have been enslaved, colonized, looted, exploited economically, subject to the vagaries of the development industry, and politically and economically subjugated in every sense of the term. Still, the contemporary results of that exploitation are blamed on the Africans' ineptitude, with racism making this conclusion seem almost natural. I do not intend to remove all vestiges of agency from African peoples on the continent or in the diaspora, but only to say that the discussion often erases or belittles history, and this exclusion is influenced and shaped by race. When one is assumed incapable and incompetent, then no deeper explanation is necessary. These same assumptions accompany American views of domestic poverty and perceptions of African American deficiencies. Black Americans are assumed to be disproportionately poor because they are inferior and unable to compete, not because of segregation, racism and a history of profound oppression. For one brief moment, Katrina reminded Americans of its oft forgotten "other" and crystallized how that "other" is treated in a wealthy nation that could do much better. Racism has again relegated them to the periphery, however, as New Orleans continues to lie in ruins and its inhabitants scattered across the nation. Maybe, we are not so distant from our discarded brothers and sisters after all, but perhaps this is just too painful to contemplate. Perchance in this respect Du Bois and others were correct; we will live or die together, whether we like it or not. We must build and re-build our deep-rooted connections and understand the joint roots of our different, but connected, oppressions.

Notes

1. Sherrie Armstrong Tomlinson, "No New Orleans Left Behind: An Examination of the Disparate Impact of Hurricane Katrina on Minorities," *Connecticut Law Review* 38 (2006): 1153; "The Creole City," http://www.neworleansonline

.com/neworleans/multicultural/multiculturalhistory/creole.html, accessed May 27, 2007; Arnold R. Hirsch and Joseph Logsdon, "The People and Culture of New Orleans," http://www.neworleansonline.com/neworleans/history/people.html, accessed May 27, 2007; Arthur Hardy, "History of Mardi Gras," http://www.neworleansonline.com/neworleans/mardigras/mardigrashistory/mghistory.html, accessed May 27, 2007; Clyde Woods, "Do You Know What It Means to Miss New Orleans? Katrina, Trap Economics, and the Rebirth of the Blues," *American Quarterly* 57 (2005): 1005, 1008–9; U.S. House of Representatives, Select Bipartisan Committee to Investigate the Preparation for and Response to Hurricane Katrina, "A Failure of Initiative: Final Report of the Select Bipartisan Committee to Investigate the Preparation for and Response to Hurricane Katrina," 109th Congress, Washington DC: Government Printing Office, February 19, 2006), 89, http://katrina.house.gov/full_katrina_report.htm; Miranda Welbourne, "The Environmental Justice Movement's Response to Hurricane Katrina, A Critique: Problems Faced, Successes, Failures and the State of the Movement One Year Later," *Thurgood Marshall Law Review* 32 (2006): 125; Wendy B. Scott, "From an Act of God to the Failure of Man: Hurricane Katrina and the Economic Recovery of New Orleans," *Villanova Law Review* 51 (2007): 581, 584–85; Elisabeth Bumiller, "Gulf Coast Isn't the Only Thing Left in Tatters; Bush's Status with Blacks Takes a Hit," *New York Times*, September 12, 2005, A17.

2. Paul Krugman, "Tragedy in Black and White," *New York Times*, September 19, 2005, A25; Eric Lipton et al., "Storm and Crisis: Government Assistance; Breakdowns Marked Path from Hurricane to Anarchy," *New York Times*, September 11, 2005, 11; Molly Ivins, "FEMA, Our Man-made Disaster Area," *Fort Worth Star-Telegram*, September 11, 2005, E4; Larry Eichel, "Delay, Hesitation, Despair and Disaster," *Fort Worth Star-Telegram*, September 11, 2005, A24; Diane Carman, "U.S. Leaders Flunking Disasters 101," *Denver Post*, September 11, 2005, C01; "2001–2005 Dealing with Disaster: Emergency Network Worse Today," *Daytona (FL) News-Journal*, September 11, 2005, 01B; Andrew Martin, Cam Simpson, and Frank James, "Best-Laid Plans Did Little to Help New Orleans," *Newport News (VA) Daily Press*, September 11, 2005, A1; "Unprepared Again: Will We Learn Enough to Be Ready for the Next Disaster?" *Charlotte (NC) Observer*, September 11, 2005, 2P; Alan Judd and Teresa Borden, "Hurricane Katrina: Odyssey Shows FEMA's Disarray; Futile Trek: Georgians Sent to Mississippi, Dallas, Galveston, Houston," *Atlanta Journal-Constitution*, September 11, 2005, A1; "Actions Added Human Cost, Hesitancy in Response May Have Led to More Deaths," *Aberdeen (SD) American News*, September 11, 2005, A1; "Failure at FEMA: Michael Brown Makes an Appropriate Exit," *Akron (OH) Beacon Journal*, September 13, 2005, B3; Susan B. Glasser and Josh White, "Homeland Security Agency in Flux; Ill-Prepared to Handle Katrina," *Washington Post*, September

4, 2005; Joanne M. Nigg, John Barnshaw, and Manuel R. Torres, "Hurricane Katrina and the Flooding of New Orleans: Emergent Issues in Sheltering and Temporary Housing," *Annals of the American Academy of Political and Social Science* 604 (2006): 113; Kathleen Tierney, Christine Bevc, and Erica Kuligowski, "Metaphors Matter: Disaster Myths, Media Frames, and Their Consequences in Hurricane Katrina," *Annals of the American Academy of Political and Social Science* 604 (2006): 57; William L. Waugh, "The Political Costs of Failure in the Katrina and Rita Disasters," *Annals of the American Academy of Political and Social Science* 604 (2006): 10, 16; Arnold M. Howitt and Herman B. Leonard, "Katrina and the Core Challenges of Disaster Response," *Fletcher Forum of World Affairs* 30 (2006): 215; Donald F. Kettl, "Is the Worst Yet to Come?" *Annals of the American Academy of Political and Social Science* 604 (2006): 273; Jonathan P. Hook and Trisha B. Miller, "The Continuing Storm: How Disaster Recovery Excludes Those Most in Need," *California Western Law Review* 43 (2006): 21; Brenda Muñiz, "In the Eye of the Storm: How the Government and Private Response to Hurricane Katrina Failed Latinos," *National Council of La Raza*, February 28, 2006; Louise K. Comfort, "Fragility in Disaster Response: Hurricane Katrina, 29 August 2005," *Forum* 3.3 (2005): 1, 4.

3. "Hurricane Katrina Turns 'Refugee' into Word of the Year," *Washington Post*, December 16, 2005, C07; Ruth Walker, "Coming to Terms with Katrina's Diaspora," *Christian Science Monitor*, September 21, 2005, 18; Rosa Brooks, "Our Homegrown Third World," *Bergen County (NJ) Record*, September 11, 2005, 5; Robert E. Pierre and Paul Farhi, "'Refugee': A Word of Trouble," *Washington Post*, September 7, 2005, C01; Jocelyn Noveck, "The Use of Word 'Refugee' Touches a Nerve," *Seattle Times*, September 7, 2005, A16; John M. Broder, "Amid Criticism of Federal Efforts, Charges of Racism Are Lodged," *New York Times*, September 5, 2005, A9; Isabel Medina, "Confronting the Rights Deficit at Home: Is the Nation Prepared in the Aftermath of Katrina? Confronting the Myth of Efficiency," *California Western Law Review* 43 (2006): 9; Richard Bernstein, "The View from Abroad," *New York Times*, September 4, 2005, 4–5; David Carr, "The Pendulum of Reporting on Katrina," *New York Times*, September 5, 2005, C1 (explaining how news reported that a Third World country had grown inside the United States); Claudia Dreifus, "Earth Science Meets Social Science in Study of Disasters," *New York Times*, March 14, 2006, F2; Lynne Duke, "Block That Metaphor: What We Mean When We Call New Orleans 'Third World,'" *Washington Post*, October 9, 2005, B01.

4. Ruth E. Gordon and Jon H. Sylvester, "Deconstructing Development," *Wisconsin International Law Journal* 22 (2004): 1, 79 (discussing "Third World" as a pejorative term); Ruth Gordon, "Critical Race Theory and International Law: Convergence and Divergence," *Villanova Law Review* 45 (2000): 827, 834; Jan

Freeman, "Gimme Shelter," *Boston Globe*, September 11, 2005, E3; Ruth Walker, "Coming to Terms with Katrina's Diaspora"; Steven O'Brien, letter to the editor, "Aftermath of Hurricane Katrina," *Irish Times*, September 17, 2005, 15 (posting letter from Steven O'Brien, public information officer for the United Nations High Commissioner for Refugees, asking media not to use "refugee" when describing the suffering in New Orleans).

5. Havidán Rodríguez, Joseph Trainor, and Enrico L. Quarantelli, "Rising to the Challenges of a Catastrophe: The Emergent and Prosocial Behavior Following Hurricane Katrina," *Annals of the American Academy of Political and Social Science* 604 (2006): 82; Linda B. Bourque et al., "Weathering the Storm: The Impact of Hurricanes on Physical and Mental Health," *Annals of the American Academy of Political and Social Science* 604 (2006): 129; Tierney et al., "Metaphors Matter"; Nigg, Barnshaw, and Torres, "Hurricane Katrina."

6. "Climate of 2005: Summary of Hurricane Katrina," National Climatic Data Center, http://www.ncdc.noaa.gov/oa/climate/research/2005/katrina.html, accessed May 28, 2007; James Dao, "In New Orleans, Smaller May Mean Whiter," *New York Times*, January 22, 2006, sec. 4, 1; Comfort, "Fragility in Disaster Response," 3, 4; Muñiz, "In the Eye of the Storm," 1; U.S. House of Representatives, "Failure of Initiative," 92; Richard D. Knabb, Jamie R. Rhome, and Daniel P. Brown, "Tropical Cyclone Report: Hurricane Katrina, 23–30 August 2005," National Hurricane Center, December 20, 2005, at 9 http://www.nhc.noaa.gov/pdf/TCR-AL122005_Katrina.pdf.

7. Waugh, "Political Costs of Failure"; Medina, "Confronting the Rights Deficit," 11; Rachael Moshman and John Hardenbergh, "The Color of Katrina: A Proposal to Allow Disparate Impact Environmental Claims," *Sustainable Development Law and Policy* 6 (2006): 15.

8. Medina, "Confronting the Rights Deficit," 11.

9. The chronic illnesses of the poor, both white and black, and of those unattended—asthma, diabetes, heart disease, hypertension—also left many people in increased jeopardy after the hurricane hit. Susan Sirkin, "The Debacle of Hurricane Katrina: A Human Rights Response," *Fletcher Forum of World Affairs* 30 (2006): 223.

10. Sirkin, "Debacle of Hurricane Katrina," 223.

11. Dayna Bowen Matthew, "Disastrous Disasters: Restoring Civil Rights Protections for the Victims of the State in Natural Disasters," *Journal of Health and Biomedical Law* 2 (2006): 218; Waugh, "Political Costs of Failure"; Comfort, "Fragility in Disaster Response," 4.

12. Matthew, "Disastrous Disasters," 218, 220; Waugh, "Political Costs of Failure."

13. Waugh, "Political Costs of Failure"; Bourque et al., "Weathering the Storm,"

139 (noting 2002 newspaper articles warning of inadequate roads and possible problems of evacuation). Termed the "Hurricane Pam" simulation, it demonstrated that the poorest citizens would not be helped by the current evacuation plan, and locations with a median income of under $27,200 had inferior evacuation plans compared to the general population. Matthew, "Disastrous Disasters," 219; the simulation was funded by FEMA and attended by officials from Louisiana and Mississippi and federal officials as part of a federal effort to simulate the most likely of twenty-five potential disaster scenarios. The agencies simulated what they would do if a strong Category 3 hurricane, eerily similar to Katrina, directly hit New Orleans. The simulation assumed that 300,000 people would be left in the city, many buildings would be destroyed, sewer systems would be down, communications would be almost completely incapacitated, 60,000 people would die and many more would be injured, and a large flood would leave parts of Louisiana uninhabitable for over a year. Unfortunately, state and local governments had not fully addressed the issues learned from the simulation when Katrina struck, including plans to evacuate those who did not have a way to get out. A second simulation for August 2005 was abandoned due to lack of funding. Accordingly, when Katrina hit, there were no adequate plans for dealing with evacuation. U.S. House of Representatives, "Failure of Initiative," 81, 82, 106. Although original evacuation plans included using school and municipal buses to aid in evacuations, there was no plan to coordinate the agencies that would run the buses, and the plans relied on the use of personal transportation to evacuate most of the population. Nigg, "Hurricane Katrina," 114–15; Medina, "Confronting the Rights Deficit," 18; Sirkin, "Debacle of Hurricane Katrina"; Will Haygood, "Living Paycheck to Paycheck Made Leaving Impossible," *Washington Post*, September 4, 2005, A33; Scott, "From an Act of God," 584–85.

14. Waugh, "Political Costs of Failure"; Comfort, "Fragility in Disaster Response," 2; Nigg et al., "Hurricane Katrina," 125; Kettl, "Is the Worst Yet to Come?" 278.

15. Waugh, "Political Costs of Failure," 13, 14; Comfort, "Fragility in Disaster Response," 4 (discussing how neglect of levees contributed to disaster); Nigg et al., "Hurricane Katrina," 115; Bryan Bender, "Guard Feels Strain from Wars," *Albany (NY) Times Union*, September 2, 2005, A7; Jean Heller, "Q&A: Hurricane Katrina," *St. Petersburg (FL) Times*, September 3, 2005, A7; Rupert Cornwell, "Hurricane Katrina: The Questions a Shocked America Is Asking Its President," *Independent (UK)*, September 3, 2005, 2.

16. Waugh, "Political Costs of Failure."

17. Medina, "Confronting the Rights Deficit," 11, 12; Dao, "In New Orleans"; Rachel A. Van Cleave, "Property Lessons in August Wilson's *The Piano Lessons* and the Wake of Hurricane Katrina," *California Western Law Review* 43 (2006):

97–98; Comfort, "Fragility in Disaster Response," 3; Matthew, "Disastrous Disasters," 246; Welbourne, "Environmental Justice Movement's Response," 126; Stiglitz, "Lessons from 'Black Tsunami'"; Hook, "Continuing Storm," 35 (stating that Vietnamese face hurdles to recovery); Muñiz, "In the Eye"); U.S. House of Representatives, "Failure of Initiative," 445; Gwen Filosa, "Report Blames Racial, Class Divisions: New Orleans Left Its Black People, Poor at Risk," *New Orleans Times Picayune*, October 13, 2005, 2.

18. Matthew, "Disastrous Disasters," 213, 218, 220–25.

19. Sirkin, "Debacle of Hurricane Katrina."

20. L. Darnell Weeden, "Hurricane Katrina: First Amendment Censorship and the News Media," *Thurgood Marshall Law Review* 31 (2005–6): 479, 488–89; Richard T. Sylves, "President Bush and Hurricane Katrina: A Presidential Leadership Study," *Annals of the American Academy of Political and Social Science* 604 (2006): 29; Secretary Michael Chertoff of Homeland Security failed to act even though predictions for the impact of Katrina met the criteria needed to initiate the federal response. U.S. House of Representatives, "Failure of Initiative," 13, 136–77; Carr, "Pendulum of Reporting on Katrina"; Scott Collins, "Anchors, Show Hosts Take a Confrontational Stance," *Houston Chronicle*, September 3, 2005, A20; Bumiller, "Gulf Coast Isn't the Only Thing Left"; Michael A. Fletcher and Richard Morin, "Bush's Approval Rating Hits New Low," *Washington Post*, September 16, 2005; Will Lester, "Crises Pound Bush Job Rating," *Albany (NY) Times Union*, September 11, 2005, A8; Tierney, Bevc, and Kuligowski, "Metaphors Matter"; Woods, "Do You Know?" 1005–6 (quoting Vukoni Lupa-Lasaga).

21. This, of course, is a distortion. They are the images the media chooses to present and stress. When one visits the global South, there is a great deal of poverty, but there are also countless people living their lives. Gordon and Sylvester, "Deconstructing Development," 77. Gordon and Sylvester also fail to account for Western complicity in Third World problems and marginality, an involvement this author has thoroughly documented and explored. Ruth Gordon, "Saving Failed States: Sometimes a Neocolonialist Notion," *American University Journal of International Law and Policy* 12 (1997): 903, 962; Gordon, "Critical Race Theory," 835; Ruth Gordon, "Racing U.S. Foreign Policy," *National Black Law Journal* 17 (2002–4): 1, 11; Ruth Gordon, "Contemplating the wto from the Margins," *Berkeley La Raza Law Journal* 17 (2006): 95, 106.

22. Walker, "Coming to Terms."

23. Freeman, "Gimme Shelter."

24. Pierre and Farhi, "Refugee." pa vice president of msnbc, commenting on why they decided to change their terminology, made this statement.

25. The executive editor of the Associated Press defended the decision with this statement. Noveck, "'Refugee' Touches a Nerve."

26. Global Language Monitor, a nonprofit organization, termed "refugee" the word of the year, noting that it was used five times more often than any other word to describe those who were left homeless after Katrina. "Hurricane Katrina Turns 'Refugee' into Word of the Year"; Brendan Buhler, "Word Watch," *Los Angeles Times*, September 11, 2005 M2; Walker, "Coming to Terms"; Pierre and Farhi, "Refugee." News organizations that abandoned the use of the word included the *Seattle Times, Washington Post, Miami Herald, Boston Globe,* and CNN. The *New York Times* and the Associated Press both continued to use the term "refugee." Noveck, "'Refugee' Touches a Nerve." Actually, the term "refugee" has been used to refer to disaster victims in past American emergencies. Those displaced during the Dust Bowl were referred to as "Dust Bowl refugees." The term was also used to describe those displaced by wildfires, floods, and even theoretical future disasters. Freeman, "Gimme Shelter." Refugee has even been used to describe those displaced by Hurricane Andrew. Moreover, "refugee" was used before Katrina hit New Orleans. It wasn't until the term was associated with the specific images of blacks displaced by Katrina, and there were references to Africa and the Third World, that it received its negative connotation. Tom Jackson, "Enumerating Blessings after Katrina's Miss," *Tampa (FL) Tribune*, August 27, 2005, 1 (referring to all those in shelters as refugees); Gary Nurenberg, "U.S. Gulf Coast Braces for Hurricane Katrina," "Five-Hour Wait to Enter Superdome Shelter," "Evacuees Stuck in Traffic near Biloxi," "Bush Declares Emergency before Storm Hits— Part 1," *CNNNews* television broadcast, August 28, 2005, 2005 WLNR 13581945 (describing people arriving on planes in Washington from New Orleans before Katrina hit as "refugees").

27. Pierre and Farhi, "Refugee." The interviewee was Mr. Tyrone McKnight.

28. Scott, "From an Act of God," 582 (revealing author's own use of references to "Third World" and "refugees"); Brooks, "Our Homegrown Third World" (claiming that America's poor experience Third World conditions everyday; Gordon, "Racing U.S. Foreign Policy," 8–9; Gordon, "Contemplating the WTO," 106; Gordon, "Critical Race Theory," 831; Gordon and Sylvester, "Deconstructing Development," 5, 79–80; Gordon, "Saving Failed States."

29. It seemed those in the Third World had a different view. One scholar noted that Katrina made them realize that perhaps we were not so smart and they were not so stupid. Gordon, "Contemplating the WTO," 39; Broder, "Amid Criticism of Federal Efforts" (discussing Al Sharpton's view of refugees as being less than citizens); "Hurricane Katrina Turns 'Refugee' into Word of the Year." "Thus the use of the term 'refugee' to describe survivors may have served to create confusion in the minds of casual observers of television reports, by equating them with, for example, Haitian refugees seeking asylum in the United States." U.S. House of Representatives, "Failure of Initiative," 446–47; Scott, "From An Act of God,"

582; Krugman, "Tragedy in Black and White"; Charles Bowden, "Exodus: Coyotes, Pollos, and the Promised Van," *Mother Jones*, 31.5 (2006): 36 (using "Third World" as reference to immigration problems and New Orleans after Katrina); Michael Tisserand, "Living Like a Refugee," *Nation*, September 19, 2005, web exclusive article, http://www.thenation.com/doc/20050919/tisserand. A poll by the General Social Survey of the National Opinion Research Center showed that 40 percent of respondents believed "America is a better country than most other countries." It is this pride of believing Americans are superior to others around the world that makes the scenes from New Orleans, which Americans therefore connect with poor Third World countries, so disconcerting and upsetting. Duke, "Block That Metaphor."

30. Refugees are defined in international conventions and accorded certain rights and privileges. The original definition of "refugee" was established in 1951, "Convention Relating to the Status Of Refugees," July 28, 1951, art. I(A)(2), 189 U.N.T.S. 150; the 1967 Protocol Relating to the Status of Refugees extended the definition. "Protocol Relating to the Status of Refugees," January 31, 1967, 606 U.N.T.S. 267; the Convention and the Protocol are available at http://www.unhcr.org/protect/PROTECTION/3b66c2aa10.pdf. There is also a UN Office of the High Commissioner for Refugees, established in 1950, designated to deal with their plight. UN High Commissioner for Refugees, G.A. Res. 428/5, U.N. Doc. A/RES/428/5, Dec. 14, 1950, http://www.unhcr.org/basics/BASICS/420cc0432.html. The United States formally adopted the 1951 Refugee Convention and the 1967 Protocol through treaty 90–27.

31. "Third World" was first used in 1952 by politician and economist Alfred Sauvy to designate countries that were not aligned with either the dominant First World economic powers of the West or the Soviet Union and its satellites, which were referred to as the Second World. Bill Ashcroft, Gareth Griffiths, and Helen Tiffin, eds., *Key Concepts in Post-Colonial Studies* (London: Routlege, 2000), 231; Vijay Prashad, *The Darker Nations: A People's History of the Third World* (New York: New Press, 2000), 10–12.

32. Brenda Gayle Plummer, *Rising Wind Black Americans and U.S. Foreign Affairs* (Chapel Hill: University of North Carolina Press, 1996), 14; Gilbert Rist, *The History of Development* (New York: Zed Books, 1997), 81; Prashad, *Darker Nations*, 8–9; Gordon and Sylvester, "Deconstructing Development," 2.

33. Gordon and Sylvester, "Deconstructing Development," 2; Keith Aoki, "Space Invaders: Critical Geography, the 'Third World' in International Law and Critical Race Theory," *Villanova Law Review* 45 (2000): 913, 925; Ashcroft, Griffiths, and Tiffin, *Key Concepts in Post-Colonial Studies*, 231–32.

34. Anne Orford, *Reading Humanitarian Intervention: Human Rights and the Use of Force in International Law* (Cambridge: Cambridge University Press, 2003), 174.

35. Ashcroft, Griffiths, and Tiffin, *Key Concepts in Post-Colonial Studies*; Gordon, "Contemplating the WTO," 107.

36. "Refugee," *Merriam Webster Dictionary*, 11th Collegiate ed.

37. "Convention Relating to the Status of Refugees," Art. 1, Sec. A, 2.

38. *Encyclopedia of Public International Law*, Max Planck Institute for Comparative Public Law and International Law, vol. 4 (New York: Elsevier/North-Holland, 2000): 72–74; Makau Mutua, "Savages, Victims, and Saviors: The Metaphor of Human Rights," *Harvard International Law Journal* 42 (2001): 201, 210–12.

39. George E. Edwards, "International Human Rights Law Violations before, during, and after Hurricane Katrina: An International Law Framework for Analysis," *Thurgood Marshall Law Review* 31 (2006): 353, 367; James Dao, "No Fixed Address," *New York Times*, September 11, 2005, 4-1; "America Humbled," *Los Angeles Times*, September 4, 2005, at 4; O'Brien, "Aftermath of Hurricane Katrina."

40. Brooks, "Our Homegrown Third World"; Pierre and Farhi, "Refugee"; Broder, "Amid Criticism of Federal Efforts"; Duke, "Block That Metaphor." The victims were not just African American but, as are a disproportionate number of poor black people in the United States, they were generally dark-hued African Americans. Commentators have noted a difference between the lives and experiences of blacks with dark skin and African physical features, and blacks with lighter skin and more European features. Such distinctions and often discrimination are known as "colorism." Studies have shown that light-skinned blacks are, on average, more educated, have more professional and technical jobs, and are wealthier than blacks with darker skin. Taunya Lovell Banks, "Colorism: A Darker Shade of Pale," UCLA *Law Review* 47 (1999–2000): 1705, 1713, 1718–22; Trina Jones, "Shades of Brown: The Law of Skin Color," 49 *Duke Law Journal* 49 (1999–2000): 1487, 1498, 1506–8.

41. Gerald Horne, "Race from Power," in *Window on Freedom: Race, Civil Rights, and Foreign Affairs, 1945–1988*, ed. Brenda Plummer (Chapel Hill: University of North Carolina Press, 2003), 48 (quoting Dr. W. E. B. Du Bois).

42. See Plummer, *Rising Wind Black Americans*; Michael Omi and Howard Winant, *Racial Formation in the United States* (New York: Routledge, 1994; Cary Fraser, "An American Dilemma," in *Window on Freedom: Race, Civil Rights, and Foreign Affairs, 1945–1988*, ed. Brenda Plummer (Chapel Hill: University of North Carolina Press, 2003), 133–37. "African Growth and Opportunity Act," 19 U.S.C.A. §§ 3701–3706 (2006); Gordon, "Contemplating the WTO," 98 n. 13; Gordon and Sylvester, "Deconstructing Development," 65–66.

43. Some of the social distance between black Americans and Africans is grounded in the many cultural differences that transcend race, as black Americans confront the reality that race is not always the primary marker once one leaves American

shores. It may also stem from a practice that has become common among immigrant communities—viewing American blacks as inferior and at the bottom of American society. Some African immigrants have not been immune to this odious practice, and black Americans in cities with large African populations have responded in kind. See Tanya Katerí Hernández, "Multiracial Matrix: The Role of Race ideology in the Enforcement of Antidiscrimination Laws, A United States--Latin America Comparison," *Cornell Law Review* 87 (2002): 1093, 1152–53; Banks, "Colorism"; Jones, "Shades of Brown"; Gordon, "Racing U.S. Foreign Policy," 7; Gordon, "Critical Race Theory," 831–33; Ruth Gordon, "Growing Constitutions," *University of Pennsylvania Journal of Constitutional Law* 1, no. 3 (1999): 528–82; Gordon, "Contemplating the WTO."

44. For background on the genocide in Darfur, Sudan, see M. Rafiqul Islam, "The Sudanese Darfur Crisis and Internally Displaced Persons in International Law: The Least Protection for the Most Vulnerable," *International Journal of Refugee Law* 18, no. 2 (2006): 356–57; Heather Cash, "Security Council Resolution 1593 and Conflicting Principles of International Law: How the Future of the International Criminal Court Is at Stake," *Brandeis Law Journal* 45 (2007): 573.

ELEVEN

"Been in the Storm So Long"

Katrina, Reparations, and the Original Understanding of Equal Protection

D. MARVIN JONES

Though nature may treat us all equally, Katrina demonstrated that society does not. These violations arise directly from the failure of the U.S. government to eliminate apartheid practices against working-poor citizens of the United States, who are mostly African Americans or otherwise people of color. These violations are historical and continuing. The tragedies of Katrina should never have happened any place, especially in America, and they certainly should never happen again.[1]

The flooding started in the Lower Ninth Ward, a predominantly African American neighborhood. Initially, the floodwaters reached six to eight feet. On Tuesday, the second levee broke, and 80 percent of the city was flooded, with waters reaching as high as twenty feet. An estimated 50,000 to 100,000 people were stranded on roofs, in the damaged Superdome, or in the Convention Center.[2]

Over 62 percent of the dead and 80 percent of those trapped on rooftops were black. The overwhelming blackness of those stranded on rooftops, trapped in the Superdome, and floating dead in the water strongly suggest a connection between racial caste and catastrophe.

As Jesse Jackson stated: "Today I saw 5,000 African Americans on the I-10 causeway desperate, perishing, dehydrated, babies dying. It looked like Africans in the hull of a slave ship. It was so ugly and so obvious."[3] Similarly, Congresswoman Cynthia McKinney stated: "As I saw the mostly African American families ripped apart, I could only think of slavery. Families ripped apart, herded into what looked like concentration camps."[4]

The connection between slavery and the plight of blacks in the aftermath of Katrina has an objective dimension. The starting point is the apparent present-day connection between race and caste; this is reflected both in the present-day correlation between race and poverty and the continuing "segregation"—it is euphemistically referred to as concentration—of the black poor.[5]

The majority of those living below the poverty line in the city were African American. Data collected by the Brookings Institution indicated that "nearly 50,000 poor New Orleans citizens lived in neighborhoods where the poverty rate exceeded forty percent."[6] In fact, New Orleans ranked second among the nation's largest cities for the number of African American families who were clustered in "extremely poor neighborhoods" like the Lower Ninth Ward. Among the 28 percent of New Orleans' residents who lived below the poverty line, 84 percent were African American. This concentration of blacks in impoverished areas like the Ninth Ward was not accidental:

> Because of its origins as one of the oldest slave trading centers in the country, New Orleans has a unique history in both race relations and residential segregation. Slavery required blacks to live in close proximity to their white owners. This created a mixed residential pattern that was characteristic of other southern cities in the nineteenth century. The rigid caste/race system defined social distance when physical distance was lacking. In the twentieth century, the advent of civil rights and equality for blacks has

led to less patriarchal race relations but, paradoxically, greater residential segregation. Blacks have become more residentially isolated since the turn of the century.[7]

Thus, there is a context in which the close connection among race, poverty, and space, such as in the Ninth Ward, traces back to slavery.[8]

Blacks sought reparations for slavery in the past. Sigmund Freud observed that every great civilization begins with a great crime. Perhaps slavery was America's. Reparations claims are usually aimed at collecting compensation for a collective crime, which has created a kind of moral debt. But it is more than this because reparations claims resonate as actions that set the moral scales of history back in order, so that a nation that has professed a commitment to democracy can live out the true meaning of its creed.

Reparations represent the moral equivalent of a boiling, seething cauldron in which anger, historic injustice, and present inequality, of the kind Katrina showed so vividly, have all been mixed. The legal system has put a lid on the pot of this historic social claim. This lid is constructed out of two objections: reparations represent a moral rather than a legal claim, and redressing claims that date far back into history would shake asunder the foundations of the law.

The first argument is one about positivism. It sets forth the notion that only claims that fit within the narrow confines of a legal wrong will be redressed. This has been historically justified by claims that judges lack the authority to address questions of morality. These traditional rationalizations, however, rest ultimately not on abstract principle but on self-interest; to give redress to blacks would require an upheaval of traditional baselines of privileges and rights. Thus the greatest of injustices is ultimately beyond the ken of "justice" because of the greatness of the changes that would be required.

Judge Calvin Clayton argued that while individuals would respond to *Fiat justitia ruat coelem*, or "let justice be done though the heavens fall," society would not. He maintained that "[*Fiat justitia ruat clum*] is undoubtedly the logical lingo of life. But you are aware that communities do not follow such lines; your course, therefore, will place you in opposition to the community in which you live. Your conscientious convictions will cross self-interest, and the community will not allow you to carry them out."[9]

Moreover, he reasoned, "of individuals, there are not a few who earnestly desire to do something; but they are mostly without faith or hope, like me. And, from the communities from the great organizations in society no help whatever is to be expected."[10]

This line between race and morality has crystallized in recent cases in a requirement of specificity. In order to make out a modern claim of race discrimination, one has to show that racial harm can be traced to specific "identifiable decisions" and "identifiable decision makers."[11] In short, only specific actions and individuals are legally responsible for racial discrimination.

The second objection can be characterized as one about formalism: only discrete, specific, and present wrongs fit into the category of formal legal claims. Given the constraints of this narrow notion of a legal wrong, courts traditionally would not consider historical context, no matter how "obvious." This formalism is anchored in a distinction between a legal wrong, which is within the ken of courts, and a social wrong, which is not. Law professor Paul Brest argued that "an individual's claim to moral compensation loses force as the nature, extent and consequences of the wrongs inflicted become harder to identify and the wrongs recede into the past."[12] Indeed, as claims to compensation become more attenuated, they begin to compete with claims based on the vagaries of fate.[13]

The U.S. Supreme Court has dismissed the moral claims of blacks generally as incompatible with the legal system. It has stated,

> Societal discrimination, without more, is too amorphous a basis
> for imposing a racially classified remedy. . . . No one doubts that

there has been serious racial discrimination in this country. But as the basis for imposing discriminatory legal remedies that work against innocent people, societal discrimination is insufficient and over expansive. In the absence of particularized findings, a court could uphold remedies that are ageless in their reach into the past, and timeless in their ability to affect the future.[14]

At bottom, reparations claims seek to redistribute wealth and goods on the basis of historical argument. But the point here is that the law exists to prevent such redistributions. It is not that the heavens would have to fall, but that the foundations of the law foreclose these historically grounded claims. Somewhere between the objections of logical positivism, presentism, and the law's requirement for specificity and discrete identifiable discrimination, reparations claims have failed. The perpetuation of racial caste must be addressed, however. We simply have to address these historical claims through their current manifestations.[15]

What Katrina represents is an instance, which in a real sense removes the lid from the pot of historic injustice. It presents an example in which the legacy of slavery and a present legal wrong are bound up together. What is this present wrong? New Orleans was not merely the scene of a disaster, but the scene of a crime. As Barack Obama stated on the floor of the Senate, it was a crime less of "active malice" than a systemic pattern of "indifference."[16]

Katrina is not only a crime, but one in which we know all of the perpetrators. It is redressable. In the following pages I lay out why this is a crime in the most conservative tradition of criminal law and why the foundations of our constitutional order not only allow the redress of this great wrong but also how they require it.

What the Government Failed to Do

As we all saw, the New Orleans calamity was ultimately the result of . . . neglect by . . . governments. Up to five days passed and stranded, hungry, and dehydrated New Orleans residents were clinging to their rooftops exposed to the elements—and dying by the score. Those who made their way to the official evacuation points at the Superdome . . . found themselves waiting. . . . Some people needed dialysis. Some needed insulin. Some were just old and frail or newly born. Some of them died. —MICHAEL I. NIMAN, "Katrina's America: Failure, Racism, and Profiteering," *Humanist*

By September 1, 2005, crowds in the Superdome had swollen to 30,000. Patients were abandoned in hospitals. Bodies floated in the water. Other bodies lay uncollected, eaten by rats and dogs. It was as if New Orleans was "Another Country." President Bush summarized the crisis well. "Citizens drowned in their attics," he declared, "desperate mothers crying out on national TV for food and water. The breakdown of law and order. And a government, at all levels, that fell short of its responsibilities."[17]

This abandonment began long before the storm. The most egregious failure of government was its failure to prepare. To begin with, the substantial danger of a storm breaching the vital levees of New Orleans was well known at all levels of government:

In July 2004, emergency officials from FEMA [Federal Emergency Management Agency] . . . ran a $1 million computer model called "Hurricane Pam" that simulated winds of 120 miles per hour, twenty inches of rain, evacuation of one million residents, and a storm surge that overcame the city's levees. "Pam" anticipated two specific scenarios to aid in emergency planning and response: a major hurricane impacting the Gulf Coast region and hurricane-caused failure of the levees. . . . Hurricane Katrina embodied both of these scenarios, and so should have been anticipated and planned for.[18]

The failure of local government was even more specific, however. As one congressional witness testified:

> Nagin's failure to prepare was heightened by the delay in giving an evacuation order. On Saturday, August 27, 2005 the head of the National Hurricane Center told Mayor Nagin this was the worst hurricane he had ever seen. Mayor Nagin almost inexplicably waited until the next day to issue evacuation orders.[19]

Nagin also failed to prepare shelters after the storm:

> Instead of evacuation, they were transported to inhumane conditions in three locations throughout the city, called "shelters of last resort;" including the New Orleans Superdome sports arena and a highway intersection called the "Cloverleaf." The conditions were horrid. The heat, lack of power, lack of food, absence of sanitation provisions and a total lack of preparedness led to conditions described at once as "horrible," "unbearable," and "miserable."[20]

What underscores the failure to prepare, after the government knew the high level of risk involved, is that the government knew, or should have known, that poor blacks would bear a disproportionate share of any disaster to come.

Social scientists have said that officials should have been able to predict the characteristics of those who would stay behind. As Lee Clarke explained, "They would be poor, distrustful of the police and political establishment, largely African-American, with no way to get out."[21] What made Katrina's impact on poor people, who were overwhelmingly black, predictable was that this group was dependent on public transportation, which was largely nonexistent in the aftermath of the storm. For the black poor, the question would not be whether to evacuate, but how, with what car, with what money. In the face of this avoidable dilemma, hundreds of school buses remained idle and in harm's way. As Dyan French elaborated,

> Why would you get in the public media and ask a city where 80 percent of its citizens ride public transport to evacuate? What were they supposed to do? Fly? Get on a broom? After you allowed the buses to sit in the water areas, that's one thing five years in Transportation would have told me, and I wasn't at the top. You move all of your equipment and your transportation out of harm's way. You know, the president declares two days in advance that it's coming, and you don't move any of the equipment. Who is fooling whom?[22]

Part of the difficulty in preparing for the storm was the lens of race. The paradigm case of victims in need of government help is the example of the disaster victim. Blacks stranded in this way appealed implicitly to notions of equal citizenship in their appeals for rescue. Yet by referring to blacks as "refugees," the press and the government portrayed them as something less than full-fledged citizens. Race mediated the paradigmatic medium to reframe the image of disaster victims as sociopaths. People seeking food were transformed through this lens, for example, into looters. Victims getting a canoe to rescue others trapped on rooftops were transformed into thugs. This rhetorical abuse prefigured the abuse that later occurred when government first responders treated the evacuees as foreigners. This treatment was severe enough that many characterized first responders' actions as those of an occupation rather than a rescue:

> On Wednesday, August 31, two days after Hurricane Katrina, Mayor Nagin ordered most of the New Orleans police to abandon their search and rescue missions to focus on looters. The government responded as if all reports were true by sending police and

soldiers—a response that has been analogized to the response to the San Francisco earthquake of 1906, when people foraging in the remains of their own destroyed homes were assumed to be looters, and were therefore shot and killed.[23]

It is axiomatic of criminal law that failure to act, especially in the face of substantial risk, may be as consequential as direct action. The Welansky case provides a classic example of where a failure to act constituted liability for homicide.[24]

The Welansky Model

Barnett Welansky owned the Cocoanut Grove, one of the most popular nightclubs in Boston. The official capacity of the club was six hundred. Yet on November 28, 1942, fans from a football game between Holy Cross and Boston College joined the usual crowds to fill the club with more than a thousand people. Though there were five emergency exits, all of them were either obstructed from view or locked on November 28. The Piedmont Street exit and the Shawmut Street exit were locked and operated by a key that was kept in the front office. Another door, near the revolving door in the front, led to a vestibule near the front office. The door leading to the outside exit was permanently blocked by a shelf and makeshift coat rack. The fourth exit, located in the middle of the main dining room and leading to Shawmut Street, consisted of two doors, though only one was working. This door, however, was blocked by two inward swinging Venetian doors, which were fastened with a hook and further obstructed by dining tables. A fifth exit was apparently open but was only accessible through a corridor that most patrons were unlikely to know about.[25]

A fire started when a sixteen-year-old boy tried to change a light bulb. He lit a match to find the bulb, and the match ignited some coconut husk lying next to a palm tree. An inexorable chain of events followed, which included rapidly spreading fire, smoke, and pandemonium as the crowd found that exits were blocked:

> The fire spread with great rapidity across the upper part of the room, causing much heat. The crowd in the Melody Lounge rushed up the stairs, but the fire preceded them. People got on fire while on the stairway. . . . The door at the head of the Melody Lounge stairway was not opened until firemen broke it down from outside with an axe and found it locked by a key lock, so that the panic bar could not operate. Two dead bodies were found close to it, and a pile of bodies about seven feet from it. The door in the vestibule of the office did not become open, and was barred by the clothing rack.[26]

A crime occurs when a guilty mind, called *mens rea*, coincides within a voluntary act, called *actus reus*. The two must occur together.[27]

Mens Rea

What is mens rea? It is the mental state that is required for and helps to define our concept of crime. As Blackstone noted, "*Actus non facit maxim, nisi mens sit rea.*"[28] This phrase is sometimes taken to mean that in order for a person to commit a crime, he or she must be acting with wrongful intent. As Justice Oliver Wendell Holmes famously noted, "Even a dog distinguishes between being stumbled over and being kicked."[29] As James Fitzjames Stephen pointed out in 1883, the maxim also might mean "that the definition of all or nearly all crimes contains not only an outward and visible element, but a mental element." A crime is constituted not only by what we can see outwardly, but also by what takes place inside the mind. This reflects in turn a mind/body dualism dating back to Descartes.[30]

The requirement of mens rea expresses the notion that individuals are responsible for their choices, but not for actions over which they had no control. There are two broad categories of mens rea, or two types of mental state that may constitute a crime. The first relates to the "desire" to commit a crime, and the second to belief or awareness that a crime is being committed. The classic case of a "state of desire" is "intent" or "purpose."[31]

Dante, in his famous "Inferno," perhaps anticipated the Anglo-American tradition of distinguishing between grades or levels of evil. In the American hierarchy of evils the person who intends to kill is guilty of murder, but the person who merely acts "recklessly" is guilty of manslaughter. Recklessness exists where a person acts with indifference to a substantial risk. A person who is merely reckless does not specifically desire to kill, but in his or her desire to achieve an antisocial result consciously disregards a known risk and acts anyway: he does not care whom he hurts. This is the sense of wanton recklessness. While this is often expressed as indifference, there is hatefulness in the indifference, a callousness that borders on desire for harm. The paradox of this state of mind is that it combines a feeling of "indifference," that one doesn't care, with a conscious preference, or desire, for a particular result. It is the moral proximity; a cruel coziness in principle with causing the death of another human being that allows us to say the act is "wanton." The other operative element here is that the criminal not only accepts in principle that she may cause the death of another, but that she is aware of a substantial risk that she may do so. The fact that the criminal knows there is a substantial risk—a state of awareness—combines with the callous disregard of the risk—a state of desire—to constitute the concept of "wanton recklessness." Manslaughter occurs when a wanton or reckless act causes death.[32]

Welansky was charged with involuntary manslaughter because he invited people into his establishment but failed to take the most basic precautions against an obvious danger. Mere negligence does not create criminal liability. The court felt that the failure to unlock the exits and remove obstructions from them was so callous as to constitute what the court referred to as wanton or reckless conduct. To constitute wanton or reckless conduct, as distinguished from mere negligence, grave danger to others must have been apparent, and the defendant must have chosen to run the risk rather than alter his conduct so as to avoid the act or omission, which caused the harm. In turn, the reckless failure to act was the legal cause of the fire. Wanton or reckless conduct is the legal equivalent of intentional conduct.[33]

Duty of Care

In the Welansky case, there is a duty of care for the safety of business visitors invited to premises that the defendant controls. Wanton or reckless conduct in this case may consist of intentional failure to embrace this duty in disregard of the probable harmful consequences to the visitors or of their right to care. Interestingly, the elements of mens rea seem to be present in the Katrina case in "spades." The government's failure to issue timely evacuation orders, have buses ready to transport residents, deploy police to rescue residents rather than arrest them, and have escape routes all point unmistakably to a wanton recklessness even more dramatic than that of the Welansky case.

The actus reus of a systemic failure to act is also obviously present. The disaster of thousands languishing without water and food was clearly a second disaster caused by the failure of local, state, and federal government to respond to the crisis. The only issue that can be disputed is whether or not a duty of care existed. Unlike the Welansky case, the issue of "duty of care" would be a contested proposition. The U.S. Supreme Court has held that under the U.S. Constitution the state generally has no affirmative duty to protect its citizens.[34]

Unless the state creates the danger, it generally owes no duty to protect. In *DeShaney v. Winnebago County Department of Social Services*, despite the evidence of child abuse and a social worker's personal belief that "the phone would ring some day and Joshua would be dead," the department took no action either to protect the minor Joshua from his evidently abusive father or to contact Joshua's mother until repeated abuse left Joshua paralyzed and retarded. The Supreme Court stated:

> But nothing in the language of the Due Process Clause itself requires the State to protect the life, liberty, and property of its citizens against invasion by private actors. The Clause is phrased as a limitation on the State's power to act, not as a guarantee of certain minimal levels of safety and security. It forbids the State itself to deprive individuals of life, liberty, or property without "due process of law," but its language cannot fairly be extended to impose an affirmative obligation on the State. . . . The Due Process Clauses generally confer no affirmative right to governmental aid, even where such aid may be necessary to secure life, liberty, or property interests of which the government itself may not deprive the individual.[35]

DeShaney is an instantiation of the notion that mere government inaction works no deprivation of a constitutional right. This action-inaction distinction, in turn, is linked to the notion that constitutional rights are generally negative rights only.[36]

A generation of American law students has grown up learning that as James Madison noted, "if men were angels no government would be necessary." Because men are not angels the common law imposes no duty that they behave as such: there is no duty that one citizen rescue another. In a real sense this "negative right" to be free from legal obligation to rescue is a form of "liberty." This notion of liberty as a negative right has a long and deep tradition in

American law. This negative right to be free from an obligation to rescue was part of a larger framework of liberty that freed white America from moral obligations vis-à-vis slavery. However, in the DeShaney case, the court drew upon the original conception of equal protection represented an entirely different set of assumptions. Civil rights originally were conceived as exceptions to the negative rights framework. The very nature of civil rights creates a set of affirmative obligations on government. As Jacobus ten-Broek showed many years ago, the phrase "equal protection" has deep roots in abolitionist language and in the original understanding that all persons, and particularly freed slaves, were entitled to receive "protection" by the government.[37]

Even without this context, the creation of civil rights laws by the federal government presupposes the duty of the majority to protect the minority. What ought to be clear from this historical background was made explicit during congressional debates around the Civil Rights Act of 1871. This Civil Rights Act, of which Section 1 is now codified as 42 U.S.C. 1983, was prompted by the terrorism of the Ku Klux Klan against freed slaves. A member of Congress who described the situation captured the scope of the crisis:

> While murder is stalking abroad in disguise, while whippings and lynchings and banishment have been visited upon unoffending American citizens, the local administrations have been found inadequate or unwilling to apply the proper corrective. Combinations, darker than the night which hides them, conspiracies wicked as the worst of felons could devise have gone unwhipped of justice. Immunity is given to crime, and the records of the public tribunals are searched in vain for any evidence of effective redress.[38]

It was against this background that Senator Sherman proposed an amendment, which did not pass, to the Civil Rights Act of 1871 that provided a right to persons who were injured by "any persons riotously and tumultuously assembled together . . . with intent to deprive any person of any right conferred upon him by the Constitution and laws of the United States, or to deter him or punish him for exercising such right, or by reason of his race, color, or previous condition of servitude."[39] In seeking to create this right, Sherman carried forward the then-dominant idea that the right to protection by state government was a basic right of citizens, which included former slaves. Thus Sherman stated, "Let the people of property in the southern States understand that if they will not make the hue and cry and take the necessary steps to put down lawless violence in those States their property will be holden responsible, and the effect will be most wholesome."[40]

Not only did the state have a duty to protect its residents, but such a right was also guaranteed by the federal government. More specifically, the genius of the civil rights revolution that occurred during Reconstruction was to create laws that had the effect of making the majority financially liable if minority civil rights were violated.

As the Supreme Court would later state in the famous case of *Monroe v. Pape*, "Supporters were quite clear that § 1 of the Act extended a remedy not only where a State had passed an unconstitutional statute, but also where officers of the State were deliberately indifferent to the rights of black citizens."[41] As Representative Garfield stated,

> But the chief complaint is . . . [that] by a systematic maladministration of [state law], or a neglect or refusal to enforce their provisions, a portion of the people are denied equal protection under them. Whenever such a state of facts is clearly made out, I believe [§ 5 of the Fourteenth Amendment] empowers Congress to step in and provide for doing justice to those persons who are thus denied equal protection."[42]

Similarly, John Poole argued,

> Rights conferred by laws are worthless unless laws be executed.
> The right to personal liberty or personal security can be protected
> only by execution of laws upon those who violate such rights. A
> failure to punish the offender is not only to deny the person in-
> jured the protection of the laws, but also to deprive him, in ef-
> fect, of the rights themselves.[43]

Today we think of equal protection and civil rights laws as a right
of the individual against the state for its intentional acts. The original meaning of equal protection was as a guarantee "that law enforcement would be equally effective against all threats to peace
and *safety*."[44] Equal protection originally meant that individuals
would be equally protected against all threats.

Although Senator Sherman's proposed amendment did not pass,
no one doubted the basic proposition that the state had a duty to
protect its citizens. I argue after Bingham, Sherman, and Shellabarger that the duty of government to protect its citizens is one
of the rights of citizenship itself, or as a right of "equal protection" under the equal protection clause of the Fourteenth Amendment. These voices from Reconstruction resonate in terms of the
Katrina issue. If Sherman and Shellabarger are correct, then Governor Blanco and Mayor Ray Nagin had a constitutional duty to
protect those in need of evacuation who lacked transportation,
those trapped on rooftops, and those languishing without water
or food in the Superdome and elsewhere. The fact that they, in my
view, wantonly and recklessly ignored this constitutional duty, in
the face of substantial risk, was as wanton and reckless as the actions of Welansky.[45]

Of course, there will be those who will argue that no constitutional duty exists for state officials to protect their citizens; these
individuals might cite the cruel holding of *DeShaney*. The reliance

on *DeShaney* is misplaced, however. At the heart of the *DeShaney* case are two limiting concepts. The first is that civil rights are negative rights. By negative right, we mean that the government has no affirmative obligations. The second concept is a theory of interpretation that holds that these civil rights must be construed strictly because they are countermajoritarian. Civil rights statutes, nominally threatening a city with financial liability, hold the purses of the city's taxpayers hostage to the security of minorities. This places an unavoidable burden on majorities; this is countermajoritarian. Driving both of these concerns is a theory of federalism, which holds that the federal government as a government of enumerated powers is strictly limited in the restrictions it may place on states. The reasoning of *DeShaney* is inapplicable to begin with, because the case was a due process issue, and our case for a constitutional duty is rooted in equal protection concerns. Further, the underlying concern of *DeShaney* about state-federal relations is absent; this would be a state court proceeding.

It is axiomatic of civil rights law that while the state cannot give less than the federal government, the federal Constitution requires that the state is free to give more. Concomitant to this, the state in my view is free to interpret the equal protection clause to place constraints on its own state officials greater than those that the federal government would impose. So long as the court is not inconsistent or addressing a matter that is somehow preempted, the court is free constitutionally to make its own judgment.

In a word, states are not bound to interpret civil rights as negative rights only, nor to construe civil rights narrowly on the theory that they limit the liberty of the majority. Both of these traditional limitations of civil rights are themselves part of the machinery used to reconcile the tension between federal and state power. By bringing the prosecution in state court, the tension disappears.

The actions of Mayor Ray Nagin, Governor Blanco, and the

City of New Orleans should be brought before a Louisiana Grand Jury. The legislature might have to legislate into being the procedures to be followed. The deaths that occurred were clearly, in my view, proximately caused by the wanton recklessness of these defendants. Using Welansky as a template, the sole element capable of dispute is the question of whether the state officials had a constitutional duty under the equal protection clause to protect the disproportionately black citizens who were virtually abandoned at the Superdome. It is at this juncture that the voices from Reconstruction speak into our own time. What happened to the overwhelmingly black evacuees was a crime against citizenship, a way of saying we do not regard you as citizens, as part of the unity invoked by the words "We the People." These voices from Reconstruction object from their hallowed place in our history.

Conclusion

I've been in the storm so long. Been in the storm so long. Been in the storm so long. Oh gimme little time to pray.[46]—BLACK AMERICAN FREEDOM SONG, *Voices of the Civil Rights Movement: Black American Freedom Songs, 1960–1966*

The "storm" has become a metaphor for the black experience. Whether it is the aftermath of slavery or the aftermath of a physical storm, each aftermath involves a narrative of immense suffering and injustice linked to racial caste. No one is to blame for the natural disaster of Katrina. But the ongoing storm of racism found its expression in the specific treatment of black evacuees. Someone is to blame for this social disaster. We will be defined by how we address this injustice.

Perhaps there will never be a Katrina trial. As Harriet Beecher Stowe wrote many years ago, the "great organizations" rarely address

the great injustices: the greater the injustice, the less likely government will address them.[47] So it has been with slavery. So it also has
been with Katrina. Yet a trial should happen, and then the voices
of Sherman and Shellabarger will join with the voices of those who
have gone through the storm and are still going through its aftermath. These voices hearken back to the original meaning of the Fourteenth Amendment and the original meaning of equal protection.
We should heed their voices because by listening to them, we begin
a dialogue about the relationship between race and citizenship, and
between race and democracy—a dialogue that has too long been
ignored. Those who are afraid of this dialogue are merely afraid
that justice, whether for Katrina victims or for slaves, will cost too
much. The words of Judge Clayton come to mind: *Fiat justitia ruat
coelem*, "let justice be done though the heavens fall."[48]

Notes

1. See Bryan Massingale, "Katrina Catastrophe Exposes U.S. Race Reality,"
National Catholic Reporter, March 2, 2007; Leah Hodges, "Hearing of the Select
Bipartisan Committee to Investigate the Preparation for and Response to Hurricane Katrina . . . Voices inside the Storm," testimony, Federal News Service, December 6, 2005.

2. Sherrie Armstrong Tomlinson, "No New Orleanians Left Behind: An Examination of the Disparate Impact of Hurricane Katrina on Minorities," *Connecticut
Law Review* 38 (2006): 1153, 1158–59.

3. Reverend Jesse Jackson, *Anderson Cooper 360*, CNN, aired September 2,
2005.

4. Cynthia McKinney, Comments, 151 *Congressional Record* H7805, daily
ed., September 8, 2005.

5. Tomlinson, "No New Orleanians Left Behind," 1163.

6. Alan Berube and Bruce Katz, "Katrina's Window: Confronting Concentrated Poverty across America" (Washington DC: Brookings Institution, October 2005), 2, 1.

7. Daphne Spain, "Race Relations and Residential Segregation in New Orleans: Two Centuries of Paradox," spec. issue, Race and Residence in American
Cities, *Annals of the American Academy of Political and Social Science* 441, no.
1 (1979), 82–96.

8. Paul Frymer et al., "Katrina's Political Roots and Divisions: Race, Class, and Federalism," in *Understanding Katrina: Perspectives from the Social Sciences* (New York: American Politics, Social Science Research Council, September 28, 2005).

9. Quoted in Harriet Beecher Stowe, *Dred: A Tale of the Great Dismal Swamp in Two Volumes* (Chapel Hill: University of North Carolina Press, 1856), 1:444.

10. Stowe, *Dred*, 1:444.

11. See D. Marvin Jones, "No Time for Trumpets," *Michigan Law Review* 92 (1994): 2311, 2360.

12. Jones, "No Time for Trumpets," 2311, 2360.

13. Paul Brest, "The Supreme Court Term—1975 Forward: In Defense of the Anti-discrimination Principle," *Harvard Law Review* 98 (1976): 1.

14. *Wygant v. Jackson Bd. of Education*, 476 U.S. 267, at 276.

15. Legal positivism is the thesis that law depends on historical facts and not the personal morality of the judges.

16. Barack Obama, "Statement of Senator Barrack Obama on Hurricane Katrina Relief Efforts," accessed September 6, 2005, http://obama.senate.gov/statement/050906-statement_of_senator_barack_obama_on_hurricane_katrina_relief_efforts/.

17. Michael Abomowitz and Peter Whoriskey, "New Orleans Honors Its Dead," *Washington Post*, August 30, 2006, A04.

18. Tomlinson, "No New Orleanians Left Behind," 1153, 1164–65.

19. Mary Greiz Kweit and Robert Griez Kweit, "A Tale of Two Disasters," *Publius*, June 22, 2006, 8.

20. U.S. House of Representatives, Select Bipartisan Committee to Investigate the Preparation for and Response to Hurricane Katrina, "A Failure of Initiative: The Final Report of the Select Bipartisan Committee to Investigate the Preparation for and Response to Hurricane Katrina," 109th Congress, H.R. Rep. No. 109-000 (Washington DC: Government Printing Office, February 19, 2006): 311.

21. Lee Clarke, "Worst Case Katrina," in *Understanding Katrina: Perspectives from the Social Sciences* (Washington DC: American Politics, Social Science Research Council, September 12, 2005).

22. Dyan French, "Hurricane Katrina: Voices from inside the Storm, Hearing of the Select Bi-Partisan Committee to Investigate the Preparation for and Response to Hurricane Katrina," testimony, December 6, 2005, quoted in *Boston College Third World Law Journal* 27, no. 2 (Spring 2007): 263–323.

23. Tomlinson, "No New Orleanians Left Behind," 1153, 1168–69.

24. D. Marvin Jones, *Race, Sex, and Suspicion: The Myth of the Black Male* (Westport CT: Greenwood Press 2005); Cheryl I. Harris, "Whitewashing Race, Scapegoating Culture," *California Law Review* 94 (2006): 907; *Commonwealth v. (Barnett) Welansky* 316 Mass. 383, 55 N.E. 2nd 902 (1944).

25. *Commonwealth v. Welansky*, 383, 392–94.

26. *Commonwealth v. Welansky*, 383, 392–94.

27. *Commonwealth v. Welansky*, 383, 392–94.

28. See Sir Edward Coke, *The Third Part of the Institutes of the Laws of England* (1797; rpt., Buffalo NY: William S. Hein, 1986), 107.

29. Oliver Wendell Holmes, *The Common Law*, ed. Mark DeWolfe Howe (1881; New York: Little, Brown, 1963), 7.

30. Thomas C. Grey, "Holmes and Legal Pragmatism," *Stanford Law Review* 41 (1989): 787, 795–96 (noting that "British empiricism and its traditional rival, European rationalism, had implicitly shared a dualistic conception of the human being as a spiritual or immaterial mind somehow lodged in a material body").

31. Kenneth Simmons, "Rethinking Mental States," *Boston University Law Review* 72 (1992): 463, 465. In American law, however, the concept of criminal intent is amphibian: some courts have stretched the concept so that mere "awareness" of certain circumstances satisfies the requirement of actual "intent." But despite this "twisting," the term "intent" generally refers to something more than mere awareness; generally it refers to actually wanting something to happen, "a state of desire."

32. Dante Alighieri, *Dante's Inferno*, adapted by Sandow Birk and Marcus Sanders (San Francisco: Chronicle Books, 2004), originally written between 1308 and 1321.

33. For many years this court has been careful to preserve the distinction between negligence and gross negligence, on the one hand, and wanton or reckless conduct on the other.

34. If the state takes a person into custody, a duty to protect is triggered by the affirmative act of custodial arrest. However, the absence of an affirmative duty under the constitution must not obscure another basic point: if state officials do provide services or protection, it must be provided on an equal basis.

35. *DeShaney v. Winnebago County Department of Social Services*, 489 U.S. 189, 196 (1989).

36. *DeShaney v. Winnebago County Department of Social Services*, 189.

37. See Jacobus tenBroek, *Equal under Law* (New York: Collier Books, 1965), 51–55.

38. Mr. Lowe of Kansas, *Congressional Globe*, 42nd Cong., 1st sess. (1871), 574.

39. Mr. Lowe of Kansas, 761.

40. Mr. Lowe of Kansas, 761.

41. *Monroe v. Pape*, 365 U.S. 167 (1961).

42. *Congressional Globe*, 42nd Cong., 1st sess. (1871), 153.

43. *Congressional Globe*.

44. Lawrence Rosenthal, "Policing and Equal Protection," *Yale Law and Policy Review* 21 (2003): 53.

45. Arguably, the reason Sherman's amendment did not pass was not disagreement about the right of protection but about the nature and scope of the remedy. Opponents argued that the Sherman amendment would give the federal government power to create police forces and that to give the federal government such power to intervene in municipal government would destroy their ability to function as independent entities. Perhaps this is why today the federal government will not intervene where mere negligence is involved. To go into federal court one would have to show that what happened in the Katrina aftermath involved intent in the strictest sense.

46. *Voices of the Civil Rights Movement: Black American Freedom Songs, 1960–1966* (Washington DC: Smithsonian Folkways Recordings, 1997). See also Leon F. Litwack, *"Been in the Storm so Long": The Aftermath of Slavery* (New York: Vintage, 1979) for the context in which the spiritual was sung. Litwack's Pulitzer Prize–winning book has informed much of my writing about slavery.

47. Stowe, *Dred*, 444.

48. Stowe, *Dred*, 444.

Epilogue

JEREMY I. LEVITT AND MATTHEW C. WHITAKER

On August 29, 2005, an unnatural tragedy unfolded in New Orleans that will undoubtedly and indefinitely haunt the United States and its citizens. Hurricane Katrina shook up and woke up the world to the singular realization that the United States is not only vulnerable to devastating natural disasters or "Acts of God," but, perhaps more importantly, to unnatural disasters or "Acts of Politicians." Americans and onlookers from around the world were amazed to learn that the world's most powerful nation proved incapable of preventing a Category 3 hurricane from destroying one of its most popular and culturally distinct cities. They were even more curious to know how the United States could allow tens of thousands of displaced citizens, namely African Americans, to die and suffer without food, water, or medical treatment in Louisiana's smoldering hot and humid environ. The editors of this book remain bewildered by the realization that the United States can fight conventional wars in the Middle East and engage in robust peacekeeping in Eastern Europe but simultaneously prove patently incapable of providing timely emergency assistance to dying New Orleaneans at home during a national catastrophe.[1]

The editors believe that the chapters in this volume reveal two vital truths about the United States in the aftermath of Hurricane Katrina. First, the U.S. government was, and perhaps still is, unable or unwilling to manage major disasters, even four years after the tragedy of September 11, 2001. Second, the editors believe that American society remains too immature and insincere to constructively confront the vestiges of a slavocratic and segregationist history. This history was largely responsible for the New Orleans racist topography that birthed the Ninth Ward, one of the areas hit hardest by flooding. This history continues to foster racially disparate conceptions regarding whether racism lay behind the federal government's negligent response.[2]

Hurricane Katrina unmasked America and illustrated with Leonardo da Vinci–like precision "The Last Supper" of nearly 1,850 New Orleaneans and the desperate flight of over 1 million more. It painted a grotesque picture of cruel racism, abject poverty, media bias, white apathy, and government heedlessness. Unlike the murder trial of infamous football legend O. J. Simpson, all Americans seemed to believe that government incompetence lay at the center of the tragedy; similar to the Simpson trial, however, black and white America appear to disagree on whether race played a definitive role in the federal government's unacceptably late and incompetent response. Despite this dichotomy, America revealed its inability or unwillingness to protect New Orleans' predominantly black population from death and displacement. The stark clarity of this tragic failure resonates with the luminous precision of the Rembrandt masterpiece *The Anatomy Lesson of Dr. Nicholis Tulp*. This catastrophe, however, was displayed in a tragic photographic narrative that we christen "The Anatomy Lesson of American Caste."[3]

To many onlookers in the United States and abroad, Hurricane Katrina was nothing more than another example of America's arrogant ambivalence about the plight of African Americans. The federal and state government's response and malevolent media imagery and commentary were seemingly based on, and unfortunately perpetuated, old slave folklore; governmental response and media depictions suggested that persons of African descent were inhumanely durable and impervious to high levels of pain and suffering. These institutions also insinuated that black Katrina victims were criminals and refugees. As the black masses of New Orleans suffered for four hellish days, the leadership of the Federal Emergency Management Agency (FEMA) unconcernedly claimed that it was not aware of the extent of the carnage caused by Katrina or the level of human suffering that ensued. The federal government's failure to adequately protect the rights and welfare of Katrina victims raises serious questions about whether the victims have a colorful claim against the U.S. government for racial discrimination and the arguable deprivation of the basic necessities needed to sustain life (food, water, and shelter) under international human rights law. Any such claim may find an audience in, for example, the United Nations Human Rights Council and the Organization of American States Inter-American Commission on Human Rights.[4]

We should remember August 29, 2005, as the day when America's dirty laundry of poverty and race was exposed to the world in a way unseen since the civil rights era in the 1960s. The aftermath of Hurricane Katrina was American-made. While we can debate whether or not George Bush cares about black people, or whether FEMA's dawdling response was colored by racism, African Americans must awaken to the reality that nationalist-centered self-determination is the only means to equality.

Notes

1. Chester Hartman and Gregory D. Squires, eds., *There Is No Such Thing as a Natural Disaster: Race, Class, and Hurricane Katrina* (New York: Routledge,

2006), 1–12. Also see Kent B. Germany, *New Orleans after the Promises: Poverty, Citizenship, and the Search for the Great Society* (Athens: University of Georgia Press, 2007); and David Dante Troutt and Charles Ogletree, eds., *After the Storm: Black Intellectuals Explore the Meaning of Hurricane Katrina* (New York: New Press, 2007).

2. See Michael K. Brown, Martin Carnoy, Elliot Currie, Troy Duster, David B. Oppenheimer, Marjorie M. Shultz, and David Wellman, *Whitewashing Race: The Myth of a Color-Blind Society* (Berkeley: University of California Press, 2003); Neil J. Smelser, William Julius Wilson, and Faith Mitchell, eds., *America Becoming: Racial Trends and Their Consequences*, vol. 2 (Washington DC: National Academy Press, 2001), 1–20, 222–52, 371–410; and Alice O'Conner, Chris Tilly, and Lawrence D. Bobo, eds., *Urban Inequality: Evidence from Four Cities* (New York: Russell Sage Foundation, 2006), 1–33, 89–303.

3. See Brown et al., *Whitewashing Race*; Ernest van de Wetering, *Rembrandt: The Painter at Work* (Berkeley: University of California Press, 2000).

4. Douglas Brinkley, *The Great Deluge: Hurricane Katrina, New Orleans, and the Mississippi Gulf Coast* (New York: William Morrow, 2006), 1–10; John McQuaid and Mark Schleifstein, *Path of Destruction: The Devastation of New Orleans and the Coming Age of Superstorms* (New York: Little, Brown, 2006), 151–307. Also see, generally, *International Convention on the Elimination of All Forms of Racial Discrimination*, adopted and opened for signature and ratification by General Assembly resolution 2106 (XX) of December 21, 1965 (entry into force January 4, 1969, in accordance with Article 19); *International Covenant on Civil and Political Rights*, adopted and opened for signature, ratification, and accession by General Assembly resolution 2200A (XXI) of December 16, 1966 (entry into force March 23, 1976, in accordance with Article 49); and *International Covenant on Economic, Social and Cultural Rights,* adopted and opened for signature, ratification, and accession by General Assembly resolution 2200A (XXI) of December 16, 1966 (entry into force January 3, 1976, in accordance with article 27); *Human Rights Council*, adopted by General Assembly Resolution 251, sixtieth ordinary session (entry into force April 3, 2006); *American Convention on Human Rights*, adopted at the Inter-American Specialized Conference on Human Rights, San José, Costa Rica, November 22, 1969); *Statute of the Inter-American Commission on Human Rights*, approved by Resolution No. 447 taken by the General Assembly of the OAS at its ninth regular session, held in La Paz, Bolivia, October 1979.

BIBLIOGRAPHY

Primary Sources

Archival collections, government documents, oral histories and interviews, web-based reports, newspapers, web-based newspapers and periodicals.

"African Growth and Opportunity Act," 19 U.S.C.A. §§ 3701–6 (2006).

Alighieri, Dante. *Dante's Inferno*. Adapted by Sandow Birk and Marcus Sanders. San Francisco: Chronicle Books, 2004. Originally written between 1308 and 1321.

American Civil Liberties Union. "Abandoned and Abused: Complete Report." National Prison Project of the American Civil Liberties Union. August 9, 2006, 15.

American Convention on Human Rights. Adopted at the Inter-American Specialized Conference on Human Rights, San José, Costa Rica, November 22, 1969.

American Red Cross. "Hurricane." http://www.redcross.org/services/disaster/0,1082,0_587_,00.html#Plan.

Anonymous employee. Interview by Phyllis Williams, October 11, 2005. Notes on file with the ACLU Prison Project.

Ansari v. State, 913 So.2d 834 (La. 2005).

Aristotle. *The Nicomachmean Ethics*. 350 BC. Trans. W. D. Ross. New York: Oxford University Press, 1998.

Axis Reinsurance Company v. Lanza, No 05–6318 Section: J(3), 2007 U.S. Dist. LEXIS 22976, March 29, 2007.

Brown v. Board of Education, 347 U.S. 483 (1954).

Browner, Carol M. "Before the Committee on Finance." U.S. Senate.

Accessed January 28, 2007. http://www.epa.gov/history/topics/jus
tice/01.htm.

Centers for Disease Control and Prevention. "Cases of HIV Infection and
AIDS in the United States and Dependent Areas, 2005." *HIV/AIDS Surveillance Report, 2005* 17 (2006): 1–54.

———. "HIV/AIDS among African Americans." Accessed February 1, 2007.
http://www.cdc.gov/HIV/topics/aa/resources/factsheets/pdf/aa.pdf.

Civil Rights Cases, 109 U.S. 3 (1883).

"Climate of 2005: Summary of Hurricane Katrina." National Climatic
Data Center. Accessed May 28, 2007. http://www.ncdc.noaa.gov/oa/
climate/research/2005/katrina.html.

CNN. Transcript of Press Conference. August 28, 2005. http://transcripts
.cnn.com/TRANSCRIPTS/0508/28/bn.04.html.

Cohn, Nancy. "Cuba's Hurricane Response Far Superior." *truthout Perspective,* September 3, 2005. http://www.truthout.org/docs_2005/090305Y
.shtml.

Coke, Edward. *The Third Part of the Institutes of the Laws of England.*
1797. Rpt., Buffalo NY: William S. Hein, 1986.

Commonwealth v. (Barnett) Welansky, 316 Mass. 383, 55 N.E. 2nd 902
(1944).

Congressional Globe, 42nd Cong., 1st sess. (1871): 153.

"Convention Relating to the Status of Refugees." July 28, 1951, art. I(A)
(2), 189 U.N.T.S. 150. http://www.unhcr.org/protect/PROTECTION/
3b66c2aa10.pdf.

Cook v. Gusman, Civil District Court, Parish of Orleans, No.
2005–12477.

Crawford, Matthew. "Recovery Zone: Orleans Parish Sheriff Shares His
Experiences after Katrina." *CorrectionalNews.Com* (May/June 2006).
http://correctionalnews.com/ME2/Audiences.

DeShaney v. Winnebago County Department of Social Services, 489 U.S.
189, 196 (1989).

DeWolfe, D. J. "Training Manual for Mental Health and Human Service
Workers in Major Disasters." Washington DC: Substance Abuse and
Mental Health Services Administration Center for Mental Health
Services, 2000.

Ducre, Rhonda. Interview by Phyllis Williams, March 15, 2006. Notes on file with the ACLU National Prison Project.

Earth Institute at Columbia University. "Hurricane Katrina Deceased-Victims List." N.d., accessed May 18, 2007. http://www.katrinalist.columbiz.edu/stats.php.

Environmental Protection Agency. "Environmental Equity: Reducing Risks for All Communities." Accessed March 20, 2007. http://www.epa.gov/compliance/resources/publications/ej/reducing_risk_com_vol1.pdf.

———. "Superfund Risk Assessment: Human Health Risk Characterization, Waste and Clean Up Risk Assessment." Accessed November 12, 2007. http://www.epa.gov/oswer/riskassessment/superfund_hh_characterization.htm.

———. National Center for Environmental Assessment. "Human Health Guidelines." Accessed November 12, 2007. http://cfpub.epa.gov/ncea/cfm/nceaguid_human.cfm

———. Office of Inspector General. "Evaluation Report: EPA Needs to Conduct Environmental Justice Reviews of Its Programs, Policies, and Activities." Report No. 2006-P-00034. Accessed September 18, 2006. http://www.epa.gov/oig/reports/2006/20060918–2006-P-00034.pdf.

———. Office of Inspector General. "Evaluation Report: EPA Needs to Consistently Implement the Intent of the Executive Order on Environmental Justice." Report No. 2004-P-00007. Accessed March 1, 2004. http://www.epa.gov/oig/reports/2004/ 20040301–2004-P-00007.pdf.

"Evacuees, carrying what few possessions they were able to save from the floodwaters of Katrina, exit a rescue helicopter." Photo. http://www.katrinadestruction.com/images/v/survivors/14533w.jpg.html.

Executive Order No. 12898, 59 Fed. Reg. 7629 (February 16, 1994).

"Facts about Children and Poverty." CARE. 2007. http://www.care.org/campaigns/childrenpoverty/facts.asp.

Fair, Bryan K. Review of *Black Trials: Citizenship from the Beginnings of Slavery to the End of Caste*, by Mark. S. Weiner. *Washington Post*, January 5, 2005, C04.

Federal Emergency Management Agency. "Before a Hurricane." http://www.fema.gov/hazard/hurricane/hu_before.shtm.

Federal Reserve Board. "Monetary Policy Report to the Congress." *Federal Reserve Bulletin* (2000).

Freeman v. United States Department of Homeland Security, C.A. No: 06–4846 C/W 06–5689 & 06–5696 SECTION: "A" (5), D.C. E. D. LA, 2007 U.S. Dist. LEXIS 31827, April 30, 2007.

French, Dyan. "Hurricane Katrina: Voices from inside the Storm; Hearing of the Select Bi-Partisan Committee to Investigate the Preparation for and Response to Hurricane Katrina." Testimony. December 6, 2005.

Gulf Opportunity Zone Act (GOZA). Pub. L. No. 109–135, 119 Stat. 2577 (2005).

Gusman, Marlin. Interview by Phyllis Williams, March 13, 2006, New Orleans. Notes in possession of interviewer.

Heart of Atlanta Motel, Inc. v. U.S., 379 U.S. 241 (1964).

Heron, M. P., and B. L. Smith. "Deaths: Final Data for 2003." *National Vital Statistics Reports* 55 (2007): 1–96.

Hodges, Leah. "Hearing of the Select Bipartisan Committee to Investigate the Preparation for and Response to Hurricane Katrina . . . Voices inside the Storm." Testimony. Federal News Service, December 6, 2005.

Holmes, Oliver Wendell. *The Common Law*. 1881. Ed. Mark DeWolfe Howe. New York: Little, Brown, 1963.

Holy Bible, King James Version. Regency Bible. Nashville TN: Thomas Nelson, 1990.

Hooks v. Kennedy, 913 So.2d 833 (La. 2005).

Human Rights Council. Adopted by General Assembly Resolution 251, sixtieth ordinary session.

Human Rights Watch. "Shielded from Justice: Police Brutality and Accountability in the United States." http://www.hrw.org/reports98.

"Hurricane Katrina survivor image of folks walking down railroad tracks." Photo. New Orleans, August 31, 2005. http://www.katrinadestruction.com/images/v/survivors/17kd271-katrina-images.html.

In re Katrina Canal Breaches Consolidated Litigation, 471 F. Supp. 2d 684, (E.D. La. 2007).

In the Matter of Louisiana Energy Service, L.P., 69 Fed. Reg. 25 (February 6, 2004).

Internal Revenue Bulletin. IRB 2004–12.

Internal Revenue Code §§ 61.

Internal Revenue Code §§ 108.

International Convention on the Elimination of All Forms of Racial Discrimination. Adopted and opened for signature and ratification by General Assembly Resolution 2106 (XX) of December 21, 1965.

International Covenant on Civil and Political Rights. Adopted and opened for signature, ratification and accession by General Assembly Resolution 2200A (XXI) of December 16, 1966.

International Covenant on Economic, Social and Cultural Rights. Adopted and opened for signature, ratification and accession by General Assembly Resolution 2200A (XXI) of December 16, 1966.

"Investigation of Performance of the New Orleans Flood Protection Systems in Hurricane Katrina on August 29, 2005." Independent Levee Investigation Team Final System Report, July 31, 2006, accessed April 21, 2007. http://www.ce.berkeley.edu/~new_orleans/.

Jackson, Jesse. *Anderson Cooper 360*, CNN, September 2, 2005.

Jones, D. Marvin. "No Time for Trumpets." *Michigan Law Review* 92 (1994): 2311–60.

Joseph, K. Personal communication with Alyssa G. Robillard, May 23, 2007. Notes in possession of interviewer.

Kaiser Family Foundation. "Assessing the Number of People with HIV/AIDS in Areas Affected by Hurricane Katrina." Accessed September 1, 2005. http://www.kff.org/katrina/upload/7407.pdf.

———. "CDC Will Not Release Hurricane Katrina Response Report, Will Use Analysis to Improve Preparedness, Officials Say." Accessed November 1, 2006. http://www.kaisernetwork.org/daily_reports/print_report.cfm?DR_ID=40919&dr_cat=3.

———. "Giving Voice to the People of New Orleans: The Kaiser Post-Katrina Baseline Survey." Executive Summary. May 2007, accessed May 14, 2007. http://www.allhealth.org/briefingmaterials/GivingVoicetothe PeopleofNewOrleans-KaiserPost-KatrinaBaselineSurvey-718.pdf.

———. "HIV/AIDS Policy Fact Sheet."

———. "Number of Infant Deaths, 2002." N.d., accessed May 22, 2007. http://www.statehealthfacts.org/cgi-bin/healthfacts.cgi?action=comp arecategory=Health+Status&subcategory=Infants&topic=Number+of+Infant+Deaths.

———. "A Pre-Katrina Look at the Health Care Delivery System for Low-

Income People in New Orleans." 2006, accessed April 20, 2007. http://www.kff.org/uninsured/upload/7442.pdf.

KatrinaDestruction.com. http://www.katrinadestruction.com/images/v/survivors/.

Katrina Emergency Tax Relief Act (KETRA) of 2005. Pub. L. No. 109–73, 119 Stat. 2016 (2005).

Katz, Bruce. "Concentrated Poverty in New Orleans and Other American Cities." *Chronicle of Higher Education*, August 4, 2006. http://www.brookings.edu/views/op-ed/katz/20060804.htm.

Kimbrough v. Cooper, 915 So. 2d 344, 345 (La. 2005).

Knabb, Richard D., Jamie R. Rhome, and Daniel P. Brown. "Tropical Cyclone Report: Hurricane Katrina, 23–30 August 2005." National Hurricane Center. December 20, 2005. http://www.nhc.noaa.gov/pdf/TCR-AL122005_Katrina.pdf.

Lee, Charles. "Toxic Wastes and Race in the United States: A National Report on Racial and Socio-Economic Characteristics of Communities with Hazardous Waste Sites." Commission for Racial Justice, United Church of Christ, 1987.

Louisiana Justice Coalition. "Hurricane Brings Attention to Long Broken Public Defense System." http://www.lajusticecoalition.org/news/katrina.

Lowe, Mr., of Kansas. *Congressional Globe*, 42nd Cong., 1st sess. (1871), 574.

Mann, Phyllis. "Hurricane Relief Aid." *Advocate* (Louisiana Association of Criminal Defense Lawyers, Baton Rouge), Fall 2005, 3.

McCleskey v. Kemp, 481 U.S. 279 (1987).

McKinney, Cynthia. Comments. 151 *Congressional Record* H7805, daily ed., September 8, 2005.

McLaurin v. Oklahoma State Regents, 339 U.S. 637 (1950).

McWaters v. Federal Emergency Mgmt. Agency, 436 F. Supp. 2d 802 (E.D. La. 2006).

Meet the Press. NBC News, National Broadcasting Company. Transcript from September 4, 2005. http://www.msnbc.msn.com/id/9179790/.

Minino, A. M., M. P. Heron, and B. L. Smith. "Deaths: Preliminary Data for 2004." *National Vital Statistics Reports* 54 (2006): 1–50.

Missouri ex rel. Gaines v. Canada, 305 U.S. 337 (1938).

Monroe v. Pape, 365 U.S. 167 (1961).

National Center for Health Statistics. "Health, United States, 2006 with Chartbook on Trends in the Health of Americans." Washington DC: Government Printing Office, 2006.

———. "Infant Mortality Statistics from the 2004 Period Linked Birth/ Infant Death Data Set." *National Vital Statistics Reports*. National Center for Health Statistics, 2007.

National Institutes of Health. "Addressing Health Disparities: The NIH Program of Action; What Are Health Disparities?" N.d., accessed May 20, 2007. http://healthdisparities.nih.gov/whatare.html.

"The New Orleans Hurricane Protection System: What Went Wrong and Why." Report by the American Society of Civil Engineers Hurricane Katrina External Review Panel. Reston VA: American Society of Civil Engineers, 2007.

New York Trust Co. v. Eisner, 256 U.S. 345, 349 (1991).

"NRC Issues License to Louisiana Energy Services for Gas Centrifuge Uranium Enrichment Plant in New Mexico." *NRC News*, Press Release No. 06–084. Accessed June 23, 2006. http://www.nrc.gov/reading-rm/doc-collections/news/2006/06–084.html.

Nurenberg, Gary. "U.S. Gulf Coast Braces for Hurricane Katrina"; "Five-Hour Wait to Enter Superdome Shelter"; "Evacuees Stuck in Traffic Near Biloxi"; "Bush Declares Emergency before Storm Hits—Part 1." *CNNNews* television broadcast, August 28, 2005, 2005 WLNR 13581945.

Obama, Barack. "Statement of Senator Barack Obama on Hurricane Katrina Relief Efforts." Accessed September 6, 2005. http://obama.senate.gov/statement/050906-statement_of_senator_barack_obama_on_hurricane_katrina_relief_efforts/.

Office of Minority Health. "Diabetes Fact Sheet: Eliminate Disparities in Diabetes." May 11, 2007, accessed May 22, 2007. http://www.cdc.gov/omh/AMH/factsheets/diabetes.htm.

———. "Infant Mortality Fact Sheet: Eliminate Disparities in Infant Mortality." May 11, 2007, accessed May 22, 2007. http://www.cdc.gov/omh/AMH/factsheets/infant.htm.

151 Congressional Record H8197, daily ed. (September 21, 2005).

151 Congressional Record S10320, daily ed. (September 21, 2005).

Orleans Parish Criminal Sheriff's Office. "Analysis of Daily Cost Per Inmate, 2003–2006." Attached to letter from Sheriff Marlin Gusman
to Members of the New Orleans City Council, November 10, 2005.

"People standing on the overpasses and bridges to get out of the New
Orleans floodwaters, New Orleans, Louisiana, August 31, 2005."
Photo. http://www.katrinadestruction.com/images/v/survivors/
people+on+overpasses.html.

"People who did not evacuate walk through the New Orleans floodwaters to get to higher ground, New Orleans, Louisiana August 30,
2005." Photo. http://www.katrinadestruction.com/images/v/hurri
cane/SIP0515508-surreall-scene.html.

Plessy v. Ferguson, 163 U.S. 537 (1896).

Porter v. City of New Iberia, 913 So.2d 834 (La. 2005).

Prendergast, John, and David Smock. "Post-Genocidal Reconstruction:
Building Peace in Rwanda and Burundi." Special Report No. 53,
United States Institute of Peace. http://www.usip.org/pubs/special
reports/sr990915.html.

"Protocol Relating to the Status of Refugees." January 31, 1967. 606 U.N.T.S.
267. http://www.unhcr.org/protect/PROTECTION/3b66c2aa10
.pdf.

Quinn, S. C. "Hurricane Katrina: A Social and Public Health Disaster."
American Journal of Public Health 96 (2006): 204.

Reed, Renard. Interview by Phyllis Williams, June 22, 2006. Notes on file
with the ACLU National Prison Project.

"Residents are bringing their belongings and lining up to get into the Superdome." Photo. New Orleans, August 28, 2005. http://www.katrina
destruction.com/images/v/survivors/14371-afterw.jpg.html.

Richard, Brady. E-mail interview, 2006. Notes on file with the ACLU National Prison Project.

"Rooftop, New Orleans." Photo. www.ehponline.org/.../2006/114–10/
katrina_AP.jpg.

Dred Scott v. Sandford, 60 U.S. (19 How.) 393 (1856).

Shelley v. Kramer, 334 U.S. 1 (1948).

Sierra Club. "Toxic Trailers? Tests Reveal High Formaldehyde Levels in
FEMA Trailers." N.d., accessed May 22, 2007. http://www.sierraclub
.org/gulfcoast/downloads/formaldehyde_test.pdf.

Sipuel v. Board of Regents, 332 U.S. 631 (1948).

Slaughter-House Cases, 83 U.S. 36 (1872).

Smith v. Allright, 321 U.S. 649 (1944).

State of Louisiana. News. "Task Force Pelican Updates, Fatalities." Accessed October 25, 2005. http://www.gov.state.la.us/index.cfm?md=newsroom&tmp=detail&articleID=1074.

State (of Delaware) v. Benton, 187 A. 609 (Del. 1936).

State (of Louisiana) v. Citizen, 898 So.2d 325 (La. 2005).

State (of Louisiana) v. Tomlinson, 621 So. 2d 780 (La. 1993).

Statute of the Inter-American Commission on Human Rights. Approved by Resolution No. 447 taken by the General Assembly of the OAS at its ninth regular session, held in La Paz, Bolivia, October 1979.

Stevenson, Glynedale. Interview by Phyllis Williams, May 24 and June 6, 2006. Notes on file with the ACLU Prison Project.

"Survivors Search for Food and Water." New Orleans, Louisiana. Photo. http://www.katrinadestruction.com/images/v/billingscr/Survivors+search+for+food+and+water.jpg.html.

Sweatt v. Painter, 339 U.S. 629 (1950).

Sylves, Richard T. "President Bush and Hurricane Katrina: A Presidential Leadership Study." *Annals of the American Academy of Political and Social Science* 604 (2006): 26–56.

Testimonial from Inmate #144. October 27, 2005. Original on file with the ACLU National Prison Project.

Tisserand, Michael. "Living Like a Refugee." Web exclusive article. *Nation*, September 19, 2005. http://www.thenation.com/doc/20050919/tisserand.

"Toxic Wastes and Race at Twenty, 1987–2007: A Report Prepared for the United Church of Christ Justice and Witness Ministries." Accessed November 12, 2007. http://www.ucc.org/justice/pdfs/toxic20.pdf.

"Toxic Wastes and Race Revisited: An Update on the 1987 Report on the Racial and Socioeconomic Characteristics of Communities with Hazardous Waste Sites." Center for Policy Alternatives, National Association for the Advancement of Colored People, and United Church of Christ Commission for Racial Justice, 1994.

"Trapped by Floodwaters." New Orleans. AP/Wide World Photo. www.boingboing.net/images/taleoftwocities_2.jpg.

United Health Foundation. *America's Health Rankings: A Call to Action for People and Their Communities*. Minnetonka MN: United Health Foundation, 2006.

United Nations High Commissioner for Refugees. G.A. Res. 428/5, U.N. Doc. A/RES/428/5, Dec. 14, 1950. http://www.unhcr.org/basics/BASICS/420cc0432.html.

United Nations Millennium Project on World Poverty. "Investing in Development." Final Report. 2005. http://www.unmillenniumproject.org/.

United Nations Office for the Coordination of Humanitarian Affairs. "Cuba: A Model in Hurricane Risk Management." Press release. IHA/943 (Sept. 14, 2004). http://www.un.org/News/Press/docs/2004/iha943.doc.htm.

United States Army Corps of Engineers. "Decision Making Chronology for the Lake Pontchartrain and Vicinity Hurricane Protection—Draft Final Report." 2007.

———. "General Policies." Accessed July 30, 1999. http://www.usace.army.mil/publications/eng-pamphlets/ep1165-2-1/c-3.pdf.

———. Interagency Performance Evaluation Task Force. "Performance Evaluation of the New Orleans Southeast Louisiana Hurricane Protection System." Executive Summary and Overview. American Society of Civil Engineers. vol. 1. March 26, 2007.

United States Census Bureau News. "Income Climbs, Poverty Stabilizes, Uninsured Rate Increases." Washington DC: Government Printing Office, August 29, 2006.

United States Congress, Joint Committee on Taxation. "Estimates of Federal Tax Expenditures for Fiscal Years 2006–2010." 109th Cong. Washington DC: Government Printing Office, January 12, 2005.

United States Constitution. Art. 1, § 2, para. 3.

United States Department of Health and Human Services. "Health Disparities Experienced by Blacks or African Americans—United States." *Morbidity and Mortality Weekly Report* 54 (January 14, 2005): 1–3.

———. *Healthy People 2010: Understanding and Improving Health*. 2nd ed. Washington DC: Government Printing Office, 2000.

———. "Morbidity Surveillance after Hurricane Katrina—Arkansas, Louisiana, Mississippi, and Texas, September 2005." *Morbidity and Mortality Weekly Report* 55 (July 7, 2006): 727–31.

United States Department of Justice. "Prison and Jail Inmates at Midyear 2004." Bureau of Justice Statistics Bulletin. April 2005.

United States Department of Transportation. Order on Environmental Justice, 62 Fed. Reg. 72 (April 15, 1997).

United States General Accounting Office. "Siting of Hazardous Waste Landfills and Their Correlation with Racial and Economic Status of Surrounding Communities." June 1, 1983, accessed March 19, 2007. http://archive.gao.gov/d48t13/121648.pdf.

United States House of Representatives. Select Bipartisan Committee to Investigate the Preparation for and Response to Hurricane Katrina. "A Failure of Initiative: Final Report of the Select Bipartisan Committee to Investigate the Preparation for and Response to Hurricane Katrina." 109th Cong., H.R. Rep. No. 109–000. Washington DC: Government Printing Office, February 19, 2006.

United States Senate. Committee on Homeland Security and Governmental Affairs. "Hurricane Katrina: A Nation Still Unprepared." S. Rpt. 109–322. 2006.

United States v. Bridges, 86 A.F.T.R.2d (RIA) 5280 (4th Cir. 2000).

United States v. Dee, 912 F.2d 741, 744 (4th Cir. 1990).

United States v. Foster, 2002–2 U.S.T.C. (CCH) ¶ 50,785 (E.D. Va. 2002).

United States v. Haugabook, 2002 U.S. Dist. LEXIS 25314 (M.D. Ga. 2002).

United States v. Mims, 2002 U.S. Dist. LEXIS 25291 (S.D. Ga. 2002).

United States White House. "The Federal Response to Hurricane Katrina: Lessons Learned." 2006.

United Steelworkers of America, AFL-CIO-CLC v. Weber, 443 U.S. 193 (1979).

"Urgent Weather Message." National Weather Service/New Orleans, Louisiana, August 28, 2005, at 10:11 a.m.

Verchick, Robert R. M. Statement to U.S. Senate Committee on Environment and Public Works hearing. Accessed November 17, 2005. http://epw.senate.gov/hearing_statements.cfm?id=248927.

Voices of the Civil Rights Movement: Black American Freedom Songs, 1960–1966. Washington DC: Smithsonian Folkways Recordings, 1997.

World Health Organization. Constitution. Geneva, 1948.

Wygant v. Jackson Bd. of Education, 476 U.S. 267, at 276.

Secondary Sources

Journal articles, book chapters, and non-autobiographical books.

Alfieri, Anthony V. "Race Trials." Texas Law Review 76 (1998): 1293–321.

Aoki, Keith. "Space Invaders: Critical Geography, the 'Third World' in International Law and Critical Race Theory." *Villanova Law Review* 45 (2000): 913–25.

Aprill, Ellen P., and Richard Schmalbeck. "Post-Disaster Tax Legislation: A Series of Unfortunate Events." *Duke Law Journal* 56 (2006): 51–58.

Ashcroft, Bill, Gareth Griffiths, and Helen Tiffin, eds. *Key Concepts in Post-Colonial Studies.* London: Routlege, 2000.

Atkins, D., and E. M. Moy. "Left Behind: The Legacy of Hurricane Katrina." *British Medical Journal* 331 (2005): 916–18.

Baldus, David C., et al. "Comparative Review of Death Sentences: An Empirical Study of the Georgia Experience." *Journal of Criminal Law and Criminology* 74 (1983): 661.

———. "Racial Discrimination and the Death Penalty in the Post-Furman Era: An Empirical and Legal Overview, with Recent Findings from Philadelphia." *Cornell Law Review* 83 (1998): 1638–61.

Balkin, Jack. *What Brown v. Board of Education Should Have Said: The Nation's Top Legal Experts Rewrite America's Landmark Civil Rights Decision.* New York: New York University Press, 2002.

Bancroft, Frederick. *Slave Trading in the Old South.* Columbia: University of South Carolina Press, 1959.

Banks, Taunya Lovell. "Colorism: A Darker Shade of Pale." *UCLA Law Review* 47 (1999–2000): 1705–22.

Barone, Charles A. *Radical Political Economy.* Armonk NY: M. E. Sharpe, 2004.

Barry, John M. *Rising Tide: The Great Mississippi Flood of 1927 and How It Changed America.* New York: Simon and Schuster, 1998.

Becker, Gary S. *The Economics of Discrimination.* Chicago: University of Chicago Press, 1957.

Been, Vicki. "Market Dynamics and the Siting of Lulus: Questions to Raise in the Classroom about Existing Research." *West Virginia Law Review* 96 (1994): 1069.

Berube, Alan, and Bruce Katz. "Katrina's Window: Confronting Concentrated Poverty across America." Washington DC: Brookings Institution, October 2005.

Binder, Dennis, Colin Crawford, Eileen P. Gauna, et al. "A Survey of Federal Agency Response to President Clinton's Executive Order No. 12898 on Environmental Justice." *Environmental Law Reporter* 31 (2001): 11133.

Block, Walter. "Government and the Katrina Crises." *Free Market*, October 2005. http://www.mises.org/freemarket_detail.asp?control=56 5&sortorder=articledate.

Boland, R. T. "Can It Get Any Worse?" *Frontiers of Health Services Management* 23 (2006): 31–34.

Bourne, Joel K., Jr. "Gone with the Water." *National Geographic Magazine*, October 2004, 1.

Bourque, Linda B., et al. "Weathering the Storm: The Impact of Hurricanes on Physical and Mental Health." *Annals of the American Academy of Political and Social Science* 604 (2006): 129.

Bowden, Charles. "Exodus: Coyotes, Pollos, and the Promised Van." *Mother Jones* 31, no. 5 (2006): 36.

Bowers, Meredith J. "The Executive's Response to Environmental Injustice: Executive Order 12898." *Environmental Law* 1 (1995): 645.

Brest, Paul. "The Supreme Court Term—1975 Forward: In Defense of the Anti-Discrimination Principle." *Harvard Law Review* 98 (1976): 1.

Brinkley, Douglas. *The Great Deluge: Hurricane Katrina, New Orleans, and the Mississippi Gulf Coast.* New York: William Morrow, 2006.

Brodie, M., E. Weltzien, A. Drew, R. J. Blendon, and M. A. Benson. "Experiences of Hurricane Katrina Evacuees in Houston Shelters: Implications for Future Planning." *American Journal of Public Health* 96 (2006): 1402–8.

Brookings Institution. "New Orleans after the Storm: Lessons from the Past, a Plan for the Future." Washington DC: Brookings Institution, 2005.

Brown, Michael K., Martin Carnoy, Elliot Currie, Troy Duster, David B.

Oppenheimer, Marjorie M. Shultz, and David Wellman. *Whitewashing Race: The Myth of a Color-Blind Society*. Berkeley: University of California Press, 2003.

Browne-Dianis, Jennifer Lai, Marielena Hincapie, and Saket Soni, eds. *And Injustice for All: Workers' Lives in the Reconstruction of New Orleans*. Washington DC: Advancement Project, 2006.

Bullard, Robert D. *Dumping in Dixie: Race, Class, and Environmental Quality*. Boulder CO: Westview Press, 2000.

———. *Unequal Protection: Environmental Justice and Communities of Color*. San Francisco: Sierra Club Books, 1997.

Canterbery, E. Ray. *The Making of Economics*. Belmont CA: Wadsworth, 1976.

Canterbery, E. Ray, and Robert J. Burkhardt. "What Do We Mean by Asking Whether Economics Is a Science?" In *Why Economics Is Not Yet a Science*, ed. Alfred S. Eichner. Armonk NY: M. E. Sharpe, 1983.

Carr, James H. Comments on "Predatory Home Lending: Moving toward Legal and Policy Solutions." Conference at John Marshall Law School, Chicago, September 9, 2005.

Carter, Stephen L. "When Victims Happen to Be Black." *Yale Law Journal* 97 (1988): 420.

Cash, Heather. "Security Council Resolution 1593 and Conflicting Principles of International Law: How the Future of the International Criminal Court Is at Stake." *Brandeis Law Journal* 45 (2007): 573.

Cato Institute. "Did Big Government Return with Katrina?" *Cato Policy Report*, November/December 2005. http://www.cato.org/pubs/pol icy_report/v27n6/cpr-27n6-2.pdf.

Clarke, Lee. "Worst Case Katrina." In *Understanding Katrina: Perspectives from the Social Sciences*. Washington DC: American Politics, Social Science Research Council, September 12, 2005.

Cole, Luke, and Sheila Foster. *From the Ground Up: Environmental Racism and the Rise of the Environmental Justice Movement*. New York: New York University Press, 2001.

Comfort, Louise K. "Fragility in Disaster Response: Hurricane Katrina, 29 August 2005." *Forum* 3, no. 3 (2005), article 1.

Congleton, Roger D. "The Story of Katrina: New Orleans and the Political Economy of Catastrophe." *Public Choice* 127 (2006): 5–15.

Cooper, Christopher, and Robert Block. *Disaster: Hurricane Katrina and the Failure of Homeland Security*. New York: Times Books, 2006.

Corless, I. B., et al. "Symptom Status and Medication Adherence in HIV Disease." *International Conference on AIDS Abstracts* 14 (2002).

"The Creole City." Accessed May 27, 2007. http://www.neworleansonline .com/neworleans/multicultural/multiculturalhistory/creole.html.

Dalton, George. *Primitive, Archaic and Modern Economies: Essays of Karl Polanyi*. Garden City NY: Anchor Books 1968.

Daniels, Ronald J., Donald F. Kettl, and Howard Kunreuther, eds. *On Risk and Disaster: Lessons from Hurricane Katrina*. Philadelphia: University of Pennsylvania Press, 2006.

Davidson, Paul. *Post Keynesian Macroeconomic Theory*. Northampton UK: Edward Elgar, 1994.

Davies, G., et al. "Overview and Implementation of an Intervention to Prevent Adherence Failure among HIV-Infected Adults Initiating Antiretroviral Therapy: Lessons Learned from Project HEART." *AIDS Care* 18 (2006): 895–903.

Denton, Nancy, and Douglass S. Massey. *American Apartheid: Segregation and the Making of the Underclass*. Cambridge MA: Harvard University Press, 1998.

Dimitrjevic, Nenad. "Moral Responsibility for Collective Crime: Transitional Justice in the Former Yugoslavia." *Eurozine*, May 7, 2006. http:// www.eurozine.com/articles/2006–07–05-dimitrijevic-en.html.

Donatelle, Rebecca J. *Health: The Basics*. 4th ed. Boston: Allyn and Bacon, 2000.

Dreier, Peter, John Mollenkopf, and Todd Swanstrom. *Place Matters: Metropolitics for the Twenty-First Century*. Lawrence: University Press of Kansas, 2001.

Dugger, William. *Underground Economics*. Armonk NY: M. E. Sharpe, 1992.

Dyson, Michael Eric. *Come Hell or High Water: Hurricane Katrina and the Color of Disaster*. New York: Basic Books, 2006.

Edwards, George E. "International Human Rights Law Violations before, during, and after Hurricane Katrina: An International Law Framework for Analysis." *Thurgood Marshall Law Review* 31 (2006): 353–67.

Encyclopedia of Public International Law. Max Planck Institute for

Comparative Public Law and International Law. Vol. 4. New York: Elsevier/North-Holland, 2000.

Evans, Gareth. "The Responsibility to Protect and the Duty to Protect." *American Society of International Law* 98 (2004): 77.

Evans, Gareth, and Mahomed Sahnoun. "The Responsibility to Protect: Rethinking Humanitarian Intervention." *Foreign Affairs* 81 (2002): 99.

Fair, Bryan K. "The Anatomy of American Caste." *St. Louis University Public Law Review* 18, no. 2 (1999): 381.

———. "The Darker Face of *Brown*: The Promise and Reality of the Decision's Anticaste Moorings Remain Unreconciled." *Judicature* 88 (September–October 2004): 80.

———. *Notes of a Racial Caste Baby: Color Blindness and the End of Affirmative Action.* New York: New York University Press, 1997.

———. "Re(caste)ing Equality Theory: Will *Grutter* Survive Itself by 2028?" In symposium, "Race Jurisprudence and the Supreme Court: Where Do We Go from Here?" *University of Pennsylvania Journal of Constitutional Law* 7 (2005): 721, 722.

———. "Taking Educational Caste Seriously: Why *Grutter* Will Help Very Little." *Tulane Law Review* 78 (2004): 1843.

Fischetti, Mark. "Drowning New Orleans." *Scientific American*, October 2001, 6.

Franco, C., et al. "Systemic Collapse: Medical Care in the Aftermath of Hurricane Katrina." *Biosecurity and Bioterrorism* 4 (2006): 135–46.

Franklin, John Hope. *Mirror to America.* New York: Farrar, Straus and Giroux, 2005.

Franklin, John Hope, and Alfred A. Moss Jr. *From Slavery to Freedom: A History of African Americans.* 8th ed. New York: Knopf, 2000.

Fraser, Cary. "An American Dilemma." In *Window on Freedom: Race, Civil Rights, and Foreign Affairs, 1945–1988,* ed. Brenda Plummer. Chapel Hill: University of North Carolina Press, 2003.

Friedman, Milton. *Capitalism and Freedom.* Chicago: University of Chicago Press, 1962.

Frymer, Paul, et al. "Katrina's Political Roots and Divisions: Race, Class, and Federalism." In *Understanding Katrina: Perspectives from the Social Sciences.* New York: American Politics, Social Science Research Council, September 28, 2005.

Garrett, Brandon L., and Tania Tetlow. "Criminal Justice Collapse: The Constitution after Katrina." *Duke Law Journal* 56 (2006): 127–28.

Germany, Kent B. *New Orleans after the Promises: Poverty, Citizenship, and the Search for the Great Society*. Athens: University of Georgia Press, 2007.

Gordon, Ruth. "Contemplating the WTO from the Margins." *Berkeley La Raza Law Journal* 17 (2006): 95–106.

———. "Critical Race Theory and International Law: Convergence and Divergence." *Villanova Law Review* 45 (2000): 827–34.

———. "Growing Constitutions." *University of Pennsylvania Journal of Constitutional Law* 1, no. 3 (1999): 528–82.

———. "Racing U.S. Foreign Policy." *National Black Law Journal* 17 (2003): 1–11.

———. "Saving Failed States: Sometimes a Neocolonialist Notion." *American University Journal of International Law and Policy* 12 (1997): 903–62.

Gordon, Ruth, and Jon H. Sylvester. "Deconstructing Development." *Wisconsin International Law Journal* 22 (2004): 1–79.

Grad, F. P. "The Preamble of the Constitution of the World Health Organization." *Bulletin of the World Health Organization* 80, no. 12 (2002): 981–84.

Graetz, Michael J., and Deborah H. Schenk. *Federal Income Taxation: Principles and Policies*. 5th ed. Washington DC: Foundation Press, 2005.

Greenough, P. G., and T. D. Kirsch. "Public Health Response—Assessing Needs." *New England Journal of Medicine* 353 (2005): 1544.

Grey, Thomas C. "Holmes and Legal Pragmatism." *Stanford Law Review* 41 (1989): 787–96.

Hacker, Andrew. *Money: Who Has How Much and Why*. New York: Scribner, 1998.

———. *Two Nations: Black and White, Separate, Hostile, Unequal*. New York: Scribner's, 1992.

Hall, Gwendolyn Mildew. *Africans in Colonial Louisiana: The Development of Afro-Creole Culture in the Eighteenth Century*. Baton Rouge: Louisiana State University Press, 1995.

Handwerk, Brian. "Eye on the Storm: Hurricane Katrina Fast Facts." *National Geographic News*, September 6, 2005, 1.

Hardy, Arthur. "History of Mardi Gras." Accessed May 27, 2007. http://www.neworleansonline.com/neworleans/mardigras/mardigrashistory/mghistory.html.

Harper, S., et al. "Trends in the Black-White Life Expectancy Gap in the United States, 1983–2003." *Journal of the American Medical Association* 297 (2007): 1224–32.

Harris, Cheryl I. "Whitewashing Race, Scapegoating Culture." *California Law Review* 94 (2006): 907.

Hartman, Chester, and Gregory D. Squires, eds. *There Is No Such Thing as a Natural Disaster: Race, Class, and Hurricane Katrina*. New York: Routledge, 2006.

Harvey, John T. "Heuristic Judgment Theory." *Journal of Economic Issues* 32 (1998): 47.

Hernández, Tanya Kateri. "Multiracial Matrix: The Role of Race Ideology in the Enforcement of Antidiscrimination Laws, A United States–Latin America Comparison." *Cornell Law Review* 87 (2002): 1093, 1152–53.

Higginbotham, A. Leon, Jr. *In the Matter of Color: Race and the American Legal Process: The Colonial Period*. New York: Oxford University Press, 1978.

———. *Shades of Freedom: Racial Politics and Presumptions of the American Legal Process*. New York: Oxford University Press, 1996.

Hirsch, Arnold H., and Joseph Logsdon. "The People and Culture of New Orleans." Accessed May 27, 2007. http://www.neworleansonline.com/neworleans/history/people.html.

Hodgson, Geoffrey M. "What Is the Essence of Institutional Economics?" *Journal of Economic Issues* 34 (2000): 317–23.

Hook, Jonathan P., and Trisha B. Miller. "The Continuing Storm: How Disaster Recovery Excludes Those Most in Need." *California Western Law Review* 43 (2006): 21.

Horne, Gerald. "Race from Power." In *Window on Freedom: Race, Civil Rights, and Foreign Affairs, 1945–1988*, ed. Brenda Plummer. Chapel Hill: University of North Carolina Press, 2003.

Houston, Charles Hamilton. "Don't Shout Too Soon." *Crisis* 43 (1936): 14.

Howitt, Arnold M., and Herman B. Leonard. "Katrina and the Core

Challenges of Disaster Response." *Fletcher Forum of World Affairs* 30 (2006).

Huey, James. Congressional testimony before the Senate Committee on Homeland Security and Governmental Affairs. Pp. 5–7. Accessed December 15, 2005. http://hsgac.senate.gov/_files/121505Huey.pdf.

Islam, M. Rafiqul. "The Sudanese Darfur Crisis and Internally Displaced Persons in International Law: The Least Protection for the Most Vulnerable." *International Journal of Refugee Law* 18, no. 2 (2006): 356–57.

Jaksic, Vesna. "A Fresh Start: The Stories of Those Who Left." *National Law Journal*, February 13, 2007. http://www.law.com.

Jenkins, Henry. "'People from That Part of the World': The Politics of Dislocation." Culture at Large Forum with George Lipsitz. *Cultural Anthropology* 21, no. 3 (August 2006): 469–86.

Johnson, Walter. *Soul by Soul: Life in the Antebellum Slave Market.* Cambridge MA: Harvard University Press, 1999.

Jones, D. Marvin. *Race, Sex, and Suspicion: The Myth of the Black Male.* Westport CT: Greenwood Press, 2005.

Jones, Trina. "Shades of Brown: The Law of Skin Color." *Duke Law Journal* 49 (1999–2000): 1487–508.

Kessler, R. C., S. Galea, R. T. Jones, and H. A. Parker. "Mental Illness and Suicidality after Hurricane Katrina." *Bulletin of the World Health Organization* 84 (2006): 930–38.

Kettl, Donald F. "Is the Worst Yet to Come?" *Annals of the American Academy of Political and Social Science* 604 (2006): 273.

Kuhn, Thomas S. *The Structure of Scientific Revolutions.* Chicago: University of Chicago Press, 1970.

Kweit, Mary Greiz, and Robert Griez Kweit. "A Tale of Two Disasters." *Publius*, June 22, 2006, 8.

Kysar, Douglas, and Thomas McGarity. "Did NEPA Drown New Orleans? The Levees, the Blame Game, and the Hazards of Hindsight." *Duke Law Journal* 56 (2006): 179.

LaFave, Wayne R., and Austin W. Scott Jr. *Criminal Law* § 3.7(a). 2nd ed. Toronto, Ontario: Thompson, 1986.

Lambert, Thomas, and Christopher Boerner. "Environmental Inequality:

Economic Causes, Economic Solutions." *Yale Journal on Regulation* 14 (Winter 1997): 195.

Larkin, H. "Louisiana's Second Chance." *Hospitals and Health Networks* 81 (February 2007): 54–60.

Lee, Cynthia K. Y. "Race and the Victim: An Examination of Capital Sentencing and Guilt Attribution Studies." *Chicago-Kent Law Review* 73 (1998): 533.

Levitt, Jeremy. "The Responsibility to Protect: A Beaver without a Dam? Review of *The Responsibility to Protect*, by the International Commission on Intervention and State Sovereignty, and *The Responsibility to Protect: Research, Bibliography, Background*, by Thomas G. Weiss and Don Hubert (supp. vol. to *The Responsibility to Protect*). *Michigan Journal of International Law* 25 (2003): 153.

Litwack, Leon F. *"Been in the Storm So Long": The Aftermath of Slavery*. New York: Vintage, 1979.

Logue, J. N. "The Public Health Response to Disasters in the 21st Century: Reflections on Hurricane Katrina." *Journal of Environmental Health* 69 (2006): 9–13.

Marwell, Gerald, and Ruth E. Ames. "Economists Free Ride, Does Anyone Else? Experiments on the Provision of Public Goods, IV," *Journal of Public Economics* 15 (1981): 295–96.

Matthew, Dayna Bowen. "Disastrous Disasters: Restoring Civil Rights Protections for the Victims of the State in Natural Disasters." *Journal of Health and Biomedical Law* 2 (2006): 213–48.

Mauer, Marc. *Race to Incarcerate*. New York: New Press, 2006.

McQuaid, John, and Mark Schleifstein. *Path of Destruction: The Devastation of New Orleans and the Coming Age of Superstorms*. New York: Little, Brown, 2006.

Medina, Isabel. "Confronting the Rights Deficit at Home: Is the Nation Prepared in the Aftermath of Katrina? Confronting the Myth of Efficiency." *California Western Law Review* 43 (2006): 9.

Mirowski, Philip. *More Light Than Heat: Economics as Social Physics, Physics as Nature's Economics*. Cambridge: Cambridge University Press, 1989.

Moran, Beverly I., and William Whitford. "A Black Critique of the Internal Revenue Code." *Wisconsin Law Review* 1996 (1996): 751.

Moshman, Rachael, and John Hardenbergh. "The Color of Katrina: A Proposal to Allow Disparate Impact Environmental Claims." *Sustainable Development Law and Policy* 6 (2006): 15.

Muñiz, Brenda. "In the Eye of the Storm: How the Government and Private Response to Hurricane Katrina Failed Latinos." *National Council of La Raza*, February 28, 2006.

Mutua, Makau. "Savages, Victims, and Saviors: The Metaphor of Human Rights." *Harvard International Law Journal* 42 (2001): 201–12.

Myers, Martha A., and John Hagan. "Private and Public Trouble: Prosecutors and the Allocation of Court Resources." *Social Problems* 26 (1979): 439–47.

Nelson, K. "High Levels of Formaldehyde Found in Some FEMA Trailers." May 22, 2007, accessed May 23, 2007. http://www.wafb.com/Global/story.asp?s=6527613.

Niehans, Jurg. *A History of Economic Theory: Classic Contributions, 1720–1980.* Baltimore: Johns Hopkins University Press, 1990.

Nigg, Joanne M., John Barnshaw, and Manuel R. Torres. "Hurricane Katrina and the Flooding of New Orleans: Emergent Issues in Sheltering and Temporary Housing." *Annals of the American Academy of Political and Social Science* 604 (2006): 113.

Niman, Michael I. "Katrina's America: Failure, Racism, and Profiteering." *Humanist*, November–December 2005, 11–15.

O'Conner, Alice, Chris Tilly, and Lawrence D. Bobo, eds. *Urban Inequality: Evidence from Four Cities.* New York: Russell Sage Foundation, 2006.

Omi, Michael, and Howard Winant. *Racial Formation in the United States.* New York: Routledge, 1994.

Orford, Anne. *Reading Humanitarian Intervention: Human Rights and the Use of Force in International Law.* Cambridge: Cambridge University Press, 2003.

Perea, Juan F., et al. *Race and Races: Cases and Resources for a Multiracial America.* St. Paul MN: West Group, 2000.

Plummer, Brenda Gayle. *Rising Wind: Black Americans and U.S. Foreign Affairs.* Chapel Hill: University of North Carolina Press, 1996.

Polanyi, Karl. *The Great Transformation.* Boston: Beacon Press 2001.

Posner, Richard A. "Adoption and Market Theory: The Regulation of the

Market in Adoptions." *Boston University Law Review* 67 (1987): 59–61.

Pouncy, Charles R. P. "Contemporary Financial Innovation: Orthodoxy and Alternatives." *Southern Methodist University Law Review* 51 (1998): 505.

———. "Institutional Economics and Critical Race/LatCrit Theory: The Need for a Critical 'Raced' Economics." *Rutgers Law Review* 54 (2002): 841.

———. "The Rational Rogue: Neoclassical Economic Ideology in the Regulation of the Financial Professional." *Vermont Law Review* 26 (2002): 267–68.

———. "Stock Markets in Sub-Saharan Africa: Western Legal Institutions as a Component of the Neo-Colonial Project." *University of Pennsylvania Journal of International Economic Law* 23 (2002): 85–98.

Prashad, Vijay. *The Darker Nations: A People's History of the Third World.* New York: New Press, 2000.

Radelet, Michael L., and Glenn L. Pierce. "Race and Prosecutorial Discretion in Homicide Cases." *Law and Society Review* 19 (1985): 587–619.

Rechtschaffen, Clifford, and Eileen P. Gauna. *Environmental Justice: Law, Policy, and Regulation.* Durham NC: Carolina Academic Press, 2002.

Remien, R. H., A. E. Hirky, M. O. Jonson, D. W. Weinhardt, and G. M. Le. "Adherence to Medication Treatment: A Qualitative Study of Facilitators and Barriers among a Diverse Sample of HIV+ Men and Women in Four U.S. Cities." *AIDS and Behavior* 7 (2003): 61–72.

Rintamaki, L. S., T. C. Davis, S. Skripkauskas, C. L. Bennett, and M. S. Wolf. "Social Stigma Concerns and HIV Medication Adherence." *AIDS Patient Care and STDs* 20 (2006): 359–68.

Rist, Gilbert. *The History of Development.* New York: Zed Books, 1997.

Robeson, Paul, Jr. *A Black Way of Seeing.* New York: Seven Stories Press, 2006.

Rodricks, Joseph V. "Some Attributes of Risk Influencing Decision Making by Public Health and Regulatory Officials." *American Journal of Epidemiology* 154, no. 12 (2001). Accessed November 12, 2007. http://aje.oxfordjournals.org/cgi/reprint/154/12/S7.pdf.

Rodriguez, H., and B. E. Aguirre. "Hurricane Katrina and the Healthcare Infrastructure: A Focus on Disaster Preparedness, Response, and Resiliency." *Frontiers of Health Services Management* 23 (2006): 13–23.

Rodríguez, Havidán, Joseph Trainor, and Enrico L. Quarantelli. "Rising to the Challenges of a Catastrophe: The Emergent and Prosocial Behavior Following Hurricane Katrina." *Annals of the American Academy of Political and Social Science* 604 (2006): 82.

Rosenbaum, S. "U.S. Health Policy in the Aftermath of Hurricane Katrina." *Journal of the American Medical Association* 295 (2006): 437–40.

Rosenthal, Lawrence. "Policing and Equal Protection." *Yale Law and Policy Review* 21 (2003): 53.

Rudowitz, R., D. Rowland, and A. Shartzer. "Health Care in New Orleans before and after Hurricane Katrina." *Health Affairs* 25 (2006): 393–406.

Salvaggio, J. *New Orleans' Charity Hospital: A Story of Physicians, Politics, and Poverty.* Baton Rouge: Louisiana State University Press, 1992.

Satcher, D. "Our Commitment to Eliminate Racial and Ethnic Health Disparities." *Yale Journal of Health Policy, Law and Ethics* 1 (2001): 1–14.

Scott, Wendy B. "From an Act of God to the Failure of Man: Hurricane Katrina and the Economic Recovery of New Orleans." *Villanova Law Review* 51 (2007): 581–85.

Shapiro, Thomas M. *The Hidden Cost of Being African American: How Wealth Perpetuates Inequality.* New York: Oxford University Press, 2003.

Sherman, Arloc, and Issac Shapiro. *Essential Facts about the Victims of Hurricane Katrina.* Center on Budget and Policy Priorities, September 19, 2005. http://www.cbpp.org/9-19-05pov.htm.

Sherman, Howard J. "A Holistic-Evolutionary View of Racism, Sexism, and Class Inequality." In *Inequality: Radical Institutionalist Views on Race, Gender, Class, and Nation,* ed. William M. Dugger. Westport CT: Greenwood Press, 1996.

Shughart, William F., II. "Katrinanomics: The Politics and Economics of Disaster Relief." *Public Choice* 127 (2006): 31.

Simmons, Kenneth. "Rethinking Mental States." *Boston University Law Review* 72 (1992): 463–65.

Sirkin, Susan. "The Debacle of Hurricane Katrina: A Human Rights Response." *Fletcher Forum of World Affairs* 30 (2006): 223.

Slater, Cliff. "General Motors and the Demise of Street Cars." *Transportation Quarterly* 51 (1997): 45.

Smelser, Neil J., William Julius Wilson, and Faith Mitchell, eds. *America Becoming: Racial Trends and Their Consequences*. Vol. 2. Washington DC: National Academy Press, 2001.

Smith, Nathan. "Water, Water Everywhere, and Not a Bite to Eat: Sovereign Immunity, Federal Disaster Relief, and Hurricane Katrina." *San Diego Law Review* 43 (2006): 699.

Smith, Neil. "There's No Such Thing as a Natural Disaster." *Understanding Katrina: Perspectives from the Social Sciences*. http://understandingkatrina.ssrc.org/Smith/.

Sobel, Russell S., and Peter T. Leeson. "Flirting with Disaster: The Inherent Problems with FEMA." *Policy Analysis* (Cato Institute) 573 (2006): 1–9.

Spain, Daphne. "Race Relations and Residential Segregation in New Orleans: Two Centuries of Paradox." Spec. issue, Race and Residence in American Cities. *Annals of the American Academy of Political and Social Science* 441, no. 1 (1979): 82–96.

Spencer, Robyn. "Contested Terrain: The Mississippi Flood of 1927 and the Struggle to Control Black Labor." *Journal of Negro History* 79, no. 2 (1994): 171.

Stanley, Alan P. "The Rich Young Ruler and Salvation." *Bibliotheca Sacra* 163 (2006): 46–51.

Stowe, Harriet Beecher. *Dred: A Tale of the Great Dismal Swamp in Two Volumes*. Chapel Hill: University of North Carolina Press, 1856.

Sunstein, Cass R. "The Anti-Caste Principle." *Michigan Law Review* 92 (1994): 2410.

Surrey, Stanley S., and Paul R. McDaniel. *Tax Expenditures*. Cambridge MA: Harvard University Press, 1985.

Teitel, Ruti G. *Transitional Justice*. New York: Oxford University Press, 2000.

tenBroek, Jacobus. *Equal under Law*. New York: Collier Books, 1965.

Thomas, June Manning. *Redevelopment and Race: Planning a Finer City in Postwar Detroit*. Baltimore: Johns Hopkins University Press, 1997.

Tierney, Kathleen, Christine Bevc, and Erica Kuligowski. "Metaphors Matter: Disaster Myths, Media Frames, and Their Consequences in Hurricane Katrina." *Annals of the American Academy of Political and Social Science* 604 (2006): 57.

Tomlinson, Sherrie Armstrong. "No New Orleans Left Behind: An Examination of the Disparate Impact of Hurricane Katrina on Minorities." *Connecticut Law Review* 38 (2006): 1153–59.

Troutt, David Dante, and Charles Ogletree, eds. *After the Storm: Black Intellectuals Explore the Meaning of Hurricane Katrina*. New York: New Press, 2007.

Van Cleave, Rachel A. "Property Lessons in August Wilson's The Piano Lessons and the Wake of Hurricane Katrina." *California Western Law Review* 43 (2006): 97–98.

van de Wetering, Ernest. *Rembrandt: The Painter at Work*. Berkeley: University of California Press, 2000.

Walker, Samuel, et al. *The Color of Justice: Race, Ethnicity and Crime in America*. New York: Wadsworth, 2000.

Walsh, J. C., R. Horne, M. Dalton, A. P. Burgess, and B. G. Gazzard. "Reasons for Non-Adherence to Antiretroviral Therapy: Patients' Perspectives Provide Evidence of Multiple Causes." *AIDS Care* 13 (2001): 709–20.

Waugh, William L. "The Political Costs of Failure in the Katrina and Rita Disasters." *Annals of the American Academy of Political and Social Science* 604 (2006): 10–16.

Weeden, L. Darnell. "Hurricane Katrina: First Amendment Censorship and the News Media." *Thurgood Marshall Law Review* 31 (2005–6): 479–89.

Welbourne, Miranda. "The Environmental Justice Movement's Response to Hurricane Katrina, A Critique: Problems Faced, Successes, Failures and the State of the Movement One Year Later." *Thurgood Marshall Law Review* 32 (2006): 125.

West, Cornel. "Exiles from a City and from a Nation." *Observer*, September 11, 2005.

Williams, Juan. *Enough: The Phony Leaders, Dead-End Movements, and*

Culture of Failure That Are Undermining Black America—and What We Can Do about It. New York: Crown, 2006.

Wilson, J. "Health and the Environment after Hurricane Katrina." *Annals of Internal Medicine* 144 (2006): 153.

Wilson, Jim. "New Orleans Is Sinking." *Popular Mechanics*, September 11, 2001, 5.

Woods, Clyde. "Do You Know What It Means to Miss New Orleans? Katrina, Trap Economics, and the Rebirth of the Blues." *American Quarterly* 57 (2005): 1005–9.

Worika, Ibibia Lucky. "Deprivation, Despoilation and Destitution: Whither Environment and Human Rights in Nigeria's Niger Delta?" *ILSA Journal of International and Comparative Law* 8 (Fall 2001): 1.

CONTRIBUTORS

Mitchell F. Crusto is Professor of Law at Loyola University New Orleans. His legal scholarship focuses on the interdisciplinary intersections between law and society, especially business and the environment, the constitution and equality, insurance and fairness, and the law of sole proprietors and liability.

Bryan K. Fair is the Thomas E. Skinner Professor of Law at the University of Alabama School of Law. He is a contributor to National Public Radio and the Annenberg Public Policy Center at the University of Pennsylvania. He is the author of *Notes of a Racial Caste Baby: Colorblindness and the End of Affirmative Action* (1997). His current research agenda focuses on equality theory, and the central theme of his writing is equal protection jurisprudence.

Ruth Gordon is Professor of Law at Villanova University School of Law. Her primary interests are in international law. She is the author of many articles on the various roles the United Nations plays in developing countries. She has been a Riesenfeld Fellow in Public International Law at the University of California at Berkeley and a Revson Fellowship Scholar at the City College of the City University of New York Center for Legal Education and Urban Policy. She was a member of the board of directors of the American Society of International Law and the American Bar Association International Law and Practice Section, and is currently a member of the American Bar Association Committee on World Order Under Law.

Linda S. Greene is Evjue-Bascom Professor of Law at the University of Wisconsin–Madison. Her teaching and academic scholarship concentrate on the areas of constitutional law, civil procedure, legislation, civil rights, and sports law. She has worked as a civil rights attorney on the staff of the

NAACP Legal Defense and Educational Fund in New York City. She has lectured and consulted on constitutional and civil rights issues at the request of the U.S. Department of State in Austria, Mozambique, Norway, and Zimbabwe. She has served as counsel to the U.S. Senate Judiciary Committee and as associate vice chancellor of UW–Madison.

D. Marvin Jones is Professor of Law at the University of Miami School of Law and a nationally recognized expert on civil and political rights. He has published widely in the nation's most prestigious law journals, including the *Georgetown Law Journal*, the *University of Michigan Law Journal*, and the *Vanderbilt Law Journal*. His essays also appeared in various books, including *Critical White Studies: Looking behind the Mirror* (1997). In 1997 he was the James Thomas Prize by Yale University, which recognized him as one the most "innovative" legal scholars in the United States. He is the author of *Race, Sex, and Suspicion: The Myth of the Black Male* (2005). A familiar face in various media outlets, he has appeared on PBS's *Frontline*, CNN's *Burden of Proof*, Fox News's *The O'Reilly Factor*, and *The Week in Review*.

Phyllis Kotey, a retired judge, is Clinical Associate Professor of Law and director of the Juvenile Justice Clinic at Florida International College of Law. She supervises a Juvenile Delinquency and Education Advocacy clinic and teaches in the areas of children, ethics, education, and criminal practice. She served as an assistant state attorney specializing in major crimes and capital sexual battery cases and serving as chief of the county court. She served as Associate Dean of the Florida Judicial College and is a faculty member for the National Justice Institute, the National Judicial College, and various judicial conferences throughout the nation. She speaks and lectures widely on judicial ethics, criminal law, domestic violence, and custody.

Jeremy I. Levitt is Associate Dean for International Programs and Distinguished Professor of International Law at Florida A&M University College of Law. He is also Associate Professor of Law and director of the Program for Human Rights and Global Justice at the Florida International University College of Law (on leave) and is an affiliated faculty member of the African New World Studies Program at FIU. He has served as a legal consultant to the Special Court for Sierra Leone, senior legal advisor to the Carter Center's Rule of Law Project in Liberia, and legal advisor to the Liberial Truth and Reconciliation Commission. He is a noted international lawyer. His books include *Africa: Mapping New Boundaries in International Law* (2008), *The Evolution of Deadly Conflict in Liberia: From 'Paternaltarianism' to State Collapse* (2005), and *Africa: Selected Documents on Political, Conflict and Security, Humanitarian and Judicial Issues* (2003). His forthcoming book is *Illegal Peace? An Inquiry into the Legality of Power-Sharing with Africa Warlords and Rebels.*

Kenneth B. Nunn is Professor of Law at the University of Florida Levin College of Law. He specializes in criminal law and criminal procedure. He has written widely on issues relating to the criminal justice system, including juvenile justice and the impact of criminal justice policies on the African American community. His research interests include assessing the impact of race on legal institutions, studying the influence of law on the African Diaspora, and examining the connections between law, culture, and society. He lives in Gainesville, Florida, with his wife and two daughters.

Charles R. P. Pouncy is Associate Professor at the Florida International University College of Law. He teaches corporate law, comparative corporate law, nonprofit corporate law, and professional responsibility. His research focuses on critical economic theory and has explored issues relating to securities markets and organizational theory, stock markets in developing countries, critical race theory, and queer theory. Before entering the academy, he served as a senior trial attorney at the Commodity Futures Trading Commission and as a trial attorney at the U.S. Department of Labor. He is a member of the board of directors of Latina and Latino Critical Theory, Inc. ("LatCrit") and is a past member of the executive committee of the Association of American Law Schools Section on Gay and Lesbian Issues.

Alyssa G. Robillard is Assistant Professor of Health in African and African American Studies at Arizona State University. A health educator by training, she received her undergraduate degree from Xavier University of Louisiana. She earned her MSPH in health behavior and PhD in health education and health promotion from the University of Alabama at Birmingham School of Public Health. She is a certified health education specialist (CHES), whose research focuses on adolescents, media, HIV, and health issues. She was awarded the Building Bridges Award from the Association of Black Public Health Students at the Rollins School of Public Health of Emory University and the Community Service Award from the Chivers Grant Institute at Morehouse College, and she has been designated as a Health Disparities Scholar with the National Center on Minority Health and Health Disparities.

Andre L. Smith is Assistant Professor of Tax and Administrative Law at the Florida International University College of Law. He has also worked for the Democratic National Committee Office of African American Outreach and the NAACP National Voter Fund. He is the author of several articles relating to tax jurisprudence. He is currently working on "Asymmetrical Market Imperfections," in which he describes subordination of all types in terms of fair competition in the marketplace of goods and services, as well as the marketplace for ideas. He is also preparing "Original Understandings of Justice," an article that reconstructs an African jurisprudential philosophy originating in ancient Nubia and Egypt, extending through the kingdoms of Songhay, Mali, and Ghana.

Carlton Waterhouse is Assistant Professor of Law at the Florida International University College of Law, where he teaches courses in property, administrative law, critical race theory, environmental law, international environmental law, and environmental justice. His legal experience includes private practice in addition to ten years served as an attorney at the U.S. Environmental Protection Agency, where he served in the Office of Regional Counsel in Atlanta, Georgia, and the Office of General Counsel in Washington DC. He is a member of the Pennsylvania and the Georgia bar associations and speaks widely on issues related to reparations, environmental policy, civil rights, social ethics, and other matters of public policy.

Matthew C. Whitaker is an award-winning scholar, teacher, activist, and emerging voice among public intellectuals in the United States. He is currently Associate Professor of History at Arizona State University and is also an affiliate faculty in African and African American Studies and the School of Justice and Social Inquiry at ASU. He specializes in American history, African American history, the African Diaspora, civil and human rights, and social movements. His books include *African American Icons of Sport: Triumph, Courage, and Excellence (2008) and Race Work: The Rise of Civil Rights in the Urban West* (2005). His forthcoming book is *Over Jordan: A History of African Americans in the Twentieth Century*. He is the vice president of the nonprofit 501C3 African Policy Institute, and is co-Owner and CEO of the Whitaker Group, L.L.C., a consulting firm that specializes in human relations and interpersonal and intercultural communication. In 2008 he, along with several partners, was given the Excellence in Diversity Award by the National League of Cities, for their Healing Racism Community Dialogue Series in Phoenix, Arizona.

INDEX

In the Justice and Social Inquiry series

Hurricane Katrina
America's Unnatural Disaster
Edited and with an introduction by
Jeremy I. Levitt and Matthew C. Whitaker

To order or obtain more information on these
or other University of Nebraska Press titles,
visit www.nebraskapress.unl.edu.